Adult Learners Welcome Here

A Handbook for Librarians and Literacy Teachers

By
Marguerite Crowley Weibel

Foreword by
Robert Wedgeworth

Neal-Schuman Publishers, Inc.
New York   London

Published by Neal-Schuman Publishers, Inc.
100 William Street, Suite 2004
New York, NY 10038-4512

Copyright © 2007 Neal-Schuman Publishers, Inc.

Printed and bound in the United States of America.

The paper used in this publication meets the minimum requirements of American National Standard for Information Sciences – Permanence of Paper for Printed Library Materials, ANSI Z39.48-1992.

ISBN-13: 978-1-55570-578-7
ISBN-10: 1-55570-578-2

Library of Congress Cataloging-in-Publication Data

Weibel, Marguerite Crowley.
    Adult learners welcome here : a handbook for librarians and literacy teachers / Marguerite Crowley Weibel.
        p. cm.
    Includes bibliographical references and index.
    ISBN 1-55570-578-2 (alk. paper)
    1. Libraries and new literates. 2. Adult services in public libraries. 3. Literacy—Study and teaching. 4. Reading comprehension—Problems, exercises, etc. 5. Reading comprehension—Study and teaching. 6. Libraries and adult education. 7. Literacy programs. I. Title.
    Z716.45.W43 2007
    027.6—dc22
                                                                    2006035105

For Stuart, and for all who labor
to advance learning

Contents

Part III: Strengthening the Connection

Foreword

Librarians are generally ambivalent about asserting their role as educators. They recognize that their role as a guide to the resources in their collections offers strong assistance and support to the learning of users at all levels. Yet, since they are not certified by the State and do not operate from a classroom they are reluctant to consider themselves teachers. This book by Marguerite Weibel makes clear the potential for librarians and literacy teachers to exploit the resources of libraries for the benefit of adult learners.

Adult learners, adults with low literacy skills, are probably the most marginalized people in the world. They are employed less often, earn less money if they are employed, participate less in community affairs, vote less often than others, and lack the ability to assist and support their children in school. The late Dr. Frank C. Laubach called them the "silent billion" because their voices are seldom heard in public discourse.

All too often we tend to think about literacy as a set of technical skills that are necessary to obtain employment and to engage in communications with the world. It is all this and more. Literacy levels are an indicator and predictor of the quality of life an individual can and will attain. It sits at the nexus of virtually every social problem we know—poverty, disease, famine, alcohol and substance abuse. While literacy is neither a cause nor an immediate cure for these ills, improving literacy levels is an effective way to address these problems by creating the possibility for self-sustaining change for adults and their families.

Those adults who choose to improve their literacy skills often find themselves on a waiting list due to the lack of capacity of most literacy training programs. Once enrolled, the resources to support their learning tend to be limited. Weibel points out that this need not be so. In addition to the educational texts published specifically for adult learners, the nation's public libraries hold many materials suitable for this audience. She identifies examples like pictures and poetry that can reflect the life experiences of adults and thus enhance their learning process. She provides thoughtful, practical advice and suggestions for identifying additional materials as well. *Adult Learners Welcome Here* is subtitled a "handbook," but it actually serves as the basis for re-creating a service that has almost disappeared from many public libraries—the Readers Adviser—for a special group of readers.

The publication of this successor to Weibel's *Choosing and Using Books with Adult New Readers* is timely as the nation begins to address the implications of the latest reports on adult literacy levels in the United States. For librarians and literacy teachers this latest Weibel compilation provides a clear rationale for why libraries are important in the effort to support adult learners as well as well-researched illustrations on how to go about it.

Robert Wedgeworth
President and CEO of ProLiteracy Worldwide

Preface

Reading is like looking through
several windows which open to
an infinite landscape.
—Isabel Allende *p. 3*

Adult Learners Welcome Here: A Handbook for Librarians and Literary Teachers is addressed to two primary audiences: librarians and literacy teachers or tutors. It is also addressed to program directors, policy makers, community service workers, students, writers, readers, and all those who believe that the ability to read and to read well is fundamental both to any individual's chances of living a rich and fulfilling life and to the development and maintenance of a free, open, and thriving democratic society.

Those of us who are drawn into librarianship or teaching – whether that be as a professional or a volunteer – come to these positions from a variety of starting points and for a variety of reasons, but one thing we share is the fact that we are readers, not just people who like to read books for pleasure, but people who are convinced beyond a doubt of both the pleasure *and* the power of reading. Ask any group of librarians or literacy teachers to name favorite books and you will start a lively conversation. Not only will we name titles, but we will talk about characters we loved and wanted to emulate, places we'd never seen but often visited in our imaginations, stories that helped us understand something new about ourselves, our families, or the circumstances of our everyday lives, and stories that changed the way we looked at the familiar world around us. There is one more bond we share. We are deeply concerned about the crisis of literacy we see around us and want to try to do something about it.

This crisis of literacy in our country has two faces. One is the face of the native English speaker who, for reasons of poverty, family difficulties, learning disabilities, lack of adequate school facilities, or some combination of factors did not master basic literacy skills while in school. For these folks, the thought of reading does not conjure up a host of happy memories. Reading for them represents failure to achieve something in their young lives that is expected of all young people. It means embarrassment and frustration in everyday situations of their adult lives on the job, in the grocery store, at the doctor's office, helping a child with homework, filling out application forms, or trying to make up for lost time and opportunities by returning to school to acquire a level of education that will enable them to pursue their own goals and ambitions.

The other face of literacy is that of the immigrant coming to this country to build a better life for himself and his family. Some immigrants are well educated in their own language, but lack sufficient English to obtain a job that matches their education and ability. Others were poorly educated, if at all, in their home countries, and must try to master English without the experience of successfully mastering reading and writing in their native languages.

If we firmly believe that books and reading can change lives, then we need to have an equally strong conviction that it is never too late for someone, no matter what their earlier experiences might have been, to experience the transforming power of the written word.

There is no better place than the public library to find the books that have the power to help adult literacy students become readers. Libraries serve everyone who walks in the door, without regard to educational background, income, social standing, or interest. For almost two centuries, in libraries across this country, great writers have researched their books and immigrants have found resources to aid their adjustment to a new country and culture. In the library, people looking for work have read job ads and researched potential employers while busy workers have found an hour's respite from the toil of the day. In the library, families have introduced their children to the magic of the written word, and senior citizens have used their leisure time to pursue interests long set aside by the demands of a busy life. In this electronic age, people without access to computers at home rely on the facilities and resources of the public library to access the wealth of information made available by new technologies. In thousands of reading rooms in virtually every city and town across the country, people of all ages and stages of life and from every economic and social class freely go to find whatever it is they need from the treasure trove that is the library. *Adult Learners Welcome Here: A Handbook for Librarians and Literacy Teachers* is designed to help adult literacy students join this community of readers and knowledge seekers by discussing the many ways that public libraries can support and extend the efforts of literacy programs.

The Origins

Adult Learners Welcome Here: A Handbook for Librarians and Literacy Teachers grew out of an earlier book, *Choosing and Using Books with Adult New Readers*, published ten years ago by Neal-Schuman. Like the earlier volume, this new work demonstrates that the public library offers a wide array of books covering myriad genres and subject areas that can incorporated into meaningful and engaging lessons that not only teach the skills of literacy but also introduce students to the treasures of the public library. Beyond updating the extensive annotated bibliographies of books available in the general collection of most public libraries and accessible to adult literacy students, this current book offers several important new features:

- Part I, "Adult Literacy and Libraries," sets the context for discussion of literacy students and library books, reviewing the principles that support the library's role in promoting literacy, the state of literacy in the United States as we enter the twenty-first century, and the various ways in which the community at large addresses this problem. It also briefly reviews the basic skills literacy students need to develop and the various methods teachers use to help students build the skills they need to become readers.
- All the chapters of Part II, "Literacy, Lessons, and Libraries," offer sample lessons that enable librarians to understand how their books can be useful to literacy students and help teachers incorporate a wide array of texts into their literacy curriculum. These lessons cover all levels from beginning to advanced new readers and audiences of English and non-English-speaking origin alike.
    o Both the sample lessons and the bibliographies of useful books recognize the growing population of immigrants seeking assistance with English language literacy.
    o Almost all the titles in the extensive bibliographies were published after 1996.
    o All the titles in the bibliographies have been assigned subject headings.
- Part III, "Strengthening the Connection," also new to the current book, discusses how libraries, literacy programs, and other social, business, and educational agencies can work together to build a literacy coalition for their community.

Organization

Adult Learners Welcome Here: A Handbook for Librarians and Literacy Teachers is divided into three parts. Part I, "Adult Literacy and Libraries," provides a discussion that will help literacy teachers understand the role of the public library and librarians understand the nature and extent of the problem of low literacy.

- Chapter 1, "Literacy and the Public Library," places the topic as central to the mission of the public library and offers brief snapshots of diverse and successful programs that operate in conjunction with libraries.
- Chapter 2, "Literacy and the Community," examines the latest statistics released by the National Center for Educational Statistics, profiles the population of adult students, and provides an overview of the various responses of the educational community to the dilemma, including a discussion of health and family literacy programs.
- Chapter 3, "Literacy and Teaching Adults," reviews the skills that adult students need to become good readers. It includes various methods used to teach students these skills. This chapter also discusses how specific kinds of books available in the general collection of any public library can support, supplement, and extend any adult literacy curriculum, regardless of the teaching methods used.

Part II, "Literacy, Lessons, and Libraries," is the heart of this undertaking. The five chapters provide specific examples of books that can be used in various adult literacy settings, suggest sample lessons, and offer extensive annotated bibliographies of titles suitable for use both in adult literacy programs and in family literacy settings.

- Chapter 4, "Art and Photography: Reading Pictures," suggests books that offer new readers interesting, informative, amusing, beautiful, and challenging pictures to "read," discuss, and write about. Reading pictures gives students an opportunity to describe what they see, infer relationships within the image, react to a mood or an idea, connect the picture to events or people in their own lives, and imagine themselves in the circumstances of the picture. These are all skills that successful students must eventually apply to the written word.
- Chapter 5, "Poetry: Finding Wisdom and Delight," introduces students to an amazing range of poems that communicate ideas, insights, images, and experiences in simple, but not simplistic, language. Most of the poems were written for adults and are easy to read, or at least easy to understand when read aloud.
- In Chapter 6, "Literature: Sharing the Stories of the Human Family," students will discover a variety of stories that, whether real or imagined,

reveal some truth about who we are and how we live our lives. These books span several genres including fiction, audio books, collections of letters and other writings, biographies and memoirs, and picture books for all ages.

- Chapter 7, "Nonfiction: Seeking Information, Exploring Interests" delves into the world of information. For many adult literacy students, poor reading skills inevitably lead to poor performance in content areas of their school curriculum, so they miss much of what society might term "general knowledge." And they continue to miss much current information that readers obtain from newspapers, magazines, books, and online sources. The titles suggested in this chapter cover a wide range of topics, including history, science, nature, the arts, and health. Many books will come from the children's collection, a wonderful source of works on every conceivable subject written in a straightforward narrative style that does not address children as a specific audience. In many of the titles, compelling artwork and photographs, as well as other kinds of graphic formats, greatly enhance both the appeal of the book and the quality of the information presented.

- Chapter 8, "Print and Electronic Reference: Entering the Information Age," introduces basic information literacy skills as it also examines the many reference resources, both print and electronic, that the public library of the twenty-first century offers.

In Part III, "Strengthening the Connection," Chapter 9 offers suggestions for "Building a Literacy Coalition," including the library, literacy programs, and a number of partner agencies from the community at large.

The Appendices list resources, notes, and suggested readings to help librarians and literacy teachers identify books for adult new readers. Separate indexes for title, author, and subject follow.

Selection Criteria

The lists of books suggested in Chapters 4 to 8 represent only a sampling of what is available. Most of the books listed have been published since 1996, but keep in mind that libraries maintain many titles that are no longer available in bookstores or advertised in publishers' catalogs but yet are still informative and relevant to readers. This is particularly true of poetry, fiction, collections of letters, memoirs, and other kinds of literature that don't rely on factual information but on the understanding of the human heart.

Not all of the titles listed here will be available in all libraries, although they can usually be obtained through interlibrary loan. If a particular title is not readily accessible, however, a similar one might be. These bibliographies are meant as much to be suggestive of the *types* of books available as they are to list specific titles.

Books listed in the bibliographies of *Adult Learners Welcome Here: A Handbook for Librarians and Literacy Teachers* come from both the adult and children's collections. In fact, the children's collection of most public libraries is a valuable resource of books for adult literacy students. Obviously, many books written for children are not appropriate for adults. But think of collections of poetry marketed to children that contain poems written for adults. Format and appearance will certainly be a factor in deciding whether to introduce a particular book to adult students, but even if the book itself seems childish, the poems within are often not and can be extracted for presentation to adult students. In the area of nonfiction, I know many adults who seek a children's book on a particular topic that is unfamiliar to them because they are looking for a basic factual presentation of information. And then there are those books marketed as "picture books for all ages," which often tell stories of interest to adults—for example, stories of family history—and do so to the accompaniment of beautiful artwork. All of these books are potential sources of material for literacy students. Each annotation in the bibliographies identifies the area of the library where a title is likely to be found. Keep in mind that books that are shelved in the children's collection in one library may be found in the adult section in another, and that sometimes libraries have multiple copies of a book, with one or more in each section.

Finally, I have attempted to identify books that represent, by their authors and by their subject matter, the range of cultural diversity that exists both within literacy classes and in the United States. While my primary concern has always been the quality and potential usefulness of each text, I hope that all literacy students will find themselves represented in the pages of the titles listed here. I also hope they will find much in common with characters who come from times, places, and cultures different from their own. That, after all, is one of the real glories of reading.

Note on Literacy Terminology

Potential Audiences

- **ABLE:** Adult Basic Literacy Education and refers to English speaking students in basic literacy education.
- **ESOL:** English for Speakers of Other Languages.
- **GED:** General Education Development test that is often referred to as a high school equivalency certificate.

ESOL Students

Many books suggested for ESOL students are not specifically related to the problems or needs of the ESOL population. ESOL students have many interests beyond their need to improve their knowledge of English. The more they learn to read over a wide range of topics and kinds of materials, the better their reading, writing, and speaking abilities in the new language will be. Annotations also suggest subject headings.

Reading Levels

I have assigned three levels for new readers—beginning, intermediate, or advanced new reader. In some cases, the reading level is a range of two or all three of those levels. These categories are intentionally nonspecific because each student's own ability and interests should determine the choice of reading materials. The book aims to expand the possibilities of books available to all new readers, not restrict them by arbitrary measures meant to apply to a group of hypothetical students. Using broad standards such as these three categories allows tutors to consider more of the qualitative aspects of a particular book.

Level 1: Beginning New Reader

In general, the beginning new reader level corresponds roughly with early elementary grades and indicates books that contain familiar vocabulary, simple sentence structure, relatively large print, and a spacious layout that includes a lot of white space.

Level 2: Intermediate New Reader

The intermediate new reader level indicates books that introduce more vocabulary and more complex sentence structure. Fiction books at this level require the reader to make some inferences and apply other critical thinking skills, while the nonfiction books expect an understanding of some background materials or historical references.

Level 3: Advanced New Reader

The advanced new reader level includes longer stories, more complex sentence structure, greater use of imagery, metaphor, and inferential thinking, and, in factual texts, greater detail of explanation. Books at this level are generally recommended for students in pre-GED and GED programs.

A Range of Reading Levels

In some cases, the reading level is a range of two or all three. Consider the following questions:

- Does the writing flow with a rhythm and a semblance to real speech that makes it easy to read?
- Are words repeated in ways that are not boring but assist an inexperienced reader?
- Do the illustrations, photographs, drawings, and other graphic elements enhance both the look of the book and the accessibility of the information?

Perhaps most importantly,

- Does the subject of the book appeal to the student or is it about a topic he already knows something about and can thus apply his prior knowledge to help him understand the book's meaning?

Acknowledgments

There are many people who helped bring this project to fruition.

At Neal-Schuman Publishers, I thank Charles Harmon, Director of Publishing; Michael Kelley, Development Editor; and Christine O'Connor, Production Editor. Charles offered the invitation to write a new edition of my first book; Michael helped me work through title changes, format revisions, and much more—all with his constantly encouraging words. Christine turned a sometimes unwieldy manuscript into the book you hold today.

Early on in the project, I wanted to visit literacy programs functioning in public libraries. New York City seemed like the perfect destination since all three of its library systems have active, creative, and exemplary literacy programs. So I thank Susan O'Connor, Manager of the Literacy Program at the Brooklyn Public Library. At the New York Public Library, Kristin Krause McDonough connected me with staff responsible for their Centers for Reading and Writing, particularly Ken English, Literacy Program Director and Terry Sheehan, Site Director for the Seward Park Center for Reading and Writing. I also want to thank Anita Citron, Director of the Adult Learning Center of the Jamaica Branch, Queens Borough Public Library.

At the Seward Park Center for Reading and Writing, I was introduced to *The Literacy Review,* a publication of student writing produced by The Writing Program of The Gallatin School of Individualized Study, New York University, in collaboration with various adult literacy programs in New York City. I am grateful to June Foley, Writing Program Director of The Gallatin School, for permission to use three student writings from *The Literacy Review,* Volume 3, 2005.

I also thank LeRoy Boikai and Norma Wetzel of the Columbus Literacy Council, for their dedication to literacy and their support of my efforts and Dr. Laura Weisel, Executive Director of PowerPath to Basic Learning, for her counsel and expertise regarding adults with learning disabilities.

At the Prior Health Sciences Library of The Ohio State University, my working home base, I thank my director, Susan Kroll, and associate director, Pam Bradigan, for their continued support of my research efforts. I also thank my librarian colleagues who encouraged me along the way and all the staff at the ASK Desk who processed my many book requests, particularly Laura

Lingham, who contacted me directly when books arrived and often hand delivered them to my office.

I borrowed many books from the Columbus Public Library as well and particularly thank Susan Studebaker, Public Services Director, for permission to use pages from their library catalog in Chapter 8.

My permissions agent, Mary Dalton-Hoffman, was a true friend in need as well as a professional colleague and I thank her for her work requesting permissions and identifying material in the public domain.

Last but not least, I thank my family, my husband and fellow book lover, Stuart, and my now grown sons, Mathias and Brendan, who remain the delights of my life.

Part I

Adult Literacy and Libraries

Chapter 1

Literacy and the Public Library

"Libraries are all about literacy and they always will be."—Gary E. Strong
(DeCandido, 2001, 115)

My student was Albert, a 50-something black man who had grown up in the rural South and dropped out of formal schooling at an early age. We were reading a story in a workbook written for beginning level adult students, then answering the comprehension questions that followed. The questions asked about basic facts, such as the name of the man in the story, where he lived, where he worked, and why he was traveling from one place to another. As Albert read a question, then tried to remember the answer, I found myself turning the pages to check back on the story. I couldn't remember the answers either.

This incident happened almost thirty years ago, but it was the seminal experience that has informed all my subsequent efforts to link adult literacy programs with the public library. Initially embarrassed and irritated by my own lack of attention, I gradually came to understand that the material itself was at least partly to blame. It was boring. It was written in the kind of flat, simplistic language found frequently in texts for new readers but never heard in real speech. Neither the story nor the language engaged the reader's interest in any way, creating no visual images or "hooks" to help a reader remember who had done what or why. It was an exercise in reading, not the real thing.

I knew I had to find something else, something that would engage Albert's interest and imagination. I went to our local public library, knowing they had begun to collect simple story books that were written for adult new readers. These were a definite improvement, but limited both in content and numbers of titles available. I began to look beyond these high interest/low reading level books to the library's general collection. These high interest/low reading level books were a definite improvement but still limited in both content and numbers of titles available, so I began to peruse the library's general collection. In my literacy program, we frequently used the language experience technique for teaching reading. This technique produces its own reading material from conversations between tutor and student that the tutor records and the student then learns to read. With this technique in mind, I browsed through some adult "picture" books, such as photo documentaries, collections of photography on various themes, and travel books—what might be called "coffee table" books. I thought these might inspire some interesting language experience conversations, and they did. Then I started browsing the library's poetry collection and discovered writers such as Langston Hughes, whose poems talk of adult ideas, experiences, and feelings, but in language that is simple, yet rich and rhythmical, language so engaging that lines and phrases stayed with me—and with Albert—for weeks after reading them.

That experience taught me that *what* adult literacy students read is of paramount importance. Literacy students need to read material that captures their interest and carries them beyond recognizing words to understanding the meaning those words convey. To be sure, learning to read requires mastering a set of word recognition skills and practicing those skills frequently. But reading is so much more than a skill. It is a means of acquiring information we need to solve immediate problems, of discovering our past and preparing for our future, of escaping everyday life into imaginary worlds, of seeing something of ourselves in the lives of people we could never hope to meet, of reflecting on and perhaps even changing the way we live our lives. This is the transformational power of reading and the reason most of us have embraced professions, as librarians or teachers, that actively promote books and reading. Literacy students, even those at beginning levels, need to be introduced to this transformational experience, to glimpse the power as well as the utility of reading. We need to invite adult literacy students into this world of lifelong learning—gradually at first, and not at the expense of teaching basic skills but as a supplement and complement to those skills. In their literacy classes and tutoring sessions, students will learn *how* to read, but only by introducing them to the "real" books available in the public library will we help them become *readers*.

The Role of the Public Library

The public library has been called many things: the people's university, the gateway to knowledge and lifelong learning, the guardian of our democracy, and the keeper of our culture. At the heart of all these lofty attributes is a fundamental belief that a strong democratic society depends on, indeed requires, informed and knowledgeable citizens, and that the public library, free and open to all, is the essential keeper and provider of that knowledge.

That the library is free and open to all is a source of great pride among librarians and those citizens who use and support it. No proof of education, citizenship, social status, or ability to pay is required. In truth, though, the public library is only free and open to those who possess the one essential skill needed to access the information and knowledge contained within. That skill is literacy.

Yet a cursory review of the recent National Assessment of Adult Literacy (NAAL) report, produced by the National Center for Education Statistics and released in December, 2005 (ncces.ed.gov/naal), reveals that the United States faces a literacy crisis. The study indicates that approximately 14 percent of adults function at the very lowest level of literacy, meaning they have difficulty reading anything beyond familiar names, street signs, simple menus, or the headlines in a newspaper. Another 29 percent of adults function at the next level, achieving a basic functional literacy, but still lacking the skills necessary to help their children with homework beyond the first few grades of school, or to move into a higher level job that might require reading a technical manual, or to understand the message in a newspaper editorial. At the same time, we are continually reminded, in the media and in virtually every task we must perform, that technological advances bring swift and extensive change to our way of life and that as individuals and as a nation we need more information, more knowledge, and more understanding to accomplish our appointed tasks as well as fulfill our aspirations. The gap between an ill-informed and poorly educated populace and a society based on quick and efficient access to information is widening. If that gap is to be narrowed and literacy students are to become active participants in the culture of learning, then the public library, claiming "open to all" as one of its banner values, must play a pivotal role in the national effort to improve the literacy standards and learning opportunities of our citizens. It is an issue of equity: information equity. It is a position the American Library Association wholeheartedly endorses. Among the key action areas listed on ALA's Web site are:

- "Education and Continuous Learning" which includes "lifelong learning for all people through library and information services of every type."
- "Equity of Access" which includes "serving people of every age, income level, location, ethnicity, or physical ability, and providing the full range of information resources needed to live, learn, govern, and work.
- "21st Century Literacy" which includes "helping children and adults develop the skills they need—the ability to read and use computers—understanding that the ability to seek and effectively use information resources is essential in a global information society." (http://www.ala.org/ala/ourassociation/governingdocs/keyactionareas/keyactionareas.htm)

To foster effective programming in support of these action areas, ALA has established an Office for Literacy and Outreach Services. Their Web site, http://www.ala.org/ala/olos/outreachresource/servicesnewnonreaders.htm, offers many links to resources, materials, and information to support the many ways libraries can offer services to the literacy programs in their local communities or establish their own programs.

The Public Library: A Literacy Classroom

To call the public library a classroom is simply to recognize that it has been a center for lifelong learning since long before that term came into common use. It is a classroom in the broad sense of a place that fosters learning, and for almost two centuries, public libraries have been classrooms for entrepreneurs exploring business opportunities, for writers searching for facts as well as inspiration, for immigrants learning a new language, and for those with the benefit of leisure time exploring an encyclopedic range of interests. In this classroom, librarians are educators, not in the narrow sense of standing before a group of students imparting knowledge but in the broader sense of professionals who prepare a rich environment and then help their customers find and use the materials in that environment that meet their individual needs and interests. To extend that concept to a literacy classroom simply means including a new user group—adult new readers—among our population of information and knowledge seekers and offering them the traditional services of the public library: providing access to knowledge and information, advising readers, offering facilities for learning, and promoting public discourse. Let's look a little more closely at these traditional services and consider how we can extend them to this new and significant group of learners.

Providing Access

Public libraries provide access to the information and knowledge so necessary for active participation in an economy and a culture that are based on learning. Equally important, they provide access to the collective human culture as preserved in our written heritage, access that is crucial to understanding ourselves, our community, and our global neighbors.

They provide this access by collecting books and other sources of information over a wide range of subjects, by maintaining these collections long after most of the books are out of print and no longer in popular memory, and by opening their collections to everyone.

Working together with literacy tutors and students, librarians can open this treasure of knowledge to adult new readers. In any library's collection are books covering virtually every subject, books written on a wide range of reading levels and in varying formats, books intended to appeal to readers from different backgrounds and with different interests. Some of these books are already accessible to adult new readers because they are written at easy reading levels. Others can be made accessible to new readers through the use of teaching techniques such as language experience, information reading, and assisted reading, techniques that will be explained in Chapter 3.

Increasingly, public libraries also offer access to the world of electronic information by providing public computing sites equipped with word processing and other kinds of software applications, e-mail functions, electronic databases, and access to the Internet. These sites represent a significant service for those library patrons, including many literacy students, with limited or no personal access to computers and are thus a contribution toward the goal of information equity.

Advising Readers

Derived from S.R. Ranganathan's five basic laws of librarianship, the role of librarians as readers' advisors has a long and successful place in the history of the public library. Following Law #2, "Every reader his [and we'll add her] book," and #3, "Every book its reader" (Ranganathan, 1957, 9), librarians have connected customers with the books they want or need for information, enjoyment, intellectual stimulation, or personal growth. Librarians can easily extend this traditional role to adult new readers and their tutors or teachers by examining their collections and identifying books that will be appealing and appropriate to literacy students. The books suggested in the discussions and bibliographies in Chapters 4 to 8 are but a sampling of the titles and kinds of books that will help new readers practice their developing reading skills as they discover the range of topics, ideas, stories, and voices available to them in the library. Beyond suggesting individual titles to students or tutors who come into the library, librarians can advise readers in other ways as well. They can label books from the general collection, both adult and children's sections, that are appropriate for new readers; they can offer workshops to literacy teachers describing the range of materials available in the library to support any literacy program's curriculum; they can prepare bibliographies of materials to share with local literacy programs and other libraries; they can invite groups of students and teachers into the library for tours; and they can give book talks to students at local literacy programs. In the process, they will be connecting new readers with a range of books and materials the students might never have imagined available to them.

Offering Facilities to Promote a Learning Community

Libraries are popular and often preferred meeting places for tutors and students in many literacy programs across the country. As tutoring sites, however, libraries offer much more than tables and chairs. Libraries are welcoming places. They are not perceived as part of the educational establishment in the same way that schools are and therefore are not associated with past failures. They are community centers of lifelong learning that invite and accept all comers, regardless of any economic, social, or educational standing. Invited and welcomed into this environment, literacy students can begin to see themselves not as lacking a skill they think everyone else has, but as fellow learners in pursuit of their own particular area of knowledge and personal improvement.

Promoting Public Discourse

All libraries contribute to the public discourse on important social and community issues by buying and maintaining a collection of books and other materials that discuss those issues from varying perspectives and by sponsoring public programs on diverse topics of interest to their communities. Libraries can extend this role to the benefit of literacy students in two ways. First, they can lead a community, and perhaps even a national, discussion of issues related to literacy, education, and the glaring disparity between our goals of lifelong learning for all and the reality that almost half our adult population lacks sufficient literacy skills to become active participants in our economic and cultural life. Secondly, libraries can draw literacy students into their learning communities by inviting them to participate in some of the cultural and educational programs they sponsor, whether directly related to literacy or not.

For example, they can sponsor book discussion groups for students from the literacy program, they can include literacy students among the presenters in an oral history project about the local community, or they can invite speakers from the local immigrant community to share their experiences of immigration or stories of their native culture.

Model Adult Literacy Programs

Public libraries are not the only agencies offering literacy services, but as GraceAnne DeCandido points out in the introduction to her book, *Literacy & Libraries: Learning from Case Studies,* libraries offer unique and valuable assets to the literacy programs they sponsor, no matter how different those programs may be in specific details. Public libraries are permanent and respected institutions in their communities. They have accessible facilities, extensive referral systems, significant collections of books and other materials, and access through their patron base to a significant number of potential and enthusiastic tutors. (Candido, 2001, 8).

In her book, DeCandido offers many examples of library programs that support a range of literacy activities, from simply providing tutoring space to housing special collections of materials to incorporating the literacy program into the administrative structure of the library. For example:

- Leslie McGinnis describes the Second Start Adult Literacy Program at the Oakland, California, Public Library which emphasizes a learner-centered approach. In that program, learners participate in program planning, curriculum development, public relations, and other aspects of the library's literacy program as part of their instruction. (DeCandido, 2001, 16–29)
- At the Plymouth Public Library in Plymouth, Massachusetts, the literacy program is incorporated into the institutional structure of the library. As Director Dinah O'Brien explains, the coordinator of the literacy program is a full-time member of the library staff who participates in— and brings the literacy perspective to—all the traditional library functions, such as collection development, marketing, and public programming. (DeCandido, 2001, 52–59)
- At the Centers for Reading and Writing, operated by the New York Public Library (which includes the boroughs of Manhattan, Bronx, and Staten Island), Declan Fox describes the development of a theme-based curriculum focusing on issues related to health and wellness. (DeCandido,

2001, 85–89). Other Centers in the N.Y.P.L. system publish and disseminate their students' writing. (See examples in Chapters 3 and 5.)

- Gary E. Strong has always believed in the concept of the public library as the "people's university," a concept made vividly apparent at the Queens (N.Y.) Borough Public Library, situated in one of the most multicultural areas of the United States. The Q.B.P.L. program emphasizes flexibility to fit students' varying needs, offering small group instruction for ABLE students, conversation groups for ESOL students, classes and computer lab exercises for both groups, video and audio labs for language listening, a large multimedia collection of materials for literacy students, and tutor training workshops for volunteers. (DeCandido, 2001, 111)

- At the Brooklyn Public Library, the literacy program uses a group instruction model led by volunteers. As Susan K. O'Connor explains, they emphasize teaching reading through writing and thus integrate computer applications, such as word processing and photo manipulating programs, into their curriculum to help their students write their own stories and create books and other materials to share with each other and with other programs. (DeCandido, 2001, 124–134)

- Lest it appear that all literacy programs are in large cities, the Robinson Public Library District's library literacy program in Crawford County, Illinois, 240 miles south of Chicago, demonstrates that literacy needs and programs are not just an urban phenomenon. As director Konni Clayton notes, there has been a significant migration of immigrant populations into rural areas in recent years. In these small towns as remote from the public consciousness as they are from major cities, public libraries are often the only source of access to learning and to technological developments and opportunities. (DeCandido, 2001, 73–89)

These brief snapshots of just a few of the literacy programs offered in public libraries around the country attest to the fact that public libraries have embraced their role of providing access to knowledge and information for a whole new population of readers and potential readers with creativity and commitment to their mission of providing access to all.

From his position as president and chief executive officer of ProLiteracy Worldwide, a nongovernmental organization, retired librarian Robert Wedgeworth is uniquely qualified to advocate for libraries to assume a leadership role in the promotion of literacy, which he describes as "the one essential requirement for the transmission of our culture." In a presentation to librarians titled "The Literacy Challenge," Wedgeworth notes that the central role of libraries to acquire, organize, and make available for use all the records of human culture is essentially a passive role, and that we cannot be leaders if we are merely spectators. To be true champions of literacy, he says, we must adopt as our common purpose "the obligation to promote a culture of literacy." (Wedgeworth 2004, 14).

Chapter 2

Literacy and the Community

"A culture of literacy," to use Robert Wedgeworth's phrase, is sorely needed as we enter the twenty-first century, and the public library has a major role to play in promoting it. To set the context for our review of specific resources the public library has to offer the adult literacy classroom, it will be helpful first to review the extent of the literacy problem in the United States and the various ways this problem is being addressed. In this chapter, we will:

- review recent statistics that describe the state of literacy among the adult population;
- present a general profile of adult literacy students;
- review the range of community responses to the state of literacy; and
- consider two specialized literacy programs: family literacy and health literacy.

The State of Literacy

The latest survey of adult literacy, the National Assessment of Adult Literacy (NAAL), conducted by the National Center for Education Statistics over a fourteen-month period from May, 2003, until July, 2004, was released in December, 2005. It is not good news. The survey questioned a representative sample of 19,714 adults ages sixteen and older living in households or in prisons. Over the eleven-year period since the previous survey in 1992, little of significance in the literacy rate of adults has changed. The statistics cited and comments quoted in the discussion below come from the Web site: http://nces.ed.gov/naal/.

Types of Literacy
The NAAL survey "measures literacy by asking respondents to demonstrate that they understand the meaning of information found in texts they are asked to read." The texts that the participants are given "were drawn from actual texts and documents," not made up for the purposes of the test. The survey was structured so that questions were given first, so students could read the questions "before the materials needed to answer [them], thus encouraging respondents to read with purpose."

The survey measures attainment of literacy in three areas:

Prose Literacy
The ability to read, search, understand, and use information found in "continuous texts," meaning texts that are written in sentence and paragraph form, such as newspaper articles or works of fiction.

Document Literacy
The ability to read, search, understand, and use information found in "non-

continuous texts," meaning texts such as a bus schedule or a chart listing the nutritional content of various foods.

Quantitative Literacy
The ability to perform and understand quantitative tasks, such as computing the amount of sales tax for a purchase or figuring out the number of calories in a meal when given a calorie chart for various food items.

For our purposes, we will examine only the results in the categories of prose and document literacy.

Levels of literacy
Based on the results of the survey, respondents are assigned to four categories:

Below Basic
At this level, students were able to perform "no more than the most simple and concrete literacy skills," such as "locating easily identifiable information in short, commonplace prose texts [or] . . . documents." For example, students might pick out a few familiar words on a newspaper page but not be able to read a brief article.

Basic
This level "indicates skills necessary to perform simple and everyday literacy activities" such as "reading and understanding information in short, commonplace prose texts [or] . . . documents." For example, students could read a short, factual newspaper story but not an editorial.

Intermediate
This level "indicates skills necessary to perform moderately challenging literacy activities" such as "reading and understanding moderately dense, less commonplace prose texts as well as summarizing, making simple inferences, determining cause and effect, and recognizing the author's purpose [or] . . . locating information in dense, complex documents and making simple inferences about the information."

Proficient
This level "indicates skills necessary to perform more complex and challenging literacy activities" such as synthesizing information or making inferences from complex texts or integrating multiple pieces of information from complex documents.

(NOTE: the three reading levels I assign to the books recommended in the bibliographies in the next section of this book, namely, beginning new reader, intermediate new reader, and advanced new reader, correspond roughly though not exactly to the *below basic, basic, and intermediate* categories of the NAAL survey. A more complete explanation of the categories appears in Chapter 3.)

In the 2003 survey, 14 percent of respondents scored in the *below basic* category and 29 percent of respondents scored in the *basic* category in prose literacy. In essence, that means 43 percent of respondents fell into categories indicating a significant limitation of literacy skills. In the document literacy category, 12 percent of respondents scored in the *below basic* category and 22 percent scored in the *basic* category, for a total of 34 percent of respondents indicating significant limitation of skill in finding and understanding information in documents. Interestingly, only 13 percent scored in the *proficient* category for either document or prose literacy, a 2 percent decrease since 1992, but that is the subject for another book.

Impediments to Literacy
In a country where universal, free education is considered to be the norm, it is still shocking to consider that more than two out of five adults have literacy levels below what would be expected from an educated populace. Why is this? An analysis of demographic information taken from a questionnaire given to all participants in the survey suggests some answers.

First Language Other Than English
The survey tested literacy in English, but included among the respondents adults whose native language was not English. Among these non-native English speakers there are, of course, some who are indeed highly literate in English, but it is also reasonable to assume that speaking a first language other than English presents a significant barrier to literacy in English. Hispanics, for example, "who represent 12 percent of the NAAL population, accounted for 39 percent of the adults with *below basic* prose literacy."

Educational Attainment
Although we know from numerous news reports on the state of education in America that graduating from high school does not guarantee that a student has achieved a high level of literacy, it is likely that *not* graduating will have a negative impact on literacy level. The credibility of this assumption is supported by the fact that 55 percent of survey takers who did not complete high school scored in the *below basic* category.

Age
Although adults age 65 or older were only 15 percent of the NAAL population, they represent 26 percent of respondents scoring in the *below basic* category. Twenty percent of respondents in that lowest category were ages 50 to 64.

Disabilities
Various disabilities are a factor as well. Of those who scored in the *below basic* category, 46 percent had at least one identified disability, and some had more than one. These disabilities include three directly related to reading, namely, hearing loss, poor vision, or learning disability. The significance of learning disabilities in the adult new reader population is discussed below.

A Profile of Adult Literacy Students

Statistics can tell us only so much about any population of adults. On the survey, they are numbers and percentages, but in real classrooms and literacy programs, they are real people coping with many of the same problems all adults face, but with the added burdens of limited reading or language ability, limited education, and often limited resources of many kinds.

Diversity of Backgrounds
Adult literacy students are a diverse group. They range in age from recent high school dropouts to senior citizens still thirsting to attain a skill that has eluded them through most of their lives. American-born students come from many ethnic backgrounds, from rural and urban environments throughout the country, and from the ranks of the employed as well as the unemployed. Many are poor and living on the margins of society, but others are reasonably successful workers and middle-class citizens. Non-English-speaking students come from many different countries and speak many different languages. Some had years of education and were accomplished citizens in their homeland; others are refugees from poverty and tyranny and had little opportunity for schooling.

Other Roles in Society
In our libraries and literacy programs, we know them as students, but in the wider community, these adults fill many other roles. They are workers, parents, grandparents, spouses, and citizens involved in their communities in numerous ways. Indeed, their desire to improve their level of literacy often stems from those roles. Some are workers who want to advance in their jobs but fear their limited literacy will prevent them from performing more diffi-

cult tasks, or perhaps cause their poor reading skills to be discovered by supervisors as yet unaware of that situation. Some are parents or grandparents who want to improve their reading so they can read to their children, help them with homework, and inspire them to higher levels of education. Some literacy students are church members who want to be able to read their Bible or other religious texts and participate more actively in their congregations. Others are motivated to improve their reading so they can learn more about their local government and thus have a voice in matters of importance to their community. Some aim to finish high school; still others hope to move on to community college, vocational school, or beyond.

Although the pressures of other responsibilities clearly pose a potential impediment to adult students, their depth of experience, in living and in language, also offers them the one advantage in learning to read they have over children, who clearly have more time and leisure to master this difficult task. Adults have a much larger speaking vocabulary than children do, a vocabulary that can become the building blocks of their reading vocabulary. They have life experiences that enable them to understand a much wider range of material, both in terms of content and complexity of ideas. And their experiences— the stuff of a lifetime—can become an endless source of inspiration for topics they want to read about and write about. Knowing that success in their literacy classes will improve prospects for future success for themselves and their families gives adult students a strong motivation to persist in their literacy classes. Students don't always realize that their everyday knowledge is an asset they bring to their new learning tasks, so it is important to remind them that their experiences, accomplishments, and skills are valuable resources they can put to use in learning to read.

The Burden of Past School Experiences

For many ABLE students, experiences associated with school and learning to read are negative ones. Some students left school early to fulfill family responsibilities. Others didn't attend regularly, often because they lived in families that were dealing with other social problems such as poverty, abuse, or addictions of one kind or another. Some students moved around a lot as children and never settled into a familiar routine in a place where they were known and appreciated. Some students had vision or hearing problems that were not detected and addressed. Many had unrecognized learning disabilities. In a time when such disabilities were not widely understood, these students were never offered any kind of remedial instruction. More likely, they were labeled "slow learners" or worse and placed in special classes where no one expected them to learn to read. Whatever the cause, students who have known failure in school come to any new learning environment with all the anxieties that the memory of their past experiences inevitably evokes. Easily discouraged, even minor setbacks or perceived lack of progress can cause ABLE students to drop out of their literacy program, especially in the first few months.

For some ESOL students, the situation is quite different. Most see the opportunity to attend school of any kind as a welcome benefit, even when attending classes is but another burden the students must bear as they adapt to life in a new language and a new culture.

The Problem of Learning Disabilities

Although the term "learning disabilities" covers a range of problems and our understanding of these problems is still at a developing stage, it is now widely recognized that some deficiencies of visual and auditory perception have a neurological basis and can present a major impediment to learning to read, even among people who are highly intelligent. Indeed, in the elementary school population, the gap between a child's obvious intelligence and his poor performance at certain tasks basic to reading is often the first indication to teachers or parents that he may have a learning disability. Thus it is becoming increasingly common in elementary schools for teachers to identify students who are struggling with early reading activities and request that they be tested for learning disabilities. Many schools also provide special tutoring to help these students.

Seeing this development in elementary schools raises an obvious question: How many adult literacy students did not learn to read because they have an undiagnosed learning disability? According to the National Institute for Literacy:

> among "adults in adult education programs, social services programs, or employment-seeking programs, [estimates] indicate that probably 40–50% of these adults, at a minimum, may have learning disabilities that have kept them from achieving academic and employment success in their lives." (http://www.nifl.gov/nifl/ld/bridges/about/project.html)

Screening for potential learning disabilities is now an important part of the initial assessment of students entering a literacy program. Two widely used programs are *PowerPath* and *Bridges to Practice*.

PowerPath, developed by Laura Weisel, is a procedure specifically designed for adults in basic literacy programs. It identifies students with possible learning disabilities and suggests specific accommodations that teachers can make to help those students overcome the visual or auditory perception problems that interfere with progress in reading instruction. (Vogel, 1998, p. 133) *Bridges to Practice,* developed by the National Institute for Literacy, provides training manuals and curriculum materials to help teachers "recognize learning disabilities, learn how to implement a screening process in the program, and learn what to do when an adult has been diagnosed with a disability." (http:// www.nifl.gov/nifl/ld/bridges/about/project.html) It is important to note that both these programs are *screening procedures,* not definitive diagnoses which can only be done by certified therapists or counselors and which are quite expensive.

The Community Response to the State of Literacy

As literacy students are a diverse group, so are the programs that serve them as well as the terminology these programs use to describe themselves and their students. Of the programs designed to teach English-speaking adults to read or improve their reading, some use the term BL for Basic Literacy, some use ABE for Adult Basic Education, and some use ABLE for Adult Basic Literacy Education. Although individual programs will differ, generally speaking, these programs serve students at the lowest levels, from beginning students to the pre-GED level. GED classes prepare students to take the GED or General Educational Development test leading to a certificate of high school equivalency. Some school systems may also offer adult high school classes, leading to an actual high school diploma as distinct from a GED.

Classes for immigrants who do not speak or read English are usually called ESL for English as a Second Language, or ESOL, meaning English for Speakers of Other Languages, a term that recognizes that for many students, English is not their second language but perhaps their third or fourth.

Throughout this book, I most frequently use the terms ABLE and ESOL to refer to the programs that serve these students and to designate books in the various bibliographies as appropriate for either or both groups. The students themselves will alternately be referred to as ABLE or ESOL students, or, more generally, as adult new readers, adult literacy students, or adult learners.

ABLE classes may be run by public school systems or by community-based programs, often referred to in the literature as CBEs. Public school programs usually receive funding through both the federal and state governments and are staffed by paid teachers, sometimes with the assistance of classroom volunteers. Community-based programs may also receive government funding, but even when they do, they usually rely heavily on corporate and private donations as well, and while they may employ paid teachers to teach classes, they generally engage many volunteers, especially for small group or one-to-one tutoring sessions. Some programs rely solely on volunteers. Many community-based programs cooperate closely with public libraries; some operate in whole or in part within the library, and in some cases the literacy program is essentially a department of the library.

Community colleges are also major sites of adult education programs, offering high school equivalency credentials, English language skills, and developmental programs in reading and writing that help students prepare for college level work. They also offer the distinct advantage of being a *college,* and therefore clearly an adult setting, one with a traditional mission of helping those students not quite ready for college or long past the usual age of going to college as they make the transition into higher education.

Yet another setting for adult literacy programs is the workplace. Many companies contract with local literacy programs to provide instruction in either basic reading or English language for their employees. Often the instruction is particularly related to the language and skills needed by the workers to perform their jobs or to advance in the company.

Instruction in ABLE and ESOL programs may be given in a classroom, small group settings, or one-to-one tutoring sessions. Some programs offer all three possibilities. ABLE students often prefer the relative anonymity of one-to-one tutoring, at least at first, but many programs are discovering that small group sessions offer students something beyond basic instruction. In the course of learning and discussing topics together, students come to realize that not only are they not alone in their dilemma but they have experiences, skills, and ideas that can help other students. Some programs separate ABLE and ESOL students, while others combine the two groups within small groups or classrooms, again offering the advantages of student interaction—in this case regarding language and cultural issues as well as instructional ones.

Specialized Literacy Programs

Family Literacy
The belief that parents' active involvement in the developing literacy skills of their children significantly improves a child's literacy progress seems like common sense, but it is also well documented. In a study cited by the National Center for Family Literacy (www.famlit.org), children who were read to frequently were nearly twice as likely as children who were not read to as fre-

quently to show progress in all the obvious measures of emergent literacy: knowing all the letters of the alphabet, counting to 20, writing their name, and reading or pretending to read. Parents who lack the literacy skills necessary to read to their children not only suffer the psychological burden of not being able to help their children develop this most basic skill, they actually jeopardize their children's chances of early success in school, thus perpetuating a cycle of poor reading skills. Family literacy programs address that problem by developing programs in which parents and their children learn together in ways that benefit each generation. As described by the National Center for Family Literacy, these programs have four components:

- Children's Education—offering activities designed to promote the literacy development of children.
- Parent Time—teaching parents how to help their children with reading and other school activities.
- Parent and Child Together Time—offering parents and their children interactive literacy activities in a supportive environment.
- Adult Education—helping parents gain the literacy skills they need for their own advancement as workers and community members, as well as parents.

Some particular family literacy programs that operate around the country are:

- Even Start—a federally funded program that aims to break the cycle of poverty and illiteracy by working with low-income and low-literacy families.
- FACE—the Family and Child Education program serving the American Indian population.
- Hispanic Family Learning Institute—an organization applying the principles and practices of family literacy to programs for the Hispanic community.

The National Center for Family Literacy serves all these programs, as well as many individual programs operating in libraries and literacy organizations around the country, by offering assistance with training for staff and tutors and by publishing training manuals and other materials, many of which are available through their Web site.

Libraries have much to offer family literacy programs. Most public libraries already offer children's programming—for example, story times—that involve parents. Obviously libraries can extend invitations to these activities to local family literacy programs; they can also bring the programming into the family literacy site itself. They can offer programs that teach parents how to read to children in ways that engage the child in a discussion of a book they've read together. Libraries have a wealth of materials to support and extend the activities of family literacy programs, from simple board books, to alphabet and counting books, easy picture books, collections of poetry for children, and nonfiction books explaining topics that children and adults can learn about together. Sample titles of such books are suggested in the annotated bibliographies at the ends of Chapters 5, 6, and 7.

Health Literacy

Health literacy isn't so much a program as it is a subject area, but a subject that is of the utmost importance. There are many initiatives under way addressing this issue from different perspectives. Within the medical community, for example, there are numerous efforts to produce patient education materials that are written in plain English and at accessible reading levels. One example is the Health Literacy initiative of the American Medical Association: http:// www.ama-assn.org/ama/pub/category/8115.html. Adult education organizations are also addressing this problem, producing materials to help teachers and tutors in literacy programs around the country introduce health topics into the curriculum. The Health and Literacy Compendium, for example, developed by World Education in conjunction with the National Institute for Literacy, offers an annotated bibliography of print materials and Web sites for use with adults with limited literacy skills. They have also produced the book *Family Health and Literacy* for family literacy programs that wish to add health issues to their curriculum. Their book is available to download from their Web site: http://www.worlded.org/us/health/docs/family/.

The public library has always been a source for health information. Most libraries have a range of medical textbooks in their reference and circulating collections, some intended for a clinical audience and others intended for a family or nonmedical readership. Several of these books are listed in the discussion of print and electronic references sources in Chapter 8. That chapter also discusses electronic databases and public access Web sites with health information. The children's collection of any public library will also have several books about health-related topics, many of which will be both appealing and informative for adults. The bibliography at the end of Chapter 7, Nonfiction, suggests a few sample titles.

However they are structured, successful adult literacy programs recognize that each adult literacy student is an individual with a unique combination of skills and limitations, fears and expectations, and a life situation presenting many challenges that bear on his or her decision to approach the door of that literacy program for the first time and face a dilemma they perceive to be a major impediment on their life's journey.

Chapter 3

Literacy and Teaching Adults

> Why are we reading, if not in hope of beauty laid bare,
> life heightened and its deepest mystery probed?
> —Annie Dillard

This chapter is divided into three parts. The first two parts offer a brief review of the process of teaching adult literacy students to read. The first part, "What We Teach," reviews the basic skills students need to become better readers. The second part, "How We Teach," reviews the various methods teachers use to help students achieve that goal. The third section, "What the Library Offers," discusses how library resources can support, supplement, and extend those efforts.

What We Teach

Basic Skills

In a research project administered by the National Institute for Literacy and designed to establish research-based principles for reading instruction in adult basic education, The Partnership for Reading (a collaborative effort of several government agencies concerned with educational issues) identified four principle components of reading instruction: alphabetics, fluency, vocabulary, and comprehension. The discussion of those skills that follows comes from the project's publication, *The Partnership for Reading*. (Kruidenier, 2002, 2)

Alphabetics

To master alphabetics means to know the letters of an alphabet and to understand how those letters represent various sounds that are combined to create words. Thus, alphabetics consists of two parts. The first is "phonemic awareness," which means understanding "how words are made up of smaller sounds." Phonemic awareness means the ability to hear the word *bat* and recognize that it is made up of three sounds, *buh/a/t*. The second element of alphabetics is phonics and word analysis, which means understanding "how letters and combinations of letters are used to represent these sounds." For example, through phonics we recognize that /*ch*/ makes the sound at the beginning of the words *church, chain, children.*

Fluency

Developing fluency means gaining the skill to recognize words by sight quickly, without needing to "sound them out," and eventually applying the same ability to strings of words in phrases and sentences.

Vocabulary

Building vocabulary means knowing the meaning of a growing number of words and recognizing them in print. For adult literacy students in the early stages of reading instruction, building vocabulary essentially means translating their spoken vocabulary into a reading vocabulary. As they become better readers, both their spoken and reading vocabularies increase.

Comprehension

The ability "to understand and use the ideas and information contained" in the text being read is the ultimate goal of all reading.

How We Teach

As The Partnership for Reading points out, alphabetics and fluency are "enabling" skills needed to support the ultimate goal of reading, which is comprehension. (Kruidenier, 2002, 2–3) To a degree, methods of teaching reading can be viewed from two perspectives, those that emphasize the "enabling" skills and those that emphasize comprehension and reading for meaning.

Teaching Methods that Emphasize Alphabetics
Methods that emphasize alphabetics teach phonetic structures such as long and short vowels, hard consonants and soft consonants, blends, and so on in an ordered sequence. Practice materials generally present lists of words that illustrate the phonetic structure being taught, followed by sentences and short paragraphs that include the words just presented. So, for example, students would be given a list of words illustrating the */short i/* sound such as:

Jim, Kim, Tim, hit, sit, sister

followed by sentences using these words:

Jim hit the ball far.
Kim will sit in that chair.
Tim has a baby sister.

In a similar but slightly different approach, sometimes called the "linguistic method," students are taught to recognize the sound and spelling patterns of syllables or words rather than to identify isolated sounds such as */short i/*. With this approach, words are grouped into "families" that make the patterns obvious, as in: *bake, cake, lake, make, and take.* Again, students are given word lists, then asked to read numerous sentences using those words to reinforce the pattern. Even though the sentences are about adults or adult issues, the focus is on the word recognition skills being taught, not on the actual meaning of the sentence.

Teaching Methods that Emphasize Vocabulary
Building a reading vocabulary of words recognized by sight requires frequent repetition of words to be learned. Basically there are two groups of sight words that students must practice to gain familiarity and fluency. One is a group of frequently used words, many of which don't fit into any phonetic pattern,

words like *the, this, that, was, were, you, your,* etc. The second is a group of those words familiar or pertinent to a particular student that are gradually becoming part of the student's reading vocabulary as well as her spoken vocabulary. Such a list might include names from that student's family or words related to her job as well as new words she is learning from the materials she is reading. Teaching techniques that promote sight word recognition include brief but frequent reviews of words using flash cards, finding particular words in advertisements, food labels, newspaper articles, or any printed materials available, and creating sentences containing specified words.

Of course, building vocabulary also means adding new words to both the student's spoken and reading vocabularies. Various activities such as keeping lists of "words of the day" or "words related to weather" etc., helping students recognize root words, and teaching dictionary skills will help students increase the number of words they recognize in print and can use in everyday speech.

Teaching Methods that Emphasize Meaning

Alphabetic skills are necessary, but not sufficient in and of themselves, especially for adult students who need to see the meaningful connection between the skills they are learning in their literacy classes and the needs and ambitions of their lives outside that classroom. Finding meaningful reading materials that will engage adult students but are written at a level within reach of their reading ability, however, is always a challenge for tutors and teachers in literacy programs. Four techniques of teaching reading that address that challenge are the language experience technique, the related information reading technique, the assisted reading technique, and reading aloud to students. All are widely used in adult literacy programs and all offer students the opportunity to read materials directly related to their own lives and interests.

Language Experience Technique

- Engage the student in a conversation about a topic of interest to him.
- Write down what the students says, using his words and speech patterns as much as possible, but with correct spelling.
- Read the sentences you have written to the student, first reading the piece as a whole, then one sentence at a time.
- Ask the student to read the sentences, perhaps with your assistance at first.
- Based on your student's ability, choose words and phrases from the story to teach some of the alphabetic skills. For example, take a word from the

story that contains a particular consonant blend, help the student see and hear that blend, then create a list of other words containing that same blend. Have the student practice reading words from the list, then make sentences for each of the words.

Sample Lesson Using Language Experience Technique

The sample language experience story below comes from a literacy student at one of the New York Public Library's Centers for Reading and Writing. (Sobezak, 22). In a wonderful example of collaboration between a literacy program and another community organization, this story, along with several others from literacy programs in New York City, was published in *The Literacy Review,* a journal of literacy student writing published by the undergraduate students in the Writing Program of New York University's Gallatin School of Individualized Study. The suggested exercises that follow the story demonstrate how student-created materials can provide opportunities for a range of skill-building exercises.

Birds
By Alicja Sobczak

That was a really nice day. A little bit rainy, but still it was nice and fresh. I was at work putting the laundry into the washer. I saw a man in the park across the street. He was taking out the food from the garbage can. I thought: It is for himself.

We have bagels at work. I grabbed one. I didn't care about my manager and owners. I ran quickly to give him a bagel. He was appreciative. He loves birds. He fed them the bagel.

Suggested Activities
1. Teaching alphabetics: Use the two words *putting* and *taking* as examples to review spelling patterns for adding *ing* to words.
2. Building vocabulary: With the student, create a list of words related to weather. Depending on the student's level, consider making several lists. For example, a list of nouns that name types of weather: rain, snow, sleet, etc; a list of adjectives describing weather: rainy, wet, sunny, etc; a list of adjectives describing how weather makes us feel: fresh, happy, gloomy, etc.

> 3. Discussing meaning: Ask students how they felt when they heard that the man gave the bagel to the birds. Were they surprised? Were there any clues given in the story to predict the ending? Did their feelings toward the man change?

The great virtue of language experience stories is their immediate relevance and familiarity to the student, reinforcing the connection between words on a page and a student's language and life. Sometimes teachers worry that when students read from language experience stories they are simply memorizing what they've said or what they've heard the teacher read. For readers with minimal skill, this is often true, but it is not cause for concern. Literacy students who have memorized language experience stories are doing exactly what preschool children do who "read" from well-loved books they've memorized from repeated hearings. Parents and teachers are delighted to see a child attempt to read in this manner, because they recognize that the child has learned to associate particular words with the pictures and print of a particular book. Even if the association is not a one-to-one correspondence between spoken word and written word, it establishes an important link in the child's mind.

The same is true for literacy students. Even if beginning readers memorize the first language experience stories they read, they are still moving their eyes across a printed page matching spoken word to written word, and they are still seeing their own language and thought made permanent in print. These are essential first steps toward mastering reading. As their skill and confidence improve and as they create longer and more detailed stories based on sources outside their own experience, literacy students come to rely more on reading skill than on memory.

Information Reading Technique

The information reading technique is a variation of the language experience technique. It helps students make the transition from reading their own words to reading the words of others. To use the information reading technique:

- Read from some material of personal importance to the student—for example, a driver's manual or a pamphlet about a health issue.
- Read a paragraph or section at a time, then discuss the material with the student.
- Ask the student to explain the information learned in his or her own words, but encourage use of the specific vocabulary related to the topic.

- Write the student's version of the information, using the student's words, but suggesting changes if necessary to ensure accuracy.
- Read the student's version aloud.
- Ask the student to read the simplified version of the information, with your assistance if necessary.
- Develop word recognition and comprehension activities based on the text the student has written.

Sample Lesson Using Information Reading Technique

The example below uses text from the Web site of the National Institute of Diabetes and Digestive and Kidney Diseases, a section of the National Institutes of Health: http://diabetes.niddk.nih.gov/dm/pubs/type1and2/what.htm. As in the lesson above, the suggested exercises that follow the text demonstrate how teachers can build a range of skill-building exercises.

What Diabetes Is

Diabetes means that your blood glucose (often called blood sugar) is too high. Your blood always has some glucose in it because your body needs glucose for energy to keep you going. But too much glucose in the blood isn't good for your health.

How do you get high blood glucose?

Glucose comes from the food you eat and is also made in your liver and muscles. Your blood carries the glucose to all the cells in your body. Insulin is a chemical (a hormone) made by the pancreas. The pancreas releases insulin into the blood. Insulin helps the glucose from food get into your cells. If your body doesn't make enough insulin or if the insulin doesn't work the way it should, glucose can't get into your cells. It stays in your blood instead. Your blood glucose level then gets too high, causing pre-diabetes or diabetes.

Suggested Activities
1. Discuss the information with students and help them create sentences that repeat the main points of the two paragraphs. For example:

> a. Blood glucose is the name for blood sugar.
> b. When you have diabetes your blood glucose is too high.
> c. Your body needs blood glucose, or blood sugar, for energy.
> d. Too much blood glucose is not good for your health.
>
> 2. Once the students exhibit an understanding of the information, ask them to look at the original material to find the answers to specific questions. For example:
>   a. Where in the body is insulin made?
>   b. What does insulin do?
>   c. What happens when your body doesn't have enough insulin?
> 3. Find a diagram that labels parts of the body and add those words to the students' vocabulary list. Consider labeling in multiple languages for an ESOL class.
> 4. Have students find the words "sucrose" and "fructose" in the dictionary. Point out the common root. Have them look for examples of food labels containing either of those words.

Assisted Reading

This method can be used with any kind of material that is of interest to your student but beyond his ability to read easily on his own.

- Choose a text of interest to your student and within range of, or even slightly above, the student's reading ability.
- Read the text aloud, in meaningful phrases, pointing to each word as you go.
- When the student feels comfortable, ask him to join in by reading the words he knows and skipping over the others. You keep reading at the pace established.
- As you do this several times, the student will gain both confidence and fluency.

Reading Aloud

Although mostly associated with reading to children, reading aloud to students is an important part of the adult literacy program as well. Listening to a text read aloud engages a listener's imagination. It helps familiarize students with the more formal language of print. Perhaps, most importantly, freed from the anxiety of identifying printed words, students listening to a text read aloud can conjure up visual images or feel the emotions that those words evoke, and can therefore engage in discussions about what has been read, bringing their speaking vocabulary and life experiences to bear on a printed text beyond their reading range.

Using an Eclectic Approach

As The Partnership for Reading explains, the four basic skills of reading, alphabetics, fluency, vocabulary, and comprehension, "need to be taught together for instruction to be truly effective." (Kruidenier, 9) This means that teachers need to combine teaching methods and materials that emphasize the alphabetic skills with those that emphasize meaning. Commercially published workbooks for adult literacy students supply lots of materials for teaching the "enabling" skills of alphabetics. These graded workbooks provide students a way of measuring their progress, and for volunteer tutors, many of whom lack confidence—at least initially—in their ability to teach reading, they provide a structured outline of skill development to guide their instructional program.

But a reading program based solely on skill building exercises is not enough. Most students have difficulty transferring isolated word recognition skills to reading materials outside the classroom that have relevance to their lives. They don't see any obvious connection between mastering the consonant sounds and filling out a job application. Reading workbooks have their value, but they lack what Mike Rose calls "the real stuff of literacy," namely: conveying something meaningful, communicating information, relating narratives, shaping what we see and feel and believe into written language, listening to and reading stories, playing with the sounds of words. (Rose, 109)

To incorporate activities that emphasize meaning, particularly meaning that is directly relevant to individual students' lives, most teachers supplement workbooks with materials that are "the stuff" of everyday life: application forms, menus, food advertisements, job manuals, health information pamphlets and so on. A wide range of books from the public library can also support, supplement, and extend any reading instruction curriculum.

What the Library Offers

By using the language experience, information reading, assisted reading, and reading aloud techniques, literacy teachers can add a vast and tantalizing range of books available at any public library to the stock of materials accessible to adult literacy students of all levels. Part II explains how teachers can do this. It discusses types of books that are particularly suited for use with adult literacy students, suggests sample lessons using those books, and offers annotated bibliographies of a sampling of titles that will appeal to adult new readers. Consider, for example, the use of pictures. Looking at pictures found in art and photography books can inspire students to write language experience stories in response to images, situations, and ideas beyond their own experiences. Any public library will be an excellent source for a wide range of art and photography books. Poetry is another rich source of reading material for adult literacy students. Listening to or reading poems that address adult issues and ideas in accessible language will evoke a range of reactions that students can discuss and write about. The public library is a major resource for finding poems from the classics to hip-hop. Stories are a popular source of entertainment and edification. These stories will introduce literacy students to an intriguing cast of characters living in circumstances that are sometimes familiar and sometimes unusual, but always revealing about the varied ways we humans live our lives. Finally, in our current environment that stresses access to information, adult literacy students, both ABLE and ESOL, need to know about many issues that affect their present and future lives. They also want to use their developing reading skills to learn about topics that address their interests and arouse their curiosity. Nonfiction books covering virtually every topic imaginable can be found in the library, and many of them, particularly those in the children's collection, address their subjects in a clear, direct, and accessible style that will appeal to adults. These books also use photographs, drawings, and various charts and graphs to enhance and extend their informational value as well as their visual appeal. The modern library is also a means of access to much information that is available in electronic format, and new readers need to be introduced to those sources as well.

As Helen Lyman said in her classic book about libraries, reading, and adult literacy, *Reading and the Adult New Reader,* learning to read means "progressing from beginning literacy to an increasingly mature use of print." (Lyman, 21) All of us, good readers and beginners alike, are developing "an increasingly mature use of print." Too many students with limited reading ability put themselves in the "can't read" category while assuming that most other adults are in the "can read" category. But reading skill is not a binary function, on or off, can or can't. Being able to pick up almost any novel in the bookstore is no guarantee of being able to understand an explanation of how the changing demographics of the American population will affect the future cost and availability of health care.

All of us who consider ourselves readers know that we are travelers on a journey of lifelong learning, seeking greater understanding of ourselves and our world. Bringing adult literacy students into the library and introducing them to the treasures it contains is inviting them to join us on this journey. We may be starting from different points, but we are all headed in the same direction.

Part II

Literacy, Lessons, and Libraries

Chapter 4

Art and Photography: Reading Pictures

Lessons for the Literacy Classroom

Reading Pictures

To look at the pictures discovered in the caves of Lascaux or in the tombs of the ancient kings of Egypt is to understand that from the earliest days of human civilization, people have used pictures to tell their story. From our vantage point in the twenty-first century, we can still look at those primitive drawings and feel a connection to people who lived so long ago we can hardly measure the time. We recognize in their pictures a familiar need to record daily activities, communicate ideas, and express feelings of joy, sadness, and wonder. These distant cousins left little or no written record, but reading their pictures so many centuries later, we sense their attachment to the physical world and their quest to find meaning in its mystery, and we begin to see the origins of and connections to our own human story.

In our modern media-saturated culture, pictures are ubiquitous, and we have come to rely on them to supply much of the information we seek as well as the stories we share. Social critics often decry the prevalence of pictures over words—for example, movies and TV over books—and there are certainly troubling trends in that regard. But there are opportunities as well, enabling us to use the language of pictures to help our literacy students connect with and master the language of the written word. Reading pictures, after all, is an essential step in the development of literacy in young children, an initiation into the world of expressing and representing ideas in symbols. Although the pictures will be different, the principle remains the same when working with adult new readers. Pictures define the elements of our everyday lives. They connect us across borders of time, geography, and culture and give a human face to historical facts and figures. They strike deep emotional chords, sometimes eliciting feelings we cannot articulate in words. They tell us stories that help us find common threads in circumstances different from our own or see the familiar from new perspectives. In other words, looking at—or reading—pictures involves the same intellectual activities that reading words does.

What Art and Photography Offer Adult Literacy Students

Whether it's paintings from the great masters, photographs from magazines and newspapers, or the advertisements that surround us at every turn, we can use the objects, stories, and ideas presented in pictures to help literacy students apply their skill at "reading" those pictures to the task not only of reading words but of developing critical thinking skills. Pictures offer obvious opportunities for students to name objects, describe the activity within a picture, discern relationships among the people pictured, recognize emotions expressed and guess at those implied. For beginning level ABLE and ESOL students, such discussions present a valuable extension of the language experience technique, described in Chapter 3. Initially, students create language experience stories based on their own family, work, or everyday lives. While it is always a good idea to root initial reading experiences in the students' own circumstances, it is also important to move students beyond the familiar to a consideration of the experiences and ideas of others. Generating language experience stories from pictures will help students make that transition from thinking within the context of their known universe to considering the messages of the wider world. This is an important step toward helping students develop the skills necessary to read from a wide range of potentially unfamiliar sources.

Pictures can also serve as writing prompts. For beginning level students, even writing a label or brief caption for a picture helps them integrate writing into the very early stages of their literacy curriculum. For more advanced students, pictures can serve as practice prompts for writing exercises just as well as written prompts do for tests such as the GED writing section.

Pictures also offer students an entry into the more advanced skills of reading beyond the surface information presented to a deeper meaning that is implied. In other words, pictures offer students practice in the important skill of "reading between the lines." For example, teachers might ask students to suggest possible relationships among the people or objects in a picture, or consider the perspective or point of view conveyed by a picture, or ponder an artist's intended meaning, or imagine what might exist beyond the picture's frame. Such exercises will help students learn to make inferences and see the possibility that one picture, or one story, can be interpreted in more than one way. Similarly, asking students to respond to what is pictured in light of their own experience or memories, to compare and contrast the content or effect of similar pictures, or to express their opinions about the effectiveness, power, or beauty of an image will help them begin to develop the ability, as well as the confidence, to evaluate the information they encounter, whether in pictures or in words.

What the Library Offers: Art and Photography Books

Pictures are available from many sources, but art and photography books found in almost any public library offer an unparalleled collection of pictures from virtually every continent, century, culture, and medium. In both the adult and children's sections of the library, tutors and teachers will find books containing pictures that will appeal to adult new readers and ESOL students from diverse backgrounds and with varying levels of reading ability.

Art Books

Books displaying works of art are among the treasures of the public library for many reasons, not least because they make extraordinary art works available to millions of us who would otherwise never have a chance to see them. Whether they are reproductions of a beautiful landscape or a scene from domestic life; a documentary account of an historical event; a whimsical or critical interpretation of a time, place, or person; or a highly personal expression of imagination or emotion, these works of art represent the range of human thought and experience and offer literacy students many opportunities to build their powers of observation and understanding as well as their basic reading skills. Some works will lend themselves to detailed description, others will evoke a range of emotional responses; some will remind students of personal experiences, others will suggest new perspectives; all have the potential to stimulate student discussion not only about what appears on a canvas, but also about questions of beauty, taste, personal experience, and meaning.

Some collections of art display utilitarian creations such as hand-woven rugs or quilted coverlets, as in Paul Smith's fascinating book *Objects for Use*, a presentation of familiar objects designed as much to express beauty as to produce a usable object. Other books display works of art connected to a particular theme or activity, as David Colbert's *Baseball: The National Pastime in Art and Literature*, a collection of paintings and other works that portray the sport in ways realistic, humorous, and nostalgic. Still others introduce students to the master painters of this and previous centuries. The Rizzoli Art Series from Rizzoli Publications is a particularly attractive collection for new readers as it offers paperback books large enough to give viewers a sense of the style and scale of the originals but, with just a small number of representative works, slim enough to browse through easily or take home. The *Georgia O'Keefe* volume is discussed in the bibliography of this chapter, but most other major artists, American and otherwise, are covered by this series.

Comics are a familiar form of art that appear every day in newspapers and magazines and offer lots of opportunities for "reading pictures." In the library, you will find many collections of popular comic strips and topical cartoons that range from wry humor to family drama to philosophical musings to commentary on the state of the nation. For example, the comic strip *Peanuts* and its most recognized character, Charlie Brown, are well known not only from the comic strips of numerous newspapers but also from the many television programs that are based on the strip's characters. From the perspective of ESOL students, Charlie Brown is the kind of iconic American cultural figure that they would benefit from knowing about. Books featuring collections of *Peanuts* strips abound and will be found in most libraries. Some focus on a particular theme or character trait, such as *Charlie Brown: Not Your Average Blockhead*, while others are larger compilations of many strips, such as *Peanuts: A Golden Celebration*.

Speaking of ESOL students and their need to become familiar with American cultural figures, products, and expressions brings to mind the myriad and seemingly ubiquitous forms of advertising that appear on billboards and road signs, on television and radio, and in magazines and newspapers. Helping students learn to read the words in advertisments as well as the hidden, implied, or ironic meaning of their pictures offers teachers the opportunity to introduce students to much of the cultural as well as literal language of American life. Current magazines and newspapers available for browsing, as well as archived editions, are great sources of advertisements and public libraries offer many titles, in print and sometimes in electronic format.

Photography Books

Collections of photography books also come in a variety of formats. Consider works of photojournalism, for example, which remind us of the facts and ramifications of historical events and provide background information about the people, places, and events of popular culture. One such collection is *Americanos,* by Edward James Olmos, which presents images of Latino life in a surprising variety of locations throughout America. Geographic collections, with their photographs from neighborhoods, cities, rural landscapes, and countries around the globe can spur recollections of growing up and offer students within a class the opportunity to share their diversity of backgrounds. Tim Barnwell's *The Face of Appalachia: Portraits from the Mountain Farm* is an example of a geographic collection that includes oral histories of the people pictured as well as photographs of a land and culture rapidly disappearing. Photographs of nature, often paired with lines of poetry or brief quotations, can inspire a reflective mood and encourage students to express their feelings in either poetry or prose. Neil Folberg, for example, in his collection *Celestial Nights: Visions of an Ancient Land,* offers photographs of that distant place where the visible horizon meets the mysteries of the night sky. In a more earthly realm, collections of photography covering every sport will appeal to athletes and spectators alike and offer opportunities for descriptive writing as well as cultural commentary. *Hot Shots,* a collection of photographs from *Sports Illustrated* magazine, is one such collection that offers the added feature of a caption for every picture that is a play on words and therefore an intriguing language puzzle for English-speaking and ESOL students alike.

And don't forget the children's section of the library. Many collections of photojournalism and well illustrated nonfiction books intended to introduce young readers to the fascinating wonders and ongoing challenges of our world will also appeal to adults because of the quality of the photographs and the range of subjects covered. Other books will offer adults opportunities to share their experience and wisdom as well as their wonder of the world with the children in their lives. Yann Arthus-Betrand's *Earth From Above for Young Readers,* for example, is an extraordinary compilation of aerial photographs that present landscapes from a unique perspective, inviting viewers to see the places pictured not as isolated geographic locations but as part of a vast, beautiful, and interdependent world.

Using Art and Photography Books in the Literacy Classroom

Sample Lessons

Given that pictures can be "read" and interpreted at many levels and in many ways, these sample lessons can be adapted for use with students at all reading levels. They also offer opportunities for word recognition, vocabulary development, writing exercises, and oral language development for both ABLE and ESOL students. Suggested activities are just that—suggestions. Let your own reactions and those of your students direct your use of these and similar books.

Sample Lesson 1: Art Books From the Library's Adult Collection

Book:

Hamill, Pete. *Tools as Art: The Hechinger Collection.* Foreword by John Hechinger, New York: Harry N. Abrams, 1995.

John Hechinger is the owner of a chain of hardware stores, but it is obvious from this collection that his interest in tools goes well beyond their value as commodities to sell. The paintings and sculptures pictured here will provoke all manner of reactions from amusement to head scratching to awe at the range of creativity the human mind can reach. This collection will challenge any reader's answer to the perennial question "What is art?"

Potential Audiences

- ABLE students, beginning–advanced levels
- ESOL students, beginning–advanced levels

Suggested Activities

With ABLE or ESOL students:

- Look through the book together with students, making comments of your own and asking students for their reactions to some of the pictures.
- Make a list of some of the words used, including words to name the

---

objects pictured, words that describe objects in the picture such as colors, shapes, sizes, placement on a page, etc., and words needed to record reactions and opinions about the pictures.

- Develop a language experience story (a method described in Chapter 3) in which the students describe and react to the picture. First, help the students read their stories, then use words and phrases from the story to help students practice word recognition skills, learn new vocabulary, or practice spoken English.
- With intermediate or advanced literacy students, ask them to write their descriptions of the pictures as well as their reactions to them.
- With intermediate and advanced literacy students, ask them to write about a time or situation in which they used one of the tools pictured or, if students are so inclined, ask them to draw a picture of a tool being used in a particular situation.

Specifically with ESOL students

- Make a list of tools with the English name and its name from a student's native language. Ask the student to create a brief description, in English, of the tool's use.
- Make a list of nouns naming tools and verbs describing the action of each tool. For example: hammer—hammering, pounding; saw—sawing, cutting, etc.

Questions to Consider for Discussion or Writing

These questions could be part of an English conversation class with intermediate to advanced ESOL students or a writing assignment for intermediate to advanced Basic Literacy students or ESOL students.

1. Choose a picture from the book and imagine a scene or a story that might explain why an artist would take an ordinary object and represent it the way he or she did.
2. Do you think the pictures in this book will change the way you look at tools from now on?
3. Why do you think John Hechinger collects works of art that use tools as a subject?

Sample Lesson 2: Art Books From the Children's Collection

Book

Ancona, George. *Murals: Walls that Sing:* New York: Marshall Cavendish, 2003.

Murals have been described as the most democratic of art forms—available for all to see and possessed by no one. For this fascinating and unique book, photographer Ancona traveled through Latin America, Mexico, and the United States searching for examples of murals that revealed the character of a street, a neighborhood, a city, or a people. Including frescoes of the early *conquistadores* found in Mexico as well as street scenes from modern cities, he presents murals that tell stories, raise political awareness, express anger, or beautify a neighborhood. Presented in the context of its time, place, and message, each mural invites description, discussion, and reflection.

Potential Audiences

- ABLE students, beginning–advanced levels
- ESOL students, beginning–advanced levels

Suggested Activities

- Peruse the book with students and choose a mural to describe and discuss. Have students read about the time and place of the mural, or read the information to them if appropriate. Have students describe what they see, encouraging them to see as many details as possible, but also encouraging them to look at the work as a whole and consider the interrelationships of the people and the overall message the mural sends.
- Have students choose a particular mural from the book and attempt to "translate" or explain the message of the mural in words. Then discuss the relative power and effectiveness of the picture and the verbal explanation.
- Ask the students to identify any public messages that appear in their own environment. These could include murals of course, but also

graffiti on walls or subways and even advertisements on billboards or walls in the neighborhood. If possible, have them take pictures of these examples and bring them to class for discussion. Ask them to consider the messages within these pictures.

Questions to Consider for Discussion or Writing

1. If you could create a mural to express a message you consider important to your community, what would your message be? Describe how you would represent that message in pictures. If you are so inclined, draw some pictures that might appear in your mural.
2. What if there was a mural in your neighborhood expressing a message you did not agree with. What might you do in response to that mural?

Sample Lesson 3: Photography Books From the Library's Adult Collections

Book

Pesaresi, Marco. Underground: Travels on the Global Metro. Introduction by Francis Ford Coppola. New York: Aperture, 1998.

From the oldest underground in London to the longest in New York to the newest in Calcutta to the subway in Berlin which unites a formerly divided city in fact as well as metaphor, Pesaresi traveled the globe photographing the many rites of passage found on city subway systems. Praying, sleeping, shopping, waiting, reading, and watching, the riders of these subways pass their time in ways that are disparate yet common across the globe. His fascinating pictures offer a multitude of opportunities for students to describe the contents of a picture, comment on the human behavior, describe a mood suggested, and compare the cultural variations suggested by these fascinating glimpses of life in ten of the world's greatest cities.

Potential Audiences

- ABLE students, beginning–advanced levels
- ESOL students, beginning–advanced levels

Suggested Activities

With beginning level students:

- Have students choose a picture to describe in detail. First, have them name as many objects in the picture as possible so you can create a list of words for them to learn and to use in their description of the picture. Then have them create a language experience story describing what's happening in the picture. Once they've learned to read their description of the picture, have them write several different sentences for each of the words on the list you've created.
- Ask students to describe their own experience of riding on a subway system. They might describe one particular incident or describe how the subway is a part of their daily life. For students who've never ridden a subway, ask them to imagine their first trip. Where would they be? What would they see? How would they feel?

With intermediate and advanced level students:

- Have students write a paragraph describing a picture of their choice. Encourage them to be specific, picking up on all the details in the picture, noting the way passengers are looking or not looking at each other, for example.
- Have students create a story for one of the people in a picture of their choice. Image where that person may be going to or from, where they may live, what they might be dreaming about as they ride on the train.
- Have students discuss some of their own experiences of riding on subways, or, if they have never or rarely done so, have them write about what they would expect, whether or not they would be fearful, what they would expect to see, and so on.

Specifically with ESOL students:

- As you browse through the book with students, have them identify any objects for which they know the English name. Make a list of these words, adding others they might need to write about a subway ride.

- Have students choose one picture from the book and write a description of the picture. Encourage the students to identify as many objects as possible and to describe them as specifically as possible, including color, shape, placement in the picture, etc.
- In a class with students from multiple locations, have them discuss their experiences with subways. Prompt them with questions such as: Have you ever ridden a subway? Is your subway old or new? Is it crowded and noisy? Is it clean? Does it run all night? If you have never ridden a subway, what do you imagine it would be like?

Questions to Consider for Discussion or Writing Exercises

1. What are the advantages of a subway system? What are the disadvantages?
2. Why do you think some people prefer to drive even when there is a subway system available?
3. In some subway systems, musicians play in the stations, hoping for tips from the passengers. Do you think this is a good thing or not? Why?

Sample Lesson 4: Photography Books from the Children's Collection

Book

Arthus-Bertrand, Yann. *Earth From Above for Young Readers.* Text by Robert Burleigh. New York: Harry N. Abrams, 2001.

Dates drying in an Egyptian palm grove resemble a multicolored carpet; logs floating down the Amazon create a maze of geometric patterns; carpets laid out for sale at a Moroccan market display a range of colors to rival any artist's palette. The aerial photographs in this extraordinary collection present these and other ordinary objects from the perspective of distance, enabling viewers to see them in a wider context, not just geographically, but ecologically, as part of a vast, beautiful, and interdependent world. In this volume "for young readers," a smaller version of Arthus-Bertrand's larger work of the same title, Robert Burleigh offers commentary to explain each picture and suggest both artistic and ecological issues for discussion.

Potential Audiences

- ABLE students, beginning–advanced levels
- ESOL students, beginning–advanced levels

Suggested Activities

- Show pictures to your students without describing what they are. Ask students to guess what is actually pictured. In a class situation, encourage interchange among the students.
- Make a list of words used to describe the pictures. Depending on the level of your students, consider categorizing the words they use in discussing the pictures as nouns, verbs, and adjectives, or as words that name specific things or express particular reactions.
- With beginning level students, develop a language experience story in which the students describe and react to a particular picture, then use that story for reading practice and develop vocabulary and other exercises based on the words and phrases from the story.
- With intermediate or advanced level students, ask them to write their descriptions of the pictures as well as their reactions to them.
- In creating this book, Arthus-Bertrand hoped that viewers would consider the interconnectedness of disparate places on the same planet Earth rather than specific geographic locations. Ask your students to discuss, and write about if appropriate, whether or not they think the book achieves this end.

A Note to Librarians

There are many ways you can promote the use of art and photography books among new readers. Set up displays of these books near the new readers' collection. Connect the displays to seasonal or topical themes when possible. Consider a librarywide promotion of "picture books for adults" geared to readers at all levels. Have a display of books that are themselves works of art. When selecting new books for the library, be alert to art and photography books that will appeal to new readers as well as other patrons. Remember, too, that many older collections of art and photography still have something to say to our contemporary world. Plan a program for parents that discusses the extraordinary art work that appears in children's books. If possible, invite a book illustrator to give a presentation. Connect book displays with local exhibitions of art and photography in your area. Whenever you go to a librarians' meeting, bring home posters promoting books that would be appropriate to share with the local literacy program. When giving book talks at the local literacy program, be sure to bring a few art and photography books along. Whenever the opportunity arises, display the powerful connection between the pictures we see all around us and the words that we need to know in speech and in print to understand and explain those pictures.

A Note to Literacy Tutors
Enrich your environment with interesting pictures. Hang posters, paintings, and photographs on the walls of the literacy center. Ask your local librarian to share book posters distributed by publishing companies. Display art and photography books in classrooms, student lounges, or reception areas and encourage browsing and spontaneous discussions. Though these books are expensive when new, they are often available in used bookstores and sometimes at library book sales at much lower prices. Magazines with many pictures, such as *Life* and *National Geographic,* are also available at these sales. Invite local artists and photographers to visit your program and discuss their work. Take students to local museum exhibits and build discussions and writing assignments around the experience. Collect postcard reproductions of art works available at many museum gifts shops. With students, create and display books of their own collections of photographs, including the students' annotations, if possible. Visit the library and look for art and photography books about subjects or places of interest to the students. At every opportunity, help students to "read" the stories and information presented in the pictures that surround us everyday and to see the connection between these pictures and the words and ideas they will encounter in their reading.

Art and Photography Books for Adult Literacy Students: A Bibliography

This bibliography is a sampling of the many books offering collections of art and photography that will inspire conversations and language experience stories with adult literacy students. Books listed here will be found in both the adult and children's sections of the public library; each annotation lists the primary area where that title is most likely to be found. For this chapter, annotations do not suggest reading levels or particular audiences since art and photography books, by their very nature, lend themselves to a variety of uses with a variety of audiences.

Adams, Ansel. *America's Wilderness: The Photographs of Ansel Adams with the Writings of John Muir*. Philadelphia: Courage, 2002.

The majesty and grandeur of the photographs of Ansel Adams coupled with the poetic reflections of naturalist John Muir create this homage to the vast and spectacular wilderness of the American West. These photographs offer wonderful opportunities for describing shapes, textures, moods, or the memories of distant times and places they may evoke.

Adult collection.

Subjects: the American West; photography, thematic collections.

Alabisco, Vincent, ed. *Flash! The Associated Press Covers the World*. Introduction by Peter Arnett. New York: The Associated Press in conjunction with Harry N. Abrams, 1998.

More than one hundred fifty photographs culled from the archives of the Associated Press chronicle the major events and personalities of the twentieth century. General photodocumentaries such as this one offer students opportunities to name and describe people, places, and events; to learn about events of history unfamiliar to them with; and to recall stories or offer opinions from their own lives related to the events pictured.

Adult collection.

Subjects: photography, thematic collections.

The American Immigrant. New York: Life Books, Time Inc., 2004
See annotation in Chapter 7.

Ancona, George. *Murals: Walls That Sing*. New York: Marshall Cavendish, 2003.

Murals have been described as the most democratic of art forms: available for all to see and possessed by no one. For this fascinating and unique book, photographer Ancona traveled through Latin America, Mexico, and the United States searching for examples of murals that revealed the character of a street, a neighborhood, a city, or a people. Including frescoes of the early *conquistadores* found in Mexico as well as street scenes from modern cities, he presents murals that tell stories, raise political awareness, express anger, or beautify a neighborhood. Presented in the context of its time, place, and message, each mural invites description, discussion, and reflection.

Children's collection.

Subjects: art collections, Latin America and the Caribbean, urban life.

Arthus-Bertrand, Yann. ***Earth From Above for Young Readers.*** Text by Robert
Burleigh. New York: Harry N. Abrams, 2001.

Dates drying in an Egyptian palm grove resemble a multicolored carpet;
logs floating down the Amazon create a maze of geometric patterns; carpets
laid out for sale at a Moroccan market display a range of colors to rival any
artist's palette. The aerial photographs in this extraordinary collection present
these and other ordinary objects from the perspective of distance, enabling
viewers to see them in a wider context, not just geographically, but ecologically, as part of a vast, beautiful, and interdependent world. In this volume
"for young readers," a smaller version of Arthus-Bertrand's larger work of
the same title, Robert Burleigh offers commentary to explain each picture
and suggest both artistic and ecological issues for discussion.
Children's collection.

Subjects: photography, international collections; photography, thematic collections.

Barnwell, Tim. ***The Face of Appalachia: Portraits from the Mountain Farm.***
New York: W.W. Norton, 2003.

A native of Appalachia himself, Barnwell has spent the last twenty-five years
documenting the people and landscape of this once isolated area that is
now the target of development. Stunning as the black-and-white photographs of family farms, rolling hills and steep mountain passes are, the real
impact of the book lies in the oral histories provided by several of the people
in his photographs. Their stories of learning to live with the bounty and the
hardship inherent in their geography could inspire students at all levels to
create their own collections of illustrated oral histories from their families,
towns, or neighborhoods.
Adult collection.

Subjects: Appalachia; cultural traditions; photography, thematic collections.

Baseball's Best Shots: The Greatest Baseball Photography of All Time. Foreword by Johnny Bench. New York: DK, 2000.

Old and new intermingle in this collection of spectacular photographs of
plays in motion and of players' reactions of triumph and defeat. Describing
the actions pictured in this or any collection of sports photography offers
many potential lessons in using and building a vocabulary of verbs.
Adult collection.

Subjects: photography, thematic collections; sports.

Beckett, Sister Wendy. *Sister Wendy's American Collection*. New York: HarperCollins, 2000.

Treasures from six of America's great museums are presented along with the folksy but authoritative narrative that made Sister Wendy's public television shows an unexpected hit with viewers, even many who didn't consider themselves particularly interested in art. The museums are American but the art is international, representing paintings from a variety of styles, countries, and centuries, but also sculptures, pieces of pottery, pages from illustrated manuscripts, and ceramic tile work. Close-up insets of particular features of the art as well as side bars offering interesting tidbits of cultural and biographical information add to both the educational and entertainment value of this book.

Adult collection.

Subjects: art collections.

Colbert, David, ed. *Baseball: The National Pastime in Art and Literature*. Richmond, Va.: Time-Life Education, 2001.

Whether it is the physical beauty of a gifted athlete in motion, the subtle and surprising complexities of the game, or the emotional connection to summers past and present it inevitably evokes, baseball, more than any other sport, has long inspired writers and artists to try to capture its essence. This eclectic collection of art and literature inspired by a century of baseball offers students many opportunities to describe the contents of a picture, laugh at an imaginative interpretation, remember a particular time and place, question a commentator's point of view, or consider the many ways in which baseball, and sports in general, influences our national life. A similar work, *Diamonds are Forever: Artists and Writers on Baseball*, edited by Peter Gordon, is also available in many libraries.

Adult collection.

Subjects: art and literature collections, sports.

Drysdale, John. **Our Peaceable Kingdom: The Photographs of John Drysdale**. Compiled and introduced by Margaret Regan. New York: St. Martin's, 2000.

Surreal, whimsical, goofy, charming—these are some of the adjectives that come to mind when viewing these black-and-white photographs by English photographer Drysdale. The staged compositions of humans and animals, both wild and domestic, are mostly improbable but often wryly funny. Each is accompanied by a brief caption, many of which are puns or plays

on familiar phrases that could lead to interesting discussions with ESOL students.
Adult collection.
Subjects: animals; photography, thematic collections.

Folberg, Neil. ***Celestial Nights: Visions of an Ancient Land.*** New York: Aperture, 2001.

In his work as a photographer, Folberg has always been drawn toward that place where the horizon meets the stars, what he calls "the human edge of the cosmos." To capture that connection between earth and sky, he tries to include some recognizable aspect of the landscape, perhaps a tree or a brief stretch of desert, in photographs showing vast stretches of the night sky. The resulting pictures, taken in the Sinai Desert and other locations in the Middle East, the land of his birth and the wellspring of the world's three major religions, join the known and the unknown, the experienced and the imagined, the earthly and the divine.
Adult collection.
Subjects: the Middle East; nature and the universe; photography, thematic collections.

Friendship: A Celebration of Humanity. Prologue by Maeve Binchy. New York: William Morrow, 2001.

The M.I.L.K. Collection (Moments of Intimacy, Laughter, and Kinship) resulted from a global search for photographs documenting examples of friendship around the world. This volume reveals the truth of Binchy's comment in her introduction that "friendship can grow on the most unlikely and barren ground." Extraordinary pictures of friends of all sizes, shapes, colors, and ages will surely spark reminiscences of friendships past and present for all readers. Companion books on other themes of family and love are also available.
Adult collection.
Subjects: friendship; photography, thematic collections.

Gottlieb, Steve. **American Icons.** Lanham, Md.: Roberts, 2001.

From Main Street to Wall Street, from urban skyscrapers to the Grand Canyon, from midwestern college football to a pickup basketball game in the heart of the city, Gottlieb has captured images that bespeak the varied faces of our geographically and culturally diverse country. In brief essays summarizing each section of the book, he reveals some of the stories behind the pictures that he spent several years collecting.

Adult collection.

Subjects: American history and culture; photography, thematic collections.

Greenberg, Jan and Sandra Jordan. ***Chuck Close Up Close.*** New York: Dorling Kindersley, 1998.

"Art saved my life," Chuck Close says, and it is a remarkable life indeed. Labeled dumb, slow, lazy, or worse as a child with unrecognized learning disabilities, he discovered a talent for drawing. As a successful artist, he developed a rare nerve disorder that has led to severe paralysis, but he continues to find a way to paint. His paintings, many of which are large portraits, offer distinctly different views when seen from various distances and angles.

Greenberg and Jordan have produced appealing books showcasing the work of several artists, including pop icon Andy Warhol and the much-admired and sometimes parodied Vincent Van Gogh.

Children's collection.

Subjects: the arts and artists; art collections.

Halpern, Greg. ***Harvard Works Because We Do.*** Foreword by Studs Terkel. New York: Quantuck Lane, 2003.

Although it was rejected as a project for his senior thesis at Harvard, Halpern nevertheless pursued his idea of interviewing and photographing the service workers who cook, clean, and generally make life possible at one of America's most prestigious colleges. More than a series of photographs, this collection is a sociological statement about the difficulties these low-wage—but indispensable—workers face trying to raise a family in one of America's most expensive cities. An appendix discusses the Living Wage Campaign, a three-week sit-in by students that resulted in a pay increase for the service workers. Many literacy students both ABLE and ESOL, will empathize with the men and women pictured in this book.

Adult collection.

Subjects: economic and social conditions, immigrants and immigration, photography, thematic collections.

Hamill, Pete. ***Tools as Art: The Hechinger Collection.*** Foreword by John Hechinger. New York: Harry N. Abrams, 1995.

John Hechinger owns a chain of hardware stores, but it is obvious from this

collection that his interest in tools goes well beyond their value as commodities to sell. The paintings and sculptures pictured here will provoke all manner of reactions from amusement to head scratching to awe at the range of creativity the human mind can reach. Pete Hamill, acclaimed novelist and journalist, was once an aspiring artist himself, and his affection for these works shines through his introduction. This collection will challenge any reader's answer to the perennial question, "What is art?"
Adult collection.
Subjects: arts and crafts; art collections.

Heaven and Earth: Unseen by the Naked Eye. Introduction by David Malin. London: Phaidon, 2002.

From a microscopic view of an atom of gold to pictures from the far reaches of the universe relayed by traveling space craft, this book reveals mysteries of the universe too hidden, too small, too large, or too distant to be seen by the naked eye. Bridging the worlds of science and art, the photographs offer colors and shapes to inspire the imagination. But to realize what they actually reveal is to spark profound questions about who we are and how we stand in relationship to the vast and complex universe we inhabit.
Adult collection.
Subjects: inspirational stories and pictures; nature and the universe; photography, thematic collections.

Hughes, Langston. ***The Block.*** Collages by Romare Bearden. New York: Viking, with the Metropolitan Museum of Art, 1995.

See annotation in Chapter 5.

Laurance, Robin. ***Portrait of Islam: A Journey Through the Muslim World.*** New York: Thames and Hudson, 2002.

Through Africa, the Middle East, and the far reaches of Asia, and from bustling cities to vast desert stretches, photographer Laurance has captured many faces and facets of the Muslim world in his brilliantly colored photographs.
Adult collection.
Subjects: religious and spiritual themes, photography, thematic collections; international collections.

Lester, Julius. ***From Slave Ship to Freedom Road.*** Paintings by Rod Brown. New York: Dial, 1998.

When Julius Lester first saw the paintings of Rod Brown, he immediately recognized their power to tell the story of slavery as well as or better than any words he could write. The stark beauty of the twenty paintings presented here, with brief comments from Lester, underscores the brutality of the system depicted as well as the strength of those who endured it.
Adult collection.
Subjects: African American history and culture, art, slavery.

Life Sixty Years: A 60th Anniversary Celebration, 1936–1996. New York: Time-Life, 1996.

Arranged first by theme and then by decade, this expansive collection of photographs from the archives of *Life* magazine invites viewers to observe and reflect on the many changes that have occurred over these 60 years in athletics, arts and entertainment, politics, popular culture and the very way we experience everyday life. Retrospective collections of photographs such as this one offer reminders of the past to older viewers and a visual history lesson to younger ones, suggesting many potential topics for discussion about the benefits and losses inherent in what we like to think of as progress.
Adult collection.
Subjects: photography collections; photography, international thematic collections.

Logan, Fern. *The Artist Portrait Series: Images of Contemporary African American Artists.* Carbondale, Il: Southern Illinois University Press, 2001.

"What can you read in a face?" That's the question that comes to mind when looking at these stunning black-and-white portraits of African American artists. Logan helps us answer the question by giving us brief descriptions of each artist's life and career and telling us how those basic facts influenced her compositions for each picture. Whether the artists are familiar or unknown, readers will be drawn to their story and want to know more.
Adult collection.
Subjects: African Americans, the arts and artists; photography, thematic collections.

Lynes, Barbara Buhler. *Georgia O'Keeffe.* Rizzoli Art Series. New York: Rizzoli, 1993.

Georgia O'Keeffe's paintings of the landscapes and artifacts of the New Mexico desert offer a unique and deeply personal perspective on the color, texture, and evocative aura of this distinctive part of the American West, and responses to her paintings are likely to be equally personal and evocative.

Books in the Rizzoli Art Series are particularly appropriate for adult new readers. The large plates convey a sense of the scale of the originals, yet the books themselves are paperback and thin, including just enough representative works to give viewers a sense of the artist's style and content. The series includes the works of many major artists, from Americans such as O'Keeffe and Jacob Lawrence to the European masters such as Monet, Van Gogh, and Vermeer.

Adult collection.

Subjects: the American West, art collections, theater and artists.

Martz, Sandra Haldeman, ed. Scherer, Deidre, illustrator. *Threads of Experience*. Watsonville, Calif.: Papier-Mache, 1996.

See annotation in Chapter 5.

Menzel, Peter. *Material World: A Global Family Portrait.* San Francisco: Sierra Club, 1994.

For this unusual project, sixteen professional photographers traveled to 30 countries to live for a week with a local family, photographing them in various activities of everyday living. On the final day of the visit, each family was photographed outside their house, surrounded by all their material possessions. The resulting pictures presented in this book display a wide spectrum, not only of colors, customs, food, dress, and geography, but also of number and kind of possessions, economic opportunities, size and composition of families, and indications of personal values. The possibilities abound for reactions, comparisons, and discussions—including about the very nature of the project itself.

Menzel, in conjunction with Faith D'Aluisio, has also created *Hungry Planet: What the World Eats*, a photographic and socioeconomic examination of eating patterns in twenty-four countries around the globe.

Adult collection.

Subjects: economic and social conditions; families; photography, international collections; photography, thematic collections.

Olmos, Edward James; Lea Ybarra; and Manuel Monterrey. *Americanos: Latino Life in the United States.* Boston: Little, Brown, 1999.

Actor and activist Olmos coordinated this project, which sent more than 30 photographers across the United States to capture images of Latino life in all its multiple manifestations. From New York to California, including many sometimes surprising places in between, the pictures reveal the diversity of this population, which claims many countries of origin and participates in all facets of American life.

Adult collection.

Subjects: American history and culture; Latinos; photography, thematic collections.

O'Sullivan, Shawn, ed. *New York Exposed: Photographs from the Daily News.* Introduction by Pete Hamill. Captions by Richard Slovak. New York: Harry N. Abrams, 2001.

Called "New York's Picture Newspaper," the *Daily News* has long prided itself on telling the stories of New York and New Yorkers in pictures, and its still-growing archive is the largest searchable online database of photographs in the world, containing both current and historic images. This book offers a sampling of these images from every decade since the 1920s, featuring the celebrities and calamities as well as the moments of ordinary life that coexist in a huge metropolis.

Adult collection.

Subjects: photography, thematic collections; urban life.

Parks, Gordon. *Half Past Autumn: A Retrospective.* Boston: Bulfinch: Little, Brown, 1997.

First as a photographer of the ravages of the Great Depression and then on assignments all over the world for both *Life* and *Vogue* magazines, Parks has documented much of the social history of the twentieth century. Reminiscences about his remarkable journey from poverty to artistic acclaim are intertwined with his pictures, adding to our understanding of both the artist and his art.

Adult collection.

Subjects: African Americans; the arts and artists; biography and memoirs; photography, thematic collections.

Perry, Regenia A. *Harriet Powers's Bible Quilts.* Rizzoli Art Series. New York: Rizzoli, 1994.

Reflecting both the folk art common among American slaves as well as the creativity of the individual artist, the two Bible quilts presented in this book also give testimony to the use of art to tell a story, especially in cultures where the ability to read was severely limited by circumstance if not by law. Both of these quilts made by Harriet Powers, who was born a slave but lived into the twentieth century as a free woman, depict various scenes from the Bible. In a brief but informative narrative, Perry explains Powers' techniques and also places both the quilts and their maker in the context of the African and American cultures that inspired in her.

Adult collection.

Subjects: African Americans, arts and crafts, religious and spiritual themes.

Pesaresi, Marco. ***Underground: Travels on the Global Metro.*** Introduction by Francis Ford Coppola. New York: Aperture, 1998.

From the oldest underground in London to the longest in New York to the newest in Calcutta to the subway in Berlin which unites a formerly divided city in fact as well as metaphor, Pesaresi traveled the globe photographing the many rites of passage found on city subway systems. Praying, sleeping, shopping, waiting, reading, and watching, the riders of these subways pass their time in ways that are disparate yet common across the globe. The pictures offer a multitude of opportunities for students to describe the contents of a picture, comment on the human behavior, describe a mood suggested, and compare the cultural variations suggested by these fascinating glimpses of life in ten of the world's greatest cities.

Adult collection.

Subjects: photography, international collections; urban life.

Quilt National 2003: The Best of Contemporary Quilts. New York: Lark, 2003.

Every two years the Dairy Barn Cultural Arts Center in Athens, Ohio, presents an exhibition of art quilts and then produces a book displaying selections of the best. The quilts shown here take this traditional fabric art beyond mere functionality to an ever evolving level of creative expression. Some quilts re-create scenes from the natural world, others recall childhood memories; some offer personal or political commentary, and still others reach for a more abstract expression of feeling or mood. These imaginative creations present many opportunities for language lessons, including naming shapes, colors, and objects, describing patterns and pictures, reacting to feelings evoked, and expressing opinions of taste. Books displaying the quilts from the exhibitions of other years are also available.

Adult collection.

Subjects: art collections, arts and crafts.

Schulke, Flip. *Witness to Our Times: My Life as a Photojournalist.* Chicago: Cricket, 2003.

For the boy who ran away from a difficult home life at age fifteen, the camera became a means to survival and unexpected success. In his long life as a photojournalist, Schulke befriended and photographed the likes of John Kennedy, Martin Luther King, Jr., and Muhammad Ali. He documented some of the major events of the civil rights movement as well the early days of the space program. This book follows the range of his photographic journey, interwoven with his reflections on events both historic and personal over the last fifty years of the twentieth century.

Adult collection.

Subjects: American history and culture; civil rights; photography, thematic collections.

Schulz, Charles. *Charlie Brown: Not Your Average Blockhead.* New York: HarperCollins, 1997.

Classic, lovable, philosophical, and sporting are the modes and moods of Charlie Brown presented in this small and very accessible collection of one of America's most recognizable cartoon figures. Collections of a wide range of comic strips abound at public libraries.

Adult collection.

Subjects: comic strip collections.

Schulz, Charles. *Peanuts: A Golden Celebration.* New York: HarperCollins, 1999.

More comprehensive than the collection described above, this book follows the evolution of Charlie Brown and all his companions through five decades, with accompanying notes from creator Charles Schulz.

Adult collection.

Subjects: comic strip collections.

Smith, Paul J., ed. *Objects for Use: Handmade by Design.* New York: Harry N. Abrams, in association with the American Craft Museum, 2001.

When is a teapot just a teapot, and when is it a work of art? This is the essential question that this display of unique designs of everyday objects asks. Eating utensils, furniture, rugs, sports equipment, and even cleaning tools reveal their creator's attempt to marry form to function and create something beautiful. Perusing this book will inevitably lead to discussions about the human urge to create and the qualities that make the ordinary beautiful in the eyes of the creator or the user.

Adult collection.

Subjects: arts and crafts.

Smolan, Rick, and David Elliot Cohen. ***America 24/7.*** New York: DK, 2003. Responding to a request for digital photographs taken anywhere in the United States over a specific period of seven days, 25,000 photographers took pictures in private homes, urban neighborhoods, remote villages, and spectacular landscapes. The 1200 selections in this massive and fascinating book offer students pictures to describe, puzzle over, laugh at, or look at in wonder. The photographs are divided into thematic sections, each introduced by a thoughtful essay providing some additional inspiration for discussion.

Adult collection.

Subjects: photography, thematic collections.

Smolan, Rick, and David Cohen. ***Ohio 24/7.*** New York: DK, 2004. As an offshoot of the *America 24/7* project described above, Smolan and Cohen created a series of books focusing on the unique character of each state. In the case of Ohio, that character ranges from the quaint horse drawn buggies of Amish country to the nostalgia of courthouse squares in small-town America to the bustling metropolises of Cleveland and Columbus.

Adult collection.

Subjects: photography, thematic collections.

Sports Illustrated. ***Hot Shots.*** New York: Time Home Entertainment, 2004. Books offering collections of sports photography abound. Some concentrate on a particular sport, others on particular teams. *Hot Shots* is in a category all its own and is particularly appealing for several reasons. The photographs from the archives of this popular sports magazine are simply spectacular. Some display moments of grace and beauty, others of grit and grime; some are humorous, others awe-inspiring. They cover many international games as well as just about every sport played in America. Finally, and most intriguingly, each picture is labeled with a caption that is some kind of pun or verbal twist, so looking at the pictures and discussing the captions becomes a lesson in deciphering English idioms and the multiple meanings of words.

Adult collection.
Subjects: photography, thematic collections; sports.

Sullivan, George. ***Picturing Lincoln: Famous Photographs That Popularized the President.*** New York: Clarion, 2000.

> Abraham Lincoln was the first president whose face was widely known through photographs, and it continues to be one of the most recognizable and ubiquitous faces in American history. The pictures in this collection show Lincoln in a variety of settings and moods, and accompanying captions provide a unique look into the character of an enduring presence in our national story.

Children's collection.
Subjects: American history and culture; photography, thematic collections.

Wegman, William. ***Puppies.*** New York: Hyperion, 1997.

> Though once a man with no interest in pets, Wegman has become inextricably linked to the many generations of Weimaraner dogs he has photographed. Dressed in quirky costumes or posed creatively in outdoor settings, the puppies photographed in this collection represent yet another generation of the canine family that originally captured Wegman's heart, as he happily explains in his introduction to the photographs.

Children's collection.
Subjects: animals; photography, thematic collections.

Weingarten, Robert. ***Earthscapes.*** Carmel, Calif.: Center for Photographic Art, 1999.

> Although the subjects of these aerial views are recognizable, the distance from which they are seen imparts a different perspective, rendering the images more abstract and thus inviting viewers to look beyond the real or familiar to the imagined. Pictures such as these provide great prompts for creative writing exercises.

Adult collection.
Subjects: photography, international collections; photography, thematic collections.

Wright, Alison. ***Faces of Hope: Children of a Changing World.*** Foreword by Marian Wright Edelman. Novato, Calif.: New World Library, 2003.

> Photojournalist Wright has traveled the world working for various aid organizations such as UNICEF and Save the Children. Her work has been

called "spiritual photography," because although her photographs document the poverty and deprivation of children caught in political conflict, they also capture some essence of hope in these young faces in spite of the difficult hand the world has dealt them.

Adult collection.

Subjects: economic and social conditions; photography, international collections; photography, thematic collections.

Chapter 5

Poetry: Finding Wisdom and Delight

> "Poems keep alive the small moments which
> add up to a large moment: life itself."
> —Gary Soto

Lessons for the Literacy Classroom

The Language of Poetry

All the characteristics of language applied to the teaching of reading—and used to create workbooks for adults learning to read—are contained within poetry. Poetry employs rhyme, rhythm, alliteration, and repetition, all uses of language that help to reinforce the basic skills of reading, skills such as recognizing consonant sounds, vowel patterns, and sight words. But poetry offers so much more than just words to practice reading skills. As Kenneth Koch says in his book, *Making Your Own Days: The Pleasures of Reading and Writing Poetry,* poetry is in a sense a language of its own, "a language in which the sound of the words is raised to an importance equal to that of their meaning." (Koch, 1998, 20) Koch calls this use of language the "music" of poetry, and it is this language, this "music," that offers readers words and phrases that please the ear and engage the heart, that create sharp visual images, that strike chords of memory, and that elicit intense feelings. Words and phrases, that is, that offer readers the kinds of interactions with language that make reading both meaningful and memorable. As Joel Conarroe says in the introduction to his book *Six American Poets,* readers will find in poetry, "those flashes of insight, shocks of recognition, and feelings of well-being that transcendent art is capable of providing." (Conarroe, 1991, xvi)

What Poetry Offers Adult Literacy Students

It is that experience, that connection to "transcendent art," that makes reading more than just a vehicle for conveying information, that we want our new and developing readers to have. Lofty a goal as that may seem, it is both necessary if we want our students to become active and engaged readers, and not so difficult to achieve as we might imagine if we think of poetry as the gateway. Much great poetry also happens to use simple words, often to describe commonplace experiences. But written in the language of poetry, those simple words capture the attention of the reader, creating memorable phrases that stay in the mind's ear and vivid word pictures that imprint themselves on the mind's eye. Consider, for example, these two poems: "Dust of Snow" by Robert Frost and "Complete Destruction" by William Carlos Williams:

"Dust of Snow"
Robert Frost

The way a crow
Shook down on me
The dust of snow
From a hemlock tree

Has given my heart
A change of mood
And saved some part
Of a day I had rued.

We all have had the experience of being in a blue mood when something simple and unexpected catches our attention and raises our spirits, so we can picture the poet walking in the soft quiet of a snowfall, lost in his own thoughts, then shaken from his mood by the simple sensation of a "dust of snow." The structure and rhyme scheme of the poem lead us easily from one part of the scene, or story, to the next, curious to know what significance he is going to attach to such a mundane occurrence. His way of using language caught our attention.

Complete Destruction
William Carlos Williams

It was an icy day.
We buried the cat,
then took her box
and set fire to it

in the back yard.
Those fleas that escaped
earth and fire
died by the cold.

The particular details of this poem help you picture this rather mundane scene of burying the family cat, and yet there is something else here too, something ineffable that takes you beyond the realm of mere words and makes you feel the chill of that icy day and its implications of mortality. That is the language of poetry.

Simple poems can also express profound ideas. Consider the poem "Fire and Ice" also by Robert Frost:

Fire and Ice
Robert Frost

Some say the world will end in fire,
Some say in ice.
From what I've tasted of desire
I hold with those who favor fire.
But if it had to perish twice,
I think I know enough of hate
To say that for destruction ice
Is also great
And would suffice.

This poem is more abstract than "Dust of Snow," expressing an idea rather than describing a scene or incident. It also uses metaphors, a kind of language commonly found in poetry. But it is not necessary for a student to understand the *concept* of metaphor to understand the explosive power of desire or the destructive iciness that hatred can engender. In fact, the metaphors in this poem essentially explain the concept themselves by virtue of being graphic and demanding of our attention. A poem such as "Fire and Ice" thus becomes an excellent introduction to text that goes beyond literal meaning to convey profound ideas and feelings.

Almost all workbooks and skill building exercises created for adult students in literacy programs use simple words, repetition, and rhyme to reinforce recognition of phonetic patterns and sight words, all skills essential to fluent reading. But as every teacher knows, reading lists of sentences connected by similar words but having no connection in meaning can easily become a boring routine. With poetry however, repetition, rhythm, and rhyme engage the reader, evoking images, memories, and feelings. As poet and teacher Kenneth Koch says, "Repeating sounds and rhythms makes them physically apparent and demanding of attention" (Koch, 1998, 28).

We want the words our students encounter in their reading exercises to be "physically apparent and demanding of attention," knowing that such words and phrases are more likely to engage the students in the process of learning and remembering words. These are the qualities of poetry, part of its "music" and its power, that make it an essential source of reading material for adult literacy students of all levels.

What the Library Offers: Poetry Collections

Every public library holds a treasure trove of poetry to excite and interest adult new readers. Some of these books will be in the general adult collection. Much poetry written for adults uses simple language that speaks directly to readers about objects, events, and experiences common to us all. Julia Alvarez, for example, in her collection *Homecoming: New and Collected Poems,* uses the language of housework to explore her relationship with her mother and discover the ties between the life she led as a girl in the Dominican Republic and the life she currently leads as a professor in an American university. The works of many other writers, including icons of American poetry such as Robert Frost, Carl Sandburg, Langston Hughes, and William Carlos Williams, as well as contemporary writers such as Alice Walker, Martin Espada, Nikki Giovanni, and Richard Wilbur, include poems that are relatively short, accessible to readers new to poetry as well as the practice of reading, and widely anthologized.

General anthologies collected around particular themes will also contain poems spanning a range of length, sophistication, and reading levels. Consider, for example, the anthologies found in the Everyman's Library Pocket Poet Series by Alfred A. Knopf, which offers volumes on a variety of topics such as motherhood, friendship, and the American West.

Much poetry of interest to adults will also be found in the children's and young adult sections of the library. For example, books intended to introduce a young audience to some of the great writers of our country, such as Emily Dickinson, Walt Whitman, and Robert Frost, present poems written for adults but in language accessible enough for younger—or newer—readers to comprehend. Sometimes the format of these books will be appropriate for adults, but sometimes titles such as *The Poetry Of Walt Whitman for Young People* will be off-putting to an adult audience. Teachers, however, can still use the books as a source of poems that will appeal to their students and simply photocopy selected poems or find those poems in anthologies intended for an adult audience.

Thematic anthologies abound in the children's collection and many are based on subjects and include poems with strong appeal to adults. Arnold Adoff's *I Am the Darker Brother,* originally published in 1968 to bring the works of black poets to the attention of young readers, was updated in 1997 to include contemporary authors. *A Poem of Her Own: Voices of American Women Yesterday and Today,* compiled by Catherine Clinton and illustrated by Stephen Alcorn, includes poetry as old as that of the colonial Anne Bradstreet and as contemporary as the works of Sandra Cisneros.

Poetry is commonly thought of as a medium through which to express feelings, but it is equally powerful as a vehicle for telling stories or conveying information. In her collection of poems *The Other Side: Shorter Poems,* Angela Johnson reveals both the facts and human consequences of the planned destruction of the town of Shorter, Alabama. In an extraordinary book titled *A Wreath for Emmett Till,* Marilyn Nelson recalls the brutal murder of the young teenage boy and the national response that galvanized the civil rights movement. Both of these titles will be found in the children's collection.

Also in the children's collection you will find picture books that are illustrated versions of well-know poems such as Robert Frost's *Stopping by Woods on a Snowy Evening,* illustrated by Susan Jeffers, or Henry Wadsworth Longfellow's *Paul Revere's Ride: The Landlord's Tale,* illustrated by Charles Santore. Walter Dean Myers' *Harlem: A Poem,* illustrated by his son Christopher Myers, is an example of a picture book that offers not a famous poem but a new one in which the language, subject, and illustrations will appeal to readers of all ages.

As Gary Soto says in the introduction to his collection of poems titled *A Fire in My Hands,* "my poems are about commonplace, everyday things— baseball, an evening walk, a boyhood friendship, first love, fatherhood, a tree, rock 'n' roll, the homeless, dancing. The poems keep alive the small moments which add up to a large moment: life itself." (Soto, 1990, 6) These are the kinds of poems that adult new readers across a spectrum of age, background, native language, and reading ability can read, understand, learn from, and enjoy. They are the kinds of poems in which students will find simple or commonplace ideas expressed in amusing, surprising, and even profound ways, poems in which they will meet people just like themselves and people they would never meet outside the pages of a book.

The bibliography at the end of this chapter suggests these and many other titles of poetry books you can find in all sections of the public library. Of course poetry is also a rich medium for adults to share with the children in their lives, so titles of poetry books appropriate for family literacy are also suggested.

Using Poetry in the Literacy Classroom

Teaching Tips: Reading Poetry with Adult Literacy Students
In his book, *How to Read a Poem and Fall in Love with Poetry,* poet Edward Hirsch compares a poem to a "message in a bottle," sent forth by its writer to be found, read, reacted to, and embraced or discarded by any readers who happen to come upon it. (Hirsch, 1999, 2) Every poet hopes his "message" will find resonance with its readers and perhaps even affect their lives in some way, however small. But once that poem has been found, it is the readers who control the message by reading the poet's words through the lens of their own experience, adding their own meaning to the original words of the poet. This transaction between the writer and the reader may result in an interpretation that matches what the poet had in mind, or the reader may perceive a mean- ing that the writer never intended, but that exists, nonetheless, for that par- ticular reader. As Hirsch says of poetry readers, "Poems breathe deeper meaning into our lives, and . . . we in turn breathe deeper life into the poems. (Hirsch, 1999, vii)

Given the brevity and relative simplicity of much poetry, the "music" of its language, the infinite variety of its messages, its invitation to readers—or find- ers—of those messages to engage in a virtual dialogue of shared understand- ing across time and distance, and its profuse availability in the public library, poetry fits at all levels in the curriculum of any adult literacy program, whether

ABLE or ESOL. Here are some suggestions for incorporating poetry into a literacy program:

- Read as much poetry as you can and build your own collection of poems you like and think will be appealing to your students. Peruse the anthologies listed in the bibliography at the end of this chapter or ask your local librarian for suggestions. Robert Pinsky's *Americans Favorite Poems* and Edward Hirsch's *How to Read a Poem and Fall in Love with Poetry* are excellent guides to selecting and enjoying poetry for longtime poetry lovers and newcomers alike.

- Set aside a brief section of every class or tutoring session to read and talk about a poem.

- Begin with poems you like so you can talk about them easily. Don't be intimidated by length or sophistication of language when choosing poems to read to students. They understand complex language spoken to them, even if they cannot read equivalent language, and the "music" of poetry will help engage the students and facilitate understanding. As Kenneth Koch says in *Rose, Where Did You Get That Red?*, his classic book about teaching poetry to children, if you give students only poems about things they know, you will give them "nothing to understand that they have not already understood." (Koch, 1973, 12)

- Read poems aloud to your students. We know that reading aloud to children is a major factor in the total immersion in language through which they learn to speak and ultimately to read and write. While we cannot duplicate that kind of language immersion experience for adults, it remains true that actively listening to written language helps familiarize adult students with a variety of vocabulary and voices and reinforces their attempts to decipher, understand, and remember words on paper.

- After you've read a poem, discuss it informally with your students. Ask them if they like the poem or not, and why. A response such as, "It just sounds nice," is acceptable. As we said earlier, it is the "music" of poetry, the engagement with its language, that is an important part of the experience of listening to poetry, perhaps the only part at the beginning. To quote Koch again, once you enjoy and are drawn into a poem through some sensual appreciation, then "understanding is on the way, for pleasure in reading a poem is the first sign of [understanding] it. (Koch, 1998, 110)

- Draw out the students' responses by offering some of your own. Point to words or rhyme combinations you particularly like, images that stay with you long after you have read a poem, or memories a poem evokes. By detailing some of your reactions, you are also telling the students what to look for in poems and helping them develop a feel for poetry.

- Reading poems can lead to many useful language lessons, but be cautious about using the poems too mechanically. Don't just pick out obvious elements such as rhyming words or words beginning with the same consonant. Any kind of writing offers opportunities for those exercises, but poetry is special. Talk about those elements of a poem that make it striking or funny or beautiful. Ask the students to identify words or phrases that caught their attention. Have students describe the pictures a poem creates in their minds or the feelings it elicits. Ask them to describe any memories the poem recalls or the mood the poem suggests. Ask students to imagine what the poet was thinking or doing, or what his life was like, or what he would be like if they met him today. Ask if they have any questions they would like to ask the poet.

- Whenever possible, make poems or collections of poems available in your classroom or tutoring space. Encourage students to peruse these collections and choose poems they like to read aloud to you or to the class. Have students create their own collections of favorite poems.

- If students are attracted to a particular poet, find some biographical information about that person. Many biographies have been written about famous poets such as Robert Frost or Langston Hughes, some of which will be found in the children's collection of the library, though still suitable for adults. Information about many poets can also be found in reference sources such as *Contemporary Authors, Contemporary Poets,* and *Something About the Author.* Most public libraries have print copies of these sources, and many also now offer them in electronic versions as well.

- The Web is also a good source for finding poems about particular topics, information about poets, and ideas about teaching poetry. A quick Internet search on a poet's name or a poem's title will bring up a variety of information sources, some of which are created by teachers for their students but happen to be available to anyone through the Web. While some of these sites will be the personal opinions of the site creator, others will be instructive and authoritative. Both kinds can have their value.

Teaching Tips: Writing Poetry with Adult Literacy Students

A poem is what Edward Hirsch calls "a made thing," something the writer has created by responding to something he sees, feels, dreams about, or in some way becomes conscious of and inspired by. (Hirsch, 1999, 31) The amazing thing about writing a poem (and other kinds of writing as well) is that in the process of writing about something that has captured our attention, we often realize something we hadn't realized before we wrote about it. We actually learn something in the process of writing. This is an exciting experience and one that further engages students in the whole process of connecting the written word to all aspects of everyday life. As noted in Chapter 3, reading and writing are complementary activities, and the more practice you have with one, the more the other improves. This applies to reading and writing poetry as well. As Koch says, "A reader who knows how poetry is made has a better chance of responding to what is there." (Koch, 1998, 14) Encourage your students to write poems of their own. Here are a few teaching suggestions:

- Start with formulas that will be easy to work with. Sentence completion poems are a good example. Give students a phrase, for example, "I remember the day I . . . " and ask them to complete that phrase in several different ways.
- Encourage students to write in their own words, their own voice, not in a language they may think of as poetic.
- Encourage students to use specific details such as colors of clothing, objects in a room, food that was eaten, particulars about the weather, etc. Remind them that they want to create a vivid picture in the listener's or reader's mind.
- Have students write poems in the class or tutoring session, not at home, then read the poems aloud within the same class session to maintain interest and excitement.
- Teach by example, not explanation. Students don't need textbook definitions of metaphors, similes, and other poetic elements to understand and appreciate many poems. As they become more proficient readers and writers, however, an understanding of the techniques of good writing will deepen their appreciation for poetry and improve their own writing. Help students discover the prevalent use of metaphor, for example, by having them read or listen to many poems containing metaphors, then asking them to pick out and discuss the way one thing is compared to another in those poems. Help them incorporate some of these techniques in their own writing by having them try to imitate the work of good writers.
- Write poems yourself and share them with your students. If writing poetry is a new experience for you, tell that to your students. Let them

know that you have misgivings about your skill or about expressing your own thoughts. Share your successes and failures and any insights you gain from the experience. You will learn so much more from the process if you plunge in and do whatever you ask the students to do.

- When evaluating the students' poems, offer positive comments that highlight what they've done well, such as "I can hear the crunch of that snow" or "I can picture that red nail polish." All teaching requires a balance between encouraging students' efforts and helping them to improve those efforts. Remind them that their goal is not just writing words correctly, but actually conveying the meaning of those words in a way that others will understand and even remember.

Sample Lessons

Given that poetry can be experienced by listening as well as by reading, the poems in the lessons suggested here can be used with students across a range of reading levels. The universality of the experiences described also makes them appropriate for both ABLE and ESOL students. The suggested activities are simply that—suggestions. Let your own reactions and those of your students direct your discussions of these poems.

Sample Lesson 1: Poems that Create Vivid Word-Pictures

Some poems isolate a moment in time and shine a light on it, creating vivid word-pictures. In each of the two poems, the poets use words first to create an image and then, to dig deeper, to convey a mood, a perspective, or a feeling.

The Great Figure
William Carlos Williams

Among the rain
and lights
I saw the figure 5
in gold
on a red
firetruck
moving
tense
unheeded

---

to gong clangs
siren howls
and wheels rumbling
through the dark city.

Suggested Questions and Activities

1. Identify words in the poem that help you "see" and "hear" this fire truck.
2. Look at a printed copy of the poem. Why do you think the poet wrote the poem in this format, using short lines with brief phrases or single words?
3. Think of a particular scene that stands out vividly in your memory, then make a list of words or short phrases that come to mind when you picture this scene. Choose just a few words or phrases from your list to describe your memory as concretely as possible. Try to limit the number of words, lines, or sentences you use so your writing will be concise and specific.

NOTE TO TEACHERS: This poem actually inspired the artist Charles Demuth to produce a painting he titled "The Figure 5 in Gold." You can find copies of this painting on the Internet or in a variety of art books likely to be available in your public library. Show the picture to your students and have them find elements in the picture that also appear in the poem, as well as any the artist might have added to create his own image of this fire truck. Discuss with your students how the poem and the picture are similar, different, or complementary.

Latin Night at the Pawnshop

Chelsea, Massachusetts
Christmas, 1987

Martín Espada

The apparition of a salsa band
gleaming in the Liberty Loan
pawnshop window:

Golden trumpet,
silver trombone,
congas, maracas, tambourine,
all with price tags dangling
like the city morgue ticket
on a dead man's toe.

Suggested Questions and Activities

1. Describe how your mental picture of this scene changed as you listened to the poem. Did your feelings change as well?
2. Why do you think the poet wrote the date, "Christmas, 1987," under the title? How does it affect your reaction to the poem?
3. Imagine you are the owner of one of those instruments. Tell us your story. Why did the instrument wind up in the pawn shop? Be creative; don't worry about connecting your story to any reality in your life.

Sample Lesson 2: Poems that Recall a Memory from Childhood.

Memories of childhood offer a plethora of images and feelings ripe for exploration and expression in poetry, especially when they are viewed from the perspective of an adult looking back. A writing lesson used in several of the Centers for Reading and Writing of the New York Public Library provides an excellent example of reading and writing poetry based on childhood memories. Using George Ella Lyon's poem "Where I'm From," from her collection *Where I'm From, Where Poems Come From,* teachers read Lyon's poem to students, discussed it with them, then helped students write their own poems describing where *they* were from. Below is the original poem by Lyon, followed by two poems written by students.

Additional note: The two student poems quoted below were published in *The Literacy Review,* an annual journal of writing of adult literacy students in New York City published by the Gallatin Writing Program, part of the Gallatin School of Individualized Study of New York University. In addition, some students from the Seward Park Center for Reading and Writing Program of the NYPL read their poems at a year-end gathering celebrating the school year, and their reading had a powerful effect on the audience which included city officials and others who had supported the program in various ways, including financially.

Where I'm From
George Ella Lyon

I am from clothespins,
from Clorox and carbon-tetrachloride,
I am from the dirt under the back porch.
(Black, glistening,
it tasted like beets.)
I am from the forsythia bush
the Dutch elm
whose long-gone limbs I remember
as if they were my own.

I'm from fudge and eyeglasses,
    from Imogene and Alafair.
I'm from the know-it-alls
    and the pass-it-ons,
from Perk up! And Pipe down!
I'm from He restoreth my soul
    with a cottonball lamb
    and ten verses I can say myself.

I'm from Artemus and Billie's Branch,
fried corn and strong coffee.
From the finger my grandfather lost
    to the auger,
the eye my father shut to keep his sight.

Under my bed was a dress box
spilling old pictures,
a sift of lost faces
to drift beneath my dreams.
I am from those moments—
snapped before I budded—
leaf-fall from the family tree.

I'm From Fu Zhou
Xiu Chen

I am from Fu Zhou.

I'm from a special, difficult and loud
language.

I'm from locally grown jasmine tea and rice
from water fields.

I'm from sweet potatoes and Wobian (a kind
of rice soup).

I'm from the sound of flip-flops on the muddy
road.

I'm from hide-n-seek and ghost stories under
a full starry sky.

I'm from eating, with the pig laying down
right under the table.

I'm from the neighbors gossiping and
working together outside in the summer
night.

I'm from a small, beautiful island belonging
to Fu Zhou.

I'm From the Lower East Side
Miguel Padilla

I am from the Lower East Side.
I'm from a stickball game.

I'm from hide and seek and kick the can, all
played in the street.

I'm from *pernil* and *arroz con pollo.*

I'm from saints' pictures on the bedroom wall.

I'm from the statue of Jesus wearing the
crown with blood coming down his cheeks.

I'm from the neighbors hanging out on the
stoop watching the people go by.

I'm from the Lower East Side and those
were the best years of my life.

Suggested Questions and Activities:

1. For each of these three poems, make a list of the strong images that
   really caught your attention, things you can see, hear, smell, or feel in
   your mind. Pick out phrases, too, that have a rhythm or sound that
   appeals to you. Then think back on where *you* are from and make a
   list of images that come to mind, including sights, sounds, smells, feelings, people, places, clothing, food, bits of conversations. Pick a few of
   those images and write your own poem describing where you are from.

Sample Lesson 3: Poems that convey a message.

As we said earlier, quoting the poet Edward Hirsch, a poem is like a
"message in a bottle," sent out by the poet to be found—and interpreted—by readers far and wide. Like a child leaving home, the poem
goes on to live a life of its own, connected to its creator, but sometimes
meaning different things to different readers. The two poems below are
from one of America's most well known poets, Robert Frost. Read them
and consider what they mean to you.

Nothing Gold Can Stay
Robert Frost

Nature's first green is gold,
Her hardest hue to hold.

Her early leaf's a flower;
But only so an hour.
Then leaf subsides to leaf.
So Eden sank to grief,
So dawn goes down to day.
Nothing gold can stay.

Suggested Questions and Activities

1. What does Frost mean by saying "Nature's first green is gold"?
2. When he says in the last line, "Nothing gold can stay," is he referring to a color or something else?
3. Notice that "Eden" is capitalized. What is it referring to?
4. What would you say is the "message" of this poem?
5. There are many sayings or aphorisms that use the word and concept of gold such as "All that glitters is not gold." Can you think of others? Do they agree with the message of this poem?

The Road Not Taken
Robert Frost

Two roads diverged in a yellow wood,
And sorry I could not travel both
And be one traveler, long I stood
And looked down one as far as I could
To where it bent in the undergrowth;

Then took the other, as just as fair,
And having perhaps the better claim,
Because it was grassy and wanted wear;
Though as for that the passing there
Had worn them really about the same,

And both that morning equally lay
In leaves no step had trodden black.
Oh, I kept the first for another day!
Yet knowing how way leads on to way,
I doubted if I should ever come back.

I shall be telling this with a sigh
Somewhere ages and ages hence:
Two roads diverged in a wood, and I—
I took the one less traveled by,
And that has made all the difference.

Suggested Questions and Activities

1. Frost says he "kept the first for another day!" Do you think he ever came back?
2. What do you think it means to take the road "less traveled"? Can you think of a time when you or someone you know chose such a path?
2. Think of a time in your life when you had to choose one path or direction over another, then write a story in which you imagine what would have happened if you had chosen "the road not taken."

A Note to Librarians

Look for ways to make your poetry collection attractive and accessible to literacy students and their teachers. Identify poetry anthologies from the adult and children's collections that will be appropriate for adults and label them to indicate their appeal to new readers. Train librarians who purchase poetry books, for adults and for children, to recognize collections that will appeal to adult new readers, then label them as appropriate for this audience. Collect books about teaching poetry and promote them among tutors and staff of the literacy program. Create bibliographies of poetry books suitable for new readers. Give book talks highlighting poetry books at local literacy programs. Seek funding through local and state arts organizations for poets-in-residence to offer writing workshops and public readings and invite students and tutors from the local literacy program. Create library programs to celebrate National Poetry Month (April) and, again, invite participants from the literacy program. Better yet, if at all possible, involve staff and students from the literacy program to help in the planning.

A Note to Literacy Teachers

With your students, explore the many faces of poetry. The bibliography that follows is just a starting point. Identify particular poets you like and find examples of their poems. Set aside time in every class or tutoring session, however brief, to read poetry to your students and encourage them to read poems they like to you. With your students, memorize poems and recite them to each other. Consult local librarians for assistance in finding anthologies suitable for adult students. As you and your students find poems or books that excite you, share this information with other students. Have your students write reviews of books or individual poems to share with other students and even with other literacy programs. Poetry readings are growing in number and popularity in many cities. Consider organizing a group outing to such an event in your area. Personalize the bibliography presented here by adding titles discovered by you and your students. Poetry is a rich source of words, ideas, and compelling images. Help your students discover and explore this resource to its fullest.

Poetry Books for Adult Literacy Students: A Bibliography

This bibliography is divided into two parts. The first part lists collections of poetry suitable for adult students in both ABLE and ESOL programs. Books listed in this section will come from both the adult and children's sections of the public library; each annotation notes the primary area where that title is most likely to be shelved, although different libraries will make different decisions about the appropriate location, and some titles may be shelved in both areas. Annotations also suggest reading levels and audiences, such as ABLE and/or ESOL, pre-GED, or GED, although the needs and interests of individual students should ultimately determine the suitability of a particular book for a particular student or class. Note, too, that many anthologies contain poems that span the range of difficulty from beginning to advanced. Finally, each title is assigned subject headings to describe the themes or topics discussed. General collections are given the subject heading "poetry, general anthologies." As with all the bibliographies in this book, this list merely skims the surface of possibilities. Use it as a starting point, then add other titles as you and your students explore the rich resource of poetry.

The second section of the bibliography suggests poetry books suitable for adults and children to share in family literacy programs.

Adoff, Arnold, ed. *I Am the Darker Brother: An Anthology of Modern Poems by African Americans.* Rev. ed. New York: Simon & Schuster, 1997.
First appearing in 1968 when very few collections of the poetry of black Americans were available, this newly revised edition includes all the masters found in the original such as Langston Hughes, Gwendolyn Brooks,

and Paul Lawrence Dunbar, and adds twenty-one poems from more recent voices, including Rita Dove, Maya Angelou, and Alice Walker. It remains an excellent introduction to the impassioned and lyrical works of black American poets speaking from their own particular experience about the universal struggle for justice and equality.

Beginning-advanced new reader/ABLE/ESOL/pre-GED/GED/children's collection.

Subjects: African Americans, civil rights, slavery.

Alvarez, Julia. ***Homecoming: New and Collected Poems.*** New York: Penguin, 1996.

Alvarez returns to memories of her life as a "housebound girl . . . to savor it, to celebrate it, but also to leave it." In poems about making beds, washing windows, and observing the women who populated her young life, she explores her relationship to her mother and the Dominican culture that nurtured her, even as she takes measures to construct her own life on a very different pattern. These poems are wonderfully direct and understandable, yet rich in the metaphors of everyday—especially female—life.

Intermediate-advanced new reader/ABLE/ESOL/pre-GED/adult collection.

Subjects: immigration, Latin America and the Caribbean, childhood memories, mothers, women.

Brenner, Barbara, ed. ***Voices: Poetry and Art from Around the World.*** Washington, D.C.: National Geographic Society, 2000.

True to the global interests of its publisher, this collection offers poems from six continents paired with folk art, historical artifacts, and photographs from the same region. Some of the artists are well known, but many more are folk artists or aboriginal people whose work has been preserved through the efforts of local cultural societies. As Brenner says in her introduction, she wanted the poetry and art together "to convey a distinct feeling of places and the people who live there" so readers could "put together the past and the present and see how geography and history shape each other." In classes with an international population, these poems will invite students to discuss and perhaps write about aspects of their own land and culture.

Beginning-advanced new reader/ABLE/ESOL/pre-GED/children's collection.

Subjects: art and literature collections, geography, international perspectives.

Burleigh, Robert. *Hoops.* Illustrated by Stephen T. Johnson. San Diego: Harcourt Brace, 1997.

> Hoops. The game. Feel it. That is the staccato style of this ode to basketball as played with intensity and spirit by young men on city streets.

Intermediate new reader/pre-GED/ESOL/children's collection.

Subjects: sports, urban life.

Cameron, Eileen. *Canyon.* Photographs by Michael Collier. New York: Mikaya, 2002.

> Over thousands of years, from the drops of snow that fall in the mountains to the river that courses through ancient rock, water has sculpted the magnificent Grand Canyon. In this stunning collaboration of poetry and the visual arts, Collier's sweeping photographs offer visual definitions for Cameron's simple yet richly descriptive poems that explain the timeless workings of nature. Introducing words like cascades, scours, and surges, the poems present opportunities for intriguing vocabulary lessons while the photographs offer an introduction to one of the American continent's geological wonders.

Intermediate-advanced new reader/pre-GED/GED/ESOL/children's collection.

Subjects: art and literature collections, geography, nature.

Clinton, Catherine, ed. *I, Too, Sing America: Three Centuries of African American Poetry.* Illustrated by Stephen Alcorn. Boston: Houghton Mifflin, 1998.

> By referring in her title to both Walt Whitman's famous poem, "I Hear America Singing," and Langston Hughes' response in his poem, "I, Too," Clinton seeks to include twenty-five African American poets among the distinguished voices who sing of the glory and remind us of the promise of their native land. An informative introduction to each poet provides biographical, historical, and literary background to enhance understanding of the poetry. The soft formality of the illustrations underscores the beauty as well as the essential value of these works to our ever evolving culture.

Intermediate-advanced new reader/ABLE/ESOL/pre-GED/GED/children's collection.

Subjects: African Americans, civil rights, slavery.

Clinton, Catherine, ed. *A Poem of Her Own: Voices of American Women Yesterday and Today.* Illustrated by Stephen Alcorn. New York: Harry N. Abrams, 2003.

Traveling chronologically from Anne Bradstreet, North America's first poet published in English, through the varied voices of successive centuries up to our own, these poems reflect women's perspectives on a range of developments, both historical and domestic. The span of time and breadth of topics explored underscore the significance of women's contribution to the physical, historical, and cultural growth of our nation. The paintings accompanying each poem are more interpretive than literal, extending each poem's reach and offering additional ideas for discussion. The introductions to each poem, which set the historical context of the writer and her work, and the brief biographies of every poet provided at the end, are especially helpful to teachers.

Intermediate new reader/ABLE/pre-GED/children's collection.
Subjects: American history and culture, women.

Ciuraru, Carmela, ed. ***Motherhood: Poems About Mothers.*** Series title: Everyman's Library Pocket Poets. New York: Alfred A. Knopf, 2005.

Thematic sections in this collection include mothers and daughters, mothers and sons, grandmothers, and other connections and issues. The books in this Everyman's series are easy to peruse and would be especially useful to teachers looking for poems on particular topics. Some other themes covered in the series are love poems, poems of the American West, prayers, poems of friendship.

Intermediate-advanced new reader/ABLE/ESOL/adult collection.
Subjects: grandparents, mothers.

Dawes, Kwame. ***I Saw Your Face.*** Illustrated by Tom Feelings. New York: Dial, 2005.

The drawings came first. Over many years, artist Tom Feelings had been drawing the faces of the African Diaspora, black people he encountered in his world-wide travels. Seeing these drawings, and remembering his own mother's belief that she could she something of the history of Africa in every black face, poet Dawes composed a poem to honor that history, a history of many journeys, voluntary and involuntary, of suffering, of resilience, and of pride. A map at the end will help readers locate the many places mentioned in the poem.

Beginning-intermediate new reader/ABLE/pre-GED/ESOL/children's collection.
Subjects: Africa, African American history and culture, picture books for all ages.

Ehrmann, Max. ***Desiderata: Words for Life.*** Photographs by Marc Tauss. New York: Scholastic, 2003.

> The inspirational words of this poem can be found framed on walls in numerous offices and homes all over the country and perhaps the world. In this book, the poem is presented in readable and meaningful phrases, matched by evocative photographs.

Intermediate new reader/ABLE/pre-GED/children's collection.
Subjects: religious and spiritual themes.

Frost, Robert. ***Birches.*** Illustrated by Ed Young. New York: Henry Holt, 1988.

> The illustrations depicting a young boy swinging on the long limb of a birch tree give visual definition to Robert Frost's somewhat complex poem in which the narrator remembers the carefree days of his boyhood while also contemplating the sometimes painful conflicts he faces as an adult. "Birches," written by one of America's most revered poets, is an example of the kind of poetry that appears on the GED test, and an illustrated version like this one is invaluable in helping pre-GED and GED students understand and interpret the metaphorical language found in much poetry.

Intermediate-advanced new reader/pre-GED/GED/children's collection.
Subjects: language, nature and the universe, picture books for all ages.

Giovanni, Nikki. ***Blues: For All the Changes.*** New York: William Morrow, 1999.

> Giovanni is a prolific writer whose work ranges from sentimental evocations of family to fierce denunciations of injustice as she sees it. The three titles listed here are representative of both her varied styles and her vast range of interests. *Blues* is a combination of poetry and rambling, prose-like rants on topics both personal and political. Giovanni can be blunt, playful, ironic, witty, or angry, yet she always conveys a sense of gratitude and joy at the vagaries and unexpected surprises life can bring.

Intermediate-advanced new reader/ABLE/pre-GED/GED/adult collection.
Subjects: African Americans, civil rights, families, love, women.

Giovanni, Nikki. ***Quilting the Black-Eyed Pea: Poems and Not Quite Poems.*** New York: HarperCollins, 2002.

> The poems and brief stories in this collection reflect both the world Giovanni knows and the world she hopes for. Her breezy style moves as easily from

the personal to the political as from joy to anger. While this makes her writing accessible to new readers, several poems include references to specific people and events, particularly related to African American history, that may require some background information or, better yet, inspire some additional research at the library.

Intermediate-advanced new reader/ABLE/pre-GED/GED/adult collection.
Subjects: African Americans, personal reflections.

Giovanni, Nikki, ed. ***Shimmy Shimmy Shimmy Like My Sister Kate: Looking at the Harlem Renaissance Through Poems.*** New York: Henry Holt, 1995.

With her selection of poems for this collection, Giovanni celebrates that flowering of literary creativity among African Americans that occurred during the first half of the twentieth century and has come to be known as the Harlem Renaissance. Following each poem, she offers brief but deeply personal reactions to the language, the ideas, or the feelings that make the poem special for her. The combination of the poems and her commentary make this book both a highly readable guide to understanding poetry and an introduction to an important moment in the political as well as the literary history of America.

Intermediate-advanced new reader/pre-GED/GED/ESOL/children's collection.
Subjects: African Americans, African American history and culture, American history and culture.

Gordon, Ruth, ed. ***Pierced by the Sun: Poems About the Times We Feel Alone.*** New York: HarperCollins, 1995.

Whatever our age, we all have times when we feel different, alone, abandoned, or in some way adrift from where we want to be. The poems in this collection address these times and feelings in a range of voices.

Intermediate-advanced new reader/pre-GED/GED/children's collection
Subjects: general anthologies, loss, poetry.

Greenberg, Jan, ed. ***Heart to Heart: New Poems Inspired by Twentieth-Century American Art.*** New York: Harry N. Abrams, 2001.

Greenberg invited several distinguished American poets to choose an American work of art from the twentieth century and write a poem in response to the art. Some poems recount stories evoked by the art work; others go inside the art to speak in the voices of the object or persons pictured. Some poems offer impressionistic word pictures, while others examine the effect of the artist's technique. This collaboration of the visual and language arts is both a beautiful book and an inspiring example of what Greenberg describes as the "power of art to inspire language," an example that should inspire many teachers and students to browse collections of art that will inspire their own language.

Intermediate-advanced new reader/pre-GED/GED/ESOL/children's and adult collections.

Subjects: art and literature collections, the arts and artists, general anthologies, language, poetry.

Gunning, Monica. *America, My New Home.* Illustrated by Ken Condon. Honesdale, Pa.: Boyds Mills, 2004.

In simple poems, Gunning recalls her childhood experience of leaving her quiet rural home on the island of Jamaica and learning to live in a crowded, noisy American city. Although missing the starlit nights of her native village, she is enthralled by the parks, libraries, and infectious energy of American city life. Immigrants of all backgrounds will relate to her story, and the basic simplicity of her poems may entice reluctant students to recall and write about memories of their own childhoods.

Intermediate new reader/ABLE/ESOL/children's collection.

Subjects: Childhood memories, immigrants and immigration, Latin America and the Caribbean, picture books for all ages.

Hughes, Langston. *The Block.* Illustrated by Romare Bearden. New York: Viking, with the Metropolitan Museum of Art, 1995.

Romare Bearden's collage "The Block," which hangs in the Metropolitan Museum of Art in New York City, depicts one block in the New York neighborhood of Harlem with all its exuberant life, both visible on the street and imagined behind curtained windows. In a style that is jazzy, colorful, and mysterious, the collage portrays the unparalleled artistic vibrancy that flourishes there, even amidst poverty and racial conflict. In this book, sections of Bearden's collage are matched with thirteen of Hughes's poems that give voice to the people who lived, worked, prayed, and played on the streets of this famous neighborhood. Although not created together, the poems and the collage echo and deepen each other's depiction of daytime life and nighttime dreams.

Intermediate-advanced new reader/ABLE/pre-GED/children's collection.
Subjects: African Americans, art and literature collections, urban life.

Hull, Robert, ed. ***Breaking Free: An Anthology of Human Rights Poetry.*** New York: Thomson Learning, 1994.

Poets from several countries write about political repression, imprisonment, slavery, and censorship, among other topics. Though the book was intended to alert young people to the need to be ever vigilant on behalf of freedom, the poems are a moving reminder to all readers, regardless of age, of our responsibility to speak out for the human rights for all peoples.
Intermediate-advanced new reader/ABLE/ESOL/pre-GED/GED/children's collection.
Subjects: civil rights, political repression and resistance, slavery.

I Imagine Angels: Poems and Prayers for Parents and Children. Illustrations from the Metropolitan Museum of Art. New York: The Metropolitan Museum of Art and Atheneum, 2000.

Poems, songs, prayers, and psalms from traditions around the world are accompanied by works of art that reflect diverse cultures as well as a range of styles and forms of artwork.
Beginning-advanced new reader/ABLE/pre-GED/GED/ESOL/children's collection.
Subjects: arts and crafts, art and literature collections, religious and spiritual themes.

Janeczko, Paul, ed. ***Blushing: Expressions of Love in Poems and Letters.*** New York: Orchard, 2004.

The masters are here—Shakespeare, Wordsworth, Dickinson—and so are contemporary names such as Angelou, Giovanni, and Merwin. In different styles and different voices, they speak of that essential but elusive element of human life called love.

Janeczko has edited numerous books of poetry aimed primarily at young adults but suitable for readers long past the teenage years and thus very useful for adult literacy students. He is also a poet himself and has produced volumes of his own work. Two examples, one for which he is editor and one for which he is author, are described below.

Intermediate-advanced new reader/pre-GED/GED/ESOL/children's collection.
Subjects: love, personal reflections.

Janeczko, Paul, ed. ***Looking for Your Name: A Collection of Contemporary Poems***. New York: Orchard, 1993.

Poems that address contemporary issues such as AIDS, gun control, and war and peace offer a range of perspectives on everyday life as it is lived in our modern world. As Janeczko says in his Introduction, he looked for poems that considered "all that is delicate or endangered."

Intermediate-advanced new reader/pre-GED/GED/ESOL/children's collection.
Subjects: poetry, general anthologies.

Janeczko, Paul. ***Worlds Afire***. Cambridge, Mass.: Candlewick, 2004.

Blurring the distinctions between poetry and prose, fiction and nonfiction, this book offers a series of poems written as fiction but describing a real event, a disastrous circus fire that occurred in Hartford, Connecticut, in 1944. The poems are written in the imagined voices of various people present at the event, including adult and child spectators, circus performers, and rescue workers. Some of them were survivors, some not. Janeczko has captured a terrifying moment of time from many perspectives, and although the event he describes occurred long ago, his poems may elicit intriguing discussions and subsequent writing exercises about frightening experiences and heart-wrenching decisions related to difficult events of more recent history.

Intermediate-advanced new reader/pre-GED/GED/children's collection.
Subjects: disasters, loss, personal reflections.

Johnson, Angela. ***The Other Side: Shorter Poems***. New York: Orchard, 1998.

In brief, proselike poems, Johnson describes Shorter, Alabama, a town about to be torn down to accommodate the building of a dog track. The poems affectionately, and somewhat wistfully, recall a town with little material prosperity but a strong sense of community and place.

Beginning-intermediate new reader/ABLE/ESOL/children's collection.
Subjects: childhood memories, rural life, the American South.

Johnson, Angela. *Running Back to Ludie*. Illustrated by Angelo. New York: Orchard, 2001.

> In engaging, insightful, free-verse poems, a teenage girl presents a series of vignettes describing her life. Some describe experiences typical of a girl her age. Others reveal the author's deep longing for Ludie, the mother who left her so many years ago and is now in prison. Although raised in a loving home with her father and aunt, the mother's absence is an obvious presence as this young girl copes with the many challenges of growing up.

Intermediate new reader/pre-GED/children's collection.

Subjects: families, loss, mothers, women.

Johnston, Tony. *The Ancestors are Singing*. Illustrated by Karen Barbour. New York: Farrar, Straus & Giroux, 2003.

> These poems both recall the past and look thoughtfully at present-day life in Mexico, while also hinting at the challenge of maintaining traditions while fostering prospects for growth and change in current realities. Although focused on Mexico, the underlying poignancy of straddling different worlds strikes a universal chord. A helpful glossary explains the Spanish words sprinkled throughout the poems.

Beginning-intermediate new reader/ABLE/ESOL/children's collection.

Subjects: ancestry, childhood memories, Latin America and the Caribbean, loss.

Lewis, J. Patrick. *Freedom Like Sunlight: Praisesongs for Black Americans*. Illustrated by John Thompson. Mankato, Minn.: Creative Editions, 2000.

> Lewis offers 13 poems to commemorate and celebrate the life work of famous African Americans in politics, sports, and the arts. Together with full-page illustrations, the relatively brief poems capture the essence of each subject's character as well as the value of his or her contributions. Brief biographies at the end of the book give additional information. Poetry is not often thought of as a means of conveying information, but these poems, along with the illustrations, do so in striking and memorable ways. Reading these poems may inspire students to write similar tributes to people they know or admire.

Intermediate-advanced new reader/ABLE/ESOL/pre-GED/children's collection.

Subjects: African Americans, American history and culture, the arts and artists, civil rights, sports.

Longfellow, Henry Wadsworth. ***Paul Revere's Ride: The Landlord's Tale.*** Illustrated by Charles Santore. New York: HarperCollins, 2003.

As Santore explains in his author's note, this "landlord's tale" was a bit of local folklore often recalled in the mid-1800s by men gathered around the fire at the Wayside Inn in Massachusetts. One of those men was the poet Henry Wadsworth Longfellow, and he included the story in a series of poems he published called *Tales of the Wayside Inn.* With its often quoted line, "One if by land, two if by sea," this classic of American literature is the kind of poem that could appear on a GED test but also in ads and other bits of popular culture. A book such as this offers an excellent way to introduce this famous poem to newcomers to America as well as students preparing for the GED. Echoing the poem's galloping rhythms, Santore's illustrations beautifully detail the action and thus help explain the events described.

Advanced new reader/ABLE/ESOL/GED/children's collection.

Subjects: American history and culture, picture books for all ages.

———————

Marsalis, Wynton. ***Jazz ABZ: An A to Z Collection of Jazz Portraits.*** Illustrated by Paul Rogers.

See annotation in Chapter 7.

———————

Martz, Sandra Haldeman, ed. ***Threads of Experience.*** Fabric and thread images by Diedre Scherer. Watsonville, Calif.: Papier-Mache, 1996.

Although classed as poetry, it is really the images that make this book unique. Using scraps of fabric and decorative stitching, Scherer creates portraits of elderly men and women that are stunning for their ingenuity as well as for the emotional depth they convey. The poems accompanying each image come from elderly writers reflecting on the people and places, joys and sorrows that have marked their journeys through life.

Martz has edited several books for this publisher in which ordinary people explore the meaning of everyday events through poetry and fiction. *If I Had a Hammer: Women's Work in Poetry, Fiction, and Photography* (1990) is a good example.

Intermediate-advanced new reader/ABLE/ESOL/pre-GED/adult collection.

Subjects: arts and crafts, art and literature collections, personal reflections.

———————

Meltzer, Milton. ***Hour of Freedom: American History in Poetry.*** Illustrated by Marc Nadel. Honesdale, Pa.: Boyds Mills, 2003.

In his Introduction, Meltzer says, "Rarely have historians opened their pages

to poets. Yet poets' sense of the past, as well as of the life around them, can do much to extend and deepen the range of our own experience." With this collection of poems, folk songs, spirituals, and anthems that sing about the events, people, and beliefs that have shaped American history from colonial days to the dawning of the twenty-first century, Meltzer clearly adds the poet's voice to our nation's story. This book would be an excellent supplement to any study of American history, whether as part of a pre-GED or GED class, a citizenship class, or a class of ESOL students interested in becoming familiar with some of the cultural artifacts of their new home.
Intermediate-advanced new reader/ABLE/ESOL/pre-GED/GED/citizenship class/ children's collection.
Subjects: American history and culture.

Myers, Walter Dean. *Angel to Angel: A Mother's Gift of Love.* New York: HarperCollins, 1998.
Having lost his own mother at the age of two, Myers grew up in the company of a variety of mother figures, and the concept of motherhood clearly fascinates him. In this collection, he pairs photographs of mothers and their children with poems addressing the many facets and configurations of motherhood. These deeply personal poems express feelings of loss, gratitude, admiration, and love.
Intermediate new reader/ABLE/ESOL/children's collection.
Subjects: African Americans, loss, mothers, personal reflections.

Myers, Walter Dean. *Blues Journey.* Illustrated by Christopher Myers. New York: Holiday House, 2003.
In an introductory note, Myers explains that the distinctly American musical form known as the blues derives from the "call and response" singing and five-note, or pentatonic, scale of African music. Using this musical pattern, these poems tell of the difficulties endured by blacks as they moved from rural life to city life in the late nineteenth and twentieth centuries. Myers's son Christopher's illustrations reflect both the melancholy and the hope found in the poems and the music they echo.
Beginning-intermediate new reader/ABLE/children's collection.
Subjects: African Americans, civil rights, music, picture books for all ages.

Myers, Walter Dean. *Harlem: A Poem.* Illustrated by Christopher Myers. New York: Scholastic, 1997.
In free verse that incorporates the rhythms of jazz and the blues, Myers's

poem offers a kind of syncopated survey of African American history as it evokes memories of his childhood home of Harlem, then weaves in references to Africa, to the American South, to civil rights leaders, and to black singers and artists. Christopher Myers illustrates his father's poem with rich but muted colors suggestive of summer nights and smoky night clubs. Given its many historical references, this illustrated poem would enrich any reading and discussion of books about the black experience in America.

Intermediate new reader/ABLE/pre-GED/GED/children's collection.

Subjects: African Americans, American history and culture, picture books for all ages, urban life.

Myers, Walter Dean. *Here in Harlem: Poems in Many Voices.* New York: Holiday House, 2004.

Writing in the fictional voices of the mail carrier, the maid, the jazz singer, and many other characters based on the real people who populated the Harlem of his youth, Myers re-creates the very character of the old neighborhood itself. The poems vary in style but are within reach of most intermediate and all advanced new readers and may inspire some students to re-create in writing some of the remembered characters of their own early days.

Intermediate-advanced new reader/ABLE/pre-GED/GED/children's collection.

Subjects: African Americans, urban life.

Nelson, Marilyn. *Carver: a Life in Poems.* Asheville, N.C.: Front Street, 2001.

An extraordinary idea beautifully executed, this book captures the basic facts, the essence of character, and the historical significance of George Washington Carver in a series of biographical poems. Born a slave in 1864 and raised by his mother's white mistress after his mother was kidnapped from the plantation, Carver developed an early and deep intellectual curiosity and attachment to the natural world. He eventually became a botanist and professor at Tuskegee Institute. Explanatory footnotes will help readers understand the details woven into these captivating poems that, in their beauty and originality, offer fitting tribute to a remarkable life. As a work of both literature and history, this book would be an excellent choice for a GED class.

Advanced new reader/pre-GED/GED/children's collection.

Subjects: African Americans, biography and memoirs, nature and the universe, slavery.

Nelson, Marilyn. *A Wreath for Emmett Till.* Illustrated by Philippe Lardy. Boston: Houghton Mifflin, 2005.

The wreath of the title is a series of fifteen interwoven sonnets in which the last line of one becomes the first line of the next. As she says in her introduction, Nelson used this highly structured form because "the strict form became a kind of insulation, a way of protecting myself from the intense pain of the subject matter." With searing emotion and powerful symbolism (all explained in notes), these poems tell the story of the young Till's brutal murder, his mother's decision to have him mourned in an open casket displaying the horror of his wounds for the world to see, and the outrage that fueled the fires of a burgeoning civil rights movement. An unforgettable account of a single horrific crime, the poems also speak to the brutalities and hatred we read about in today's headlines. This book would be an excellent choice for a GED or developmental reading class. The poem makes several allusions to other works of literature as well as historical events (all explained in the notes) which could become part of a broader discussion of issues raised in this work.

Advanced new reader/pre-GED/GED/children's collection.

Subjects: African Americans, American history and culture, civil rights.

Nye, Naomi Shihab, ed. *Is This Forever, or What?* Poems and Paintings from Texas. New York: Greenwillow, 2004.

The 140 poets and painters represented in this book are all from Texas, but the ideas and sentiments they express are not limited by the 2,842 miles of the Texas border. The poems cover many topics of adult interest, the pictures represent the variety of life and landscape you'd expect from a country-size state like Texas, and the combinations of words and pictures offer many perspectives for discussing what is stated and what is implied.

Nye is both a prolific poet herself as well as a collector of poetry, especially of poems that reflect her experiences as a native of Palestine who now lives in Texas but travels frequently to her homeland.

Advanced new reader/pre-GED/GED/children's collection.

Subjects: art and literature collections, general anthologies.

Nye, Naomi Shihab. *19 Varieties of Gazelle: Poems of the Middle East.* New York: Greenwillow, 2002.

In these poems, Nye, a native of Palestine, reflects on the experiences and conflicts, both physical and emotional, of living first in the Middle East

and then as an Arab American in the United States. The details are specific to her situation, but the balancing act of holding onto something precious from the past while assimilating into the present is a universal experience, even for those who've never left their homeland.
Advanced new reader/pre-GED/ESOL/GED/children's collection.
Subjects: Arab Americans, immigrants and immigration, the Middle East.

Nye, Naomi Shihab, ed. *The Space Between Our Footsteps: Poems and Paintings from the Middle East.* New York: Simon & Schuster, 1998.
The "Middle East" is a term we hear in the news almost every day, but familiarity with the term does not necessarily indicate knowledge or understanding of the place and its people. In calling for contributions of poetry and paintings for this collection, Nye acted on her belief, as she explains in the introduction, that "human beings *everywhere* hunger for deeper-than-headline news about one another. Poetry and art are some of the best ways this heartfelt "news" may be exchanged.
Intermediate-advanced new reader/pre-GED/GED/ESOL/adult collection.
Subjects: art and literature collections, the arts and artists, international perspectives, the Middle East, poetry, general anthologies.

Nye, Naomi Shihab, ed. *What Have You Lost? Poems.* Photographs by Michael Nye. New York: Greenwillow, 1999.
An international assembly of poets examines the experience of loss, both of mundane objects, such as keys and wallets, and the more profound losses of memory and the meaning of language.
Intermediate-advanced new reader/ABLE/ESOL/pre-GED/children's collection.
Subjects: loss, personal reflections.

Philip, Neil, ed. *Earth Always Endures: Native American Poems.* Photographs by Edward S. Curtis. New York: Viking, 1996.
The chants, prayers, and songs come from various Native American traditions, but they all share a belief in the oneness of creation. Black-and-white photographs reveal a depth of spirit in the people and a vastness of the places that Native Americans call home.
Beginning-advanced new reader/ABLE/pre-GED/ESOL/children's collection.
Subjects: Native Americans, religious and spiritual themes.

Philip, Neil, ed. *It's A Woman's World: A Century of Women's Voices in Poetry.* New York: Dutton, 2000.

These poems of love and marriage, of motherhood and sisterhood, of embracing nature and enduring political oppression, all share an underlying theme of newly found freedom to explore one's self in the wider world. Of course, such freedom is not universally available to all women, even in the twenty-first century, and that fact is remembered and lamented as well. Most of the poets are American, but women from Asian, African, European, and aboriginal cultures are also represented.

Intermediate-advanced new reader/ABLE/ESOL/pre-GED/children's collection.
Subjects: international perspectives, love, mothers, women.

Pinsky, Robert, and Maggie Dietz, eds. *Americans' Favorite Poems: The Favorite Poem Project.* New York: W.W. Norton, 2000.

This is a truly exceptional book, not just because of the wealth of beautiful poems it contains, but even more so because of the heartfelt and often illuminating introductions offered by the ordinary Americans who selected the poems as their favorites. The poems chosen are eclectic and rich—no greeting card sentimentality here. Reading the introductions, you find not an academic deconstruction but a real life experience in which one particular poem mattered deeply to one particular person. These personal testaments can serve as a model for students writing or expressing their own responses to the poems they read or hear.

Beginning-advanced new readers/ABLE/ESOL/pre-GED/GED/adult collection.
Subjects: poetry, general anthologies.

Pinsky, Robert, and Maggie Dietz, eds. *Poems to Read: A New Favorite Poem Project Anthology.* New York: W.W. Norton, 2002.

A second and similar volume of favorite poems, although this time the poems are arranged thematically. Most of the poems were submitted by the general public, along with their personal comments, but others have been chosen by the editors who wanted to create an anthology to "offer the reader ways to learn more about the satisfactions of poetry."

Beginning-advanced new readers/ABLE/ESOL/pre-GED/GED/adult collection.
Subjects: poetry, general anthologies.

Rochelle, Belinda, ed. ***Words with Wings: A Treasury of African-American Poetry and Art.*** New York: HarperCollins, 2001.

The poets and artists may come from different places, different times, or even different points of view, yet in the pairing of their poems and paintings, editor Rochelle has matched words and pictures that enhance and echo each other and say ever more strongly what each tries to say alone. And though the voices heard and characters depicted are African Americans, the messages are universal.

Beginning-intermediate new reader/ABLE/pre-GED/ESOL/children's collection.
Subjects: African American history and culture, art and literature collections, the arts and artists, inspirational stories and pictures.

Rosenberg, Liz, ed. ***Earth-Shattering Poems.*** New York: Henry Holt, 1998.

In her introduction, Rosenberg says she chose poems that "shook me," that speak "powerfully to our most intense experiences and emotions," eliciting strong reactions even when the meaning is not clear. Though the intended audience is teenagers, the poems she selected are just as appropriate and meaningful to adults.

Beginning-advanced new reader/ABLE/pre-GED/GED/children's collection.
Subject: poetry, general anthologies.

Rosenberg, Liz, ed. ***The Invisible Ladder: An Anthology of Contemporary Poems for Young Readers.*** New York: Henry Holt, 1996.

In a section suggesting ways to use this book with students, editor Rosenberg says, "A seemingly simple poem can have as many echoes in it as a voice shouted in a cavern." She has clearly chosen poems that verify that statement, poems that introduce readers to a wider world and a deeper way of thinking about that world. Although the audience she had in mind were children new to poetry, her goals as well as the poems she chose to accomplish them are highly appropriate for adult new readers as well. This book will be particularly helpful to teachers, offering biographical notes on each poet, comments on the poet's own view of his or her work, and suggestions for teaching that are easily adaptable to adult students.

Beginning-advanced new reader/ABLE/pre-GED/ESOL/children's collection.
Subjects: poetry, general anthologies.

Rosenberg, Liz, ed. ***Light-Gathering Poems.*** New York: Henry Holt, 2000.

A "sister book" to *Earth-Shattering Poems* described above, the poems collected here offer "a healing answer, poems that in one way or another turn toward the light." Whether that "light" be beauty, happiness, kindness, determination, or courage, whatever the need, the response is one of solace and healing.

Beginning-advanced new reader/ABLE/pre-GED/GED/children's collection.
Subjects: poetry, general anthologies.

Sanchez, Sonia. **Like the Singing Coming Off the Drums**. Boston: Beacon, 1998.

In poems that read like a kind of musical street talk, Sanchez explores the many faces of love: passionate, dreamy, vulnerable, hopeful.

Intermediate-advanced new reader/ABLE/ESOL/pre-GED/adult collection.
Subjects: love, personal reflections.

Stevens, Wallace. ***Wallace Stevens.*** Series title: Poetry for Young People. Edited by John Serio. Illustrated by Robert Gantt Steele. New York: Sterling, 2004.

Wallace Stevens led a dual life, working as a lawyer for an insurance company but always thinking of himself, essentially, as a poet. A keen observer of both nature and the intricacies of human life, his "poems paint pictures of life's secrets," as the book's introduction says, with meaning lurking just below the obvious, as it is in so much we see in nature and everyday life.

This publisher's series, Poetry for Young People, presents the works of some of America's most famous and influential poets and, despite the series label, the poems included in this and all the books were written for adults. In the case of Wallace Stevens, the poems are quite sophisticated—the kind of poetry, in fact, likely to be found in the literature section of the GED. The presentation of each poem will be helpful to teachers, as it offers brief introductions to set the context and suggests possible meanings while leaving room for each reader's personal interpretation. Difficult vocabulary is also explained in notes on the same page. In some circumstances literacy teachers may decide that the appearance of the books in this series is not sufficiently "adult," but the content definitely is. Books on Walt Whitman and William Carlos Williams, also from this series, are discussed below.

Advanced new reader/pre-GED/GED/children's collection.
Subjects: the arts and artists, poetry, general anthologies.

Tadjo, Veronique, ed. ***Talking Drums: A Selection of Poems from Africa South of the Sahara.*** Illustrations by Veronique Tadjo. New York and London: Bloomsbury, 2000.

Both editor and illustrator of this stunning book, Tadjo says in her introduction that "the selection of poems is in fact a story, the story of Africa as told by some of its very best poets." Some of these stories have been handed down through the centuries via Africa's vibrant oral tradition while others chronicle the struggles of contemporary African states. Some reflect a spiritual life derived from close observance of nature while others express the anguish of a continent rife with dictatorship and civil war. Employing rhythm and repetitive chant, and accompanied by simple line drawings of African motifs, many of the poems will be accessible even to beginners; they will also be of particular interest to students newly arrived from Africa. A map, glossary, and list of poets by country add to the informational value of this delightful book.

Beginning-intermediate new reader/ABLE/ESOL/pre-GED/children's collection.
Subjects: Africa, civil rights, cultural divisions, picture books for all ages, political repression, political resistance.

Vecchione, Patrice. ***Truth and Lies: An Anthology of Poems.*** New York: Henry Holt, 2001.

As Vecchione says in her introduction, "Poetry is a particular way of telling the truth," and for this anthology, she has chosen poems that tell the truth, but in words and ways that "wake a reader up." The poems address a range of issues from the personal to the political, some in language accessible even to beginners and others that will challenge more advanced students.

Beginning-advanced new reader/ABLE/pre-GED/GED/children's collection.
Subjects: poetry, general anthologies.

Weatherford, Carole Boston. ***Remember the Bridge: Poems for a People.*** New York: Philomel, 2002.

The bridge of the title is a metaphor for the connections African Americans want to strengthen between the land their ancestors came from in chains and the history of their descendants down through the centuries to the current day. Many of the poems recall historical events from the days of slave trading and plantations; others chronicle the continuing struggle for civil rights, sometimes with reference to specific characters such as Rosa Parks or Jesse Owens; and still others laud the work of ordinary citizens who forge new roads into contemporary American society, building more and better bridges for coming generations.

Intermediate-advanced new reader/ABLE/pre-GED/GED/children's collection.

Subjects: Africa, African Americans, American history and culture, civil rights.

Whitman, Walt. *Walt Whitman.* Series title: Poetry for Young People. Edited by Jonathan Levin. Illustrated by Jim Burke. New York: Sterling, 1997.

A five-page introductory biography and brief notes framing each poem in its context offer an excellent introduction to one of America's most influential poets. From his celebratory "I Hear America Singing" to his lament for Lincoln in "Oh Captain! My Captain!" to poems chronicling his work with the wounded of the Civil War, this collection gives readers a sense of the expansive and soul-searching nature of this much studied poet.

See entry under Stevens for notes about other titles in this series.

Intermediate-advanced new reader/ABLE/pre-GED/GED/children's collection.

Subjects: American history and culture; poetry, general anthologies.

Williams, William Carlos. *William Carlos Williams.* Series title: Poetry for Young People. Edited by Christopher MacGowan. Illustrated by Robert Crockett. New York: Sterling, 2003.

By day he was the family doctor in Rutherford, New Jersey, but by night, when he wasn't delivering babies or making emergency house calls, this prize-winning poet was likely to be off to New York City and the company of other writers and artists with whom he loved to discuss the latest developments in the world of art. Much of the inspiration for his own art, however, came from those people he saw every day in his office and on the streets of Rutherford. Williams' poetry is accessible but also surprising in its inventiveness and far reaching in its depth of understanding of human nature.

See entries under Stevens and Wallace for notes about other titles in this series.

Intermediate-advanced new reader/ABLE/pre-GED/GED/children's collection.

Subjects: the arts and artists, poetry, general anthologies.

Zalben, Jane Breskin. ***Let There Be Light: Poems and Prayers for Repairing the World.*** New York: Dutton, 2002.

Drawing from traditions of Buddhism, Christianity, Islam, Judaism, Taoism, and Native American and African cultures, Zalben has gathered poems and prayers that speak to the unity of the human spirit and or responsibility to work for a better world to bequeath to future generations. Her illustrations reflect the diversity of cultures from which she draws her uplifting words.

Beginning-intermediate new reader/ABLE/ESOL/children's collection.

Subjects: poetry, general anthologies; religious and spiritual themes.

Poetry—Family Literacy

Asch, Frank. ***Cactus Poems.*** Photographs by Ted Levin. San Diego: Harcourt Brace, 1998.

This collaboration of words and pictures explores the wonder, beauty, and astonishing variety of life in the desert. Levin's photographs take you "up close and personal" with lizards, bobcats, cacti, rock formations, and more, while his brief informational notes help readers understand Asch's evocative poems.

Intermediate new reader/ABLE/pre-GED/ESOL/children's collection.

Subjects: animals, family literacy, nature and the universe.

Asch, Frank. ***Song of the North.*** Photographs by Ted Levin. San Diego: Harcourt Brace, 1999.

With song-like rhythm and repetition, this book-length poem introduces readers to the creatures of the north: the salmon, the puffin, the caribou, and more. Each verse tells us what the animals know, then asks us to consider what we know about the animals. The photographs offer many opportunities for describing pictures as well as considering the questions the simple text suggests.

Beginning-intermediate new reader/ABLE/pre-GED/ESOL/children's collection.

Subjects: animals, family literacy, nature and the universe.

Borden, Louise. *America Is* . . . Illustrated by Stacey Schuett. New York: Simon and Schuster, 2002.

Each page offers a new completion to the sentence beginning "America is . . . " The flag, farmers plowing the land, bustling cities, and other scenes show an America unified in its diversity.

Beginning-intermediate new reader/ABLE/pre-GED/ESOL/children's collection.

Subjects: American history and culture, family literacy.

Bruchac, Joseph. *The Circle of Thanks: Native American Poems and Songs of Thanksgiving*. Illustrated by Murv Jacob. Mahwah, N.J.: BridgeWater, 1996.

A descendant of the Abenaki tribe of American Indians, Bruchac has gathered poems and songs of thangsgiving from many Native American cultures and traditions, all reflecting a oneness with the natural world. The paintings of illustrator Jacob, himself a Cherokee descendant, use the colors and symbols of the various tribes to echo that perspective.

Intermediate new reader/ABLE/pre-GED/ESOL/children's collection.

Subjects: art and literature collections, cultural traditions, Native Americans.

Burleigh, Robert. *Langston's Train Ride*. Illustrated by Leonard Jenkins. New York: Orchard, 2004.

While riding the train from Ohio to Mexico to visit his father, a young Langston Hughes, mesmerized by the Mississippi at sunset and the rhythmic clacking of the wheels, was inspired to write one of his simplest but most poignant and well known poems, "The Negro Speaks of Rivers." This picture book imagines that train ride as it introduces young readers to this important poet and poem.

Intermediate new reader/ABLE/pre-GED/ESOL/children's collection.

Subjects: African Americans, African American history and culture, family literacy.

Clark, Ann Nolan. *In My Mother's House*. Illustrated by Velino Herrara. New York: Puffin, 1992.

Originally published in 1941, the poems in this book were written by the young Tewa Indian children living on the reservation where Clark worked as a teacher. This new edition combines the poems with illustrations that echo their simple grace and sense of the wholeness of life as the children knew it.

Beginning-intermediate new reader/ABLE/pre-GED/ESOL/children's collection.
Subjects: family literacy, Native Americans, rural life.

Dotlich, Rebecca Kai. *Over in the Pink House: New Jump Rope Rhymes.* Illustrated by Melanie Hall. Honesdale, Pa.: Boyds Mills, 2004.

The wonderful sing-song rhythm and repetitious patterns of jump rope rhymes makes them easy to read and inviting to read aloud. This is a particularly colorful and engaging collection, but most libraries will have several examples.

Beginning-intermediate new reader/ABLE/pre-GED/ESOL/children's collection.
Subjects: family literacy, language, urban life.

English, Karen. *Speak to Me (And I Will Listen Between the Lines).* Illustrated by Amy June Bates. New York: Farrar, Straus & Giroux, 2004.

In simple poems, 6 children describe their experiences throughout the school day. But underneath the surface of the daily routine, the students' words betray individual concerns, about the new baby at home, about wanting a best friend, and other typical childhood worries. This book actually models an excellent approach to talking with children in a way that encourages real discussion.

Beginning-intermediate new reader/ABLE/pre-GED/ESOL/children's collection.
Subjects: families, family literacy.

Fletcher, Ralph. *A Writing Kind of Day: Poems for Young Poets.* Illustrated by April Ward. Honesdale, Pa.: Boyds Mills, 2005.

As much a book about writing poetry as it is a book of poems, this is an excellent tool for teaching poetry to both children and adults in a family literacy program. Fletcher essentially teaches about poetry by offering numerous poems as examples, some that will appeal to children and some that will appeal to adults. Want to write about something in your everyday environment? Here are some examples. Want to learn how to use similes or metaphors well? Here are some examples. Fletcher knows poetry, and he knows how to teach.

Intermediate new reader/ABLE/pre-GED/children's collection.
Subjects: family literacy, language, writing.

Frost, Robert. *The Runaway*. Illustrated by Glenna Lang. Boston: David R. Godine, 1998.

In what could be interpreted as a story of parental care, Frost's poem tells the story of a runaway colt who becomes lost and bewildered by his first encounter with snow, then is led back home by another horse. Is that horse the mother? We aren't told, but in deciphering the meaning of Frost's words, with the help of Lang's illustrations, students will likely come to many discussions about a parent's—or a society's—responsibility to its children.

Several of Frost's poems have been reproduced as illustrated picture books. *Stopping by Woods on a Snowy Evening*, illustrated by Susan Jeffers, is a good example.

Intermediate-advanced new reader/pre-GED/GED/children's collection.
Subjects: families, family literacy.

Giovanni, Nikki. *The Genie in the Jar*. Illustrated by Chris Raschka. New York: Henry Holt, 1996.

Giovanni dedicated this book to the singer Nina Simone, and Raschka listened to Simone's recordings while creating the illustrations to accompany Giovanni's poem. Together, words and pictures convey the message that the best way a young girl can learn to sing her own song is from within the loving and nurturing embrace of family and community. Simple, but profound.

Beginning new reader/ABLE/ESOL/children's collection.
Subjects: African Americans, the arts and artists, families, family literacy.

Giovanni, Nikki. *The Sun is So Quiet*. Illustrated by Ashley Bryan. New York: Henry Holt, 1996.

Sweet and funny poems about winter, snow, the sun, and rainbows are easy and comforting for parents to share with children.

Beginning-intermediate new reader/ABLE/children's collection.
Subjects: family literacy, nature and the universe.

Greenfield, Eloise. *In the Land of Words: New and Selected Poems*. Illustrated by Jan Spivey Gilchrist. New York: HarperCollins, 2004.

Greenfield has collected some poems and written others that describe how memory, observation, and imagination feed poetry. She invites readers to follow her lead and write poems of their own, making this book an excellent source for building writing skills in a family literacy program.

Beginning-intermediate new reader/ABLE/pre-GED/children's collection.
Subjects: family literacy, writing.

Hoberman, Mary Ann. *You Read to Me, I'll Read to You: Very Short Stories to Read Together*. Boston: Little, Brown, 2001.
Like a verbal seesaw, this book presents easy rhyming verse for two readers—one adult and one child—on opposite sides of a page, with a few lines in the middle for both to read together. Comical illustrations echo the playful poems.
Beginning new reader/ABLE/ESOL/children's collection.
Subjects: families, family literacy.

Hooper, Patricia. *Where Do You Sleep Little One?* Illustrated by John Winch. New York: Holiday House, 2001.
In simple verse accompanied by vivid yet soothing illustrations, Hooper asks a succession of animals—the mouse, the deer, the rabbit, etc.—where they sleep. The pattern of each verse is the same, offering assistance to inexperienced readers, but the vocabulary varies for each animal, offering a vocabulary lesson as well as ideas about sleep that parents and children might enjoy discussing.
Beginning-intermediate new reader/ABLE/pre-GED/ESOL/children's collection.
Subjects: animals, family literacy, parents and children.

Hopkins, Lee Bennett, ed. *Oh, No! Where Are My Pants and Other Disasters: Poems*. Illustrations by Wolf Erlbruch. New York: HarperCollins, 2005.
The title bespeaks a humorous tone, but there are serious notes as well in these poems discussing experiences that are difficult for children: a friend moving away, making mistakes in school, losing a pet. These poems make the laughter and the sadness easy to share.
Beginning-intermediate new reader/ABLE/pre-GED/ESOL/children's collection.
Subjects: families, family literacy.

Hopkins, Lee Bennett, ed. *Wonderful Words: Poems About Reading, Writing, Speaking, and Listening*. Illustrated by Karen Barbour. New York: Simon & Schuster, 2004.
What better way to explain the idea of metaphor than to introduce Eve Merriam's poem, "Metaphor," which begins, "Morning is/a new sheet of

paper/for you to write on." All the poems in this inspired collection are about words, the beauty, utility, fun, and mystery of words that travel with us every day as we journey through familiar tasks and explore the world around us.

Intermediate new reader/ABLE/pre-GED/ESOL/children's collection.

Subjects: family literacy, language, writing.

Hudson, Wade, and Cheryl Hudson, eds. *How Sweet the Sound: African-American Songs for Children.* Illustrated by Floyd Cooper. New York: Scholastic, 1995.

Traditional chants, spirituals, popular blues and jazz tunes, and even protest songs are reproduced here with illustrations from award-winning artist Cooper. Many of the songs will be familiar, especially to African American students, making the reading easier. More than just a collection of songs, this book includes brief histories of all the songs and their composers, providing some history of African Americans in the process. Musical notations are included.

Beginning-advanced new reader/ABLE/pre-GED/children's collection.

Subjects: African American history and culture, family literacy, music.

Hughes, Langston. *Carol of the Brown King.* Illustrated by Ashley Bryan. New York: Atheneum, 1998.

This collaboration of two masters of their art joins six poems of Langston Hughes with Ashley Bryan's vibrant illustrations of an African American perspective on the Christian nativity story and its "brown" king.

Beginning-intermediate new reader/ABLE/pre-GED/ESOL/children's collection.

Subjects: family literacy, religious and spiritual themes.

Hughes, Langston. *The Sweet and Sour Animal Book.* Illustrated by students from the Harlem School of the Arts. New York: Oxford University Press, 1994.

In this newly discovered alphabet book, Hughes gives us rhyming poems for each animal that are clever and whimsical yet manage to convey some essential quality of the animal described as well as hint at similarities to the human condition. It is particularly fitting that the book is illustrated by the students of the Harlem School of the Arts, an arts school that has become an integral part of the community where Hughes himself found so much inspiration for his life's work.

Intermediate new reader/pre-GED/children's collection.
Subjects: African American artists, animals, the arts and artists, family literacy.

In Daddy's Arms I Am Tall: African Americans Celebrating Fathers. Illustrated by Javaka Steptoe. New York: Lee & Low, 1997.

Steptoe's strikingly imaginative collages add layers of color, interest, and meaning to his collection of tributes to fathers by several African American poets.

Beginning-intermediate new reader/ABLE/pre/GED/ESOL/children's collection.
Subjects: African Americans, families, family literacy, fathers.

Kay, Verla. ***Broken Feather***. Illustrated by Stephen Alcorn. New York: G.P. Putnam, 2002.

Broken Feather is a Native American boy growing into manhood as white settlers of a young and growing United States are moving west and claiming land. Kay tells his story in spare, simple verse, yet she conveys much information about the life of the Nez Perce Indians, a life they had to abandon as they were forced onto a reservation in Idaho. Alcorn's woodblock prints, infused with a rainbow of colors, add both informational and emotional import to the story. Two brief afterwords offer instructional background on the history of the Nez Perce and on the process of relief block prints that Alcorn used for the illustrations.

Beginning-intermediate new reader/ABLE/pre-GED/ESOL/children's collection.
Subjects: American history and culture, family literacy, Native Americans.

Lawrence, Jacob. ***Harriet and the Promised Land***. New York: Simon & Schuster, 1993.

With vivid colors and dramatic lines and shapes, Lawrence conveys the physical, spiritual, and emotional power of the amazing accomplishments of the woman called the Moses of her people. The simple verse accompanying the drawings tells the story of Harriet Tubman, a slave, who escaped to freedom and then returned to the South 19 times to lead others on the perilous journey North.

Beginning new reader/ABLE/ESOL/children's collection.
Subjects: African American history and culture, the arts and artists, civil rights, family literacy, slavery.

Let's Count the Raindrops. Illustrated by Fumi Kosaka. New York: Viking, 2001.
Short, simple poems, many employing rhyme, rhythm, and repetition, are matched by simple and endearing illustrations, making this collection particularly appealing to beginning level parents, both ABLE and ESOL, in a family literacy program.
Beginning new reader/ABLE/ESOL/children's collection.
Subjects: family literacy; poetry, general anthologies.

Merriam, Eve. *Spooky ABC*. Illustrated by Lane Smith. New York: Simon & Schuster, 2002.
With its simple rhyming verse and appropriately sinister, but fun, illustrations, this alphabet book offers an introduction to the language and customs of this particular holiday.
Beginning new reader/ABLE/ESOL/children's collection.
Subjects: cultural traditions, family literacy, language.

Micklos, John, Jr., ed. *Daddy Poems*. Illustrated by Robert Casilla. Honesdale, Pa: Wordsong, Boyds Mills, 2000.
The title says it all for this collection of playful and poignant poems by and about fathers.
Beginning-intermediate/ABLE/ESOL/children's collection.
Subjects: family literacy, fathers.

Moore, Lilian. *Mural on Second Avenue: And Other City Poems*. Illustrated by Roma Karas. Cambridge, Mass.: Candlewick Press, 2005.
From winter through fall and from day into night, Moore describes "small moments in the big city" that make us stop and look at familiar details with new insight. The illustrations are childlike, but the poems are adult in tone and, though not difficult, offer many words for both ABLE and ESOL students to add to their vocabulary lists.
Beginning-intermediate new reader/ABLE/ESOL/children's collection.
Subjects: family literacy, urban life.

Mora, Pat. *Confetti: Poems for Children*. Illustrated by Enrique O. Sanchez. New York: Lee & Low, 1996.
In a series of rhyming rhythmic poems, Mora celebrates the landscape and culture of the American Southwest. A sprinkling of Spanish words and colors reflective of that landscape add to the regional flavor.

Beginning-intermediate new reader/ABLE/pre-GED/ESOL/children's collection.
Subjects: family literacy, poetry, general anthologies.

Navasky, Bruno. ***Festival in My Heart: Poems by Japanese Children***. New York: Harry N. Abrams, 1993.

> The simple poems were written by children. The illustrations are Japanese works of art: ink and scroll paintings, woodblock prints, textiles, and folded paper. Together, they offer a slightly unfamiliar perspective that helps us see something new in nature and in ourselves.

Beginning new reader/ABLE/ESOL/children's collection.
Subjects: art and literature collections, the arts and artists, collections, family literacy, international perspective.

National Museum of the American Indian, Smithsonian Institution. ***When the Rain Stops: Poems by Young Native Americans***. New York: Simon & Schuster, 1999.

> Young Native Americans were shown images of art works and artifacts from the National Museum of the American Indian, then asked to write poems in response. Many of those art works are pictured in this book, paired with poems that directly or indirectly relate. The pairing of pictures and poems will spark lively discussions, as well as suggest ways that students might respond to the artifacts of their own environment.

Beginning-intermediate new reader/ABLE/pre-GED/ESOL/children's collection.
Subjects: art and literature, collections, family literacy, Native Americans, theatre and artists.

Shange, Ntozake. ***Ellington Was Not a Street***. Illustrated by Kadir Nelson. New York: Simon & Schuster, 2000.

> As a young girl growing up, Shange knew men who "changed the world," African American leaders who came to her father's house to visit, to party, and to discuss their political situation. Paul Robeson, W.E.B. DuBois, and Dizzy Gillespie are among the figures introduced in this reflective poem and beautifully portrayed in Nelson's illustrations. More than a poem, this picture book serves to introduce students, whether African American or not, to some of the major figures of American history and culture of the twentieth century. Additional biographical information appears at the end.

Intermediate new reader/ABLE/pre-GED/ESOL/children's collection.
Subjects: African American history and culture, African Americans, American history and culture, family literacy.

Weatherford, Carole Boston. *Sidewalk Chalk: Poems of the City*. Illustrated by Dimitrea Tokunbo. Honesdale, Pa.: Boyds Mills, 2001.

Corner restaurants, barbershops, a market, a church, and sidewalk games are among the subjects of the breezy rhyming poems in this family-oriented collection.

Beginning-intermediate new reader/ABLE/pre-GED/children's collection.
Subjects: family literacy, urban life.

———————————

Yolen, Jane, ed. *Sky Scape/City Scape: Poems of City Life*. Illustrations by Ken Condon. Honesdale, Pa.: Honesdale, 1996.

Parks, fire escapes, subways, pigeons, playgrounds and the noise, jumble, cacophony, and excitement of city life are reflected in the poems Yolen selected as well as in Condon's brightly colored illustrations.

Beginning-intermediate new reader/ABLE/ESOL/children's collection.
Subjects: family literacy, urban life.

———————————

Chapter 6

Literature: Sharing the
Stories of the Human Family

"Their story, yours, mine—it's what we all carry with us on this trip we take, and we owe it to each other to respect our stories and learn from them."—William Carlos Williams

Lessons for the Literacy Classroom

The Power of Stories

We all crave stories. Stories tell us who we are as individuals and as members of families, social groups, and nations. Children the world over are instinctively drawn to the fairy tales and legends of their culture, because these stories address the many fears and questions that children have but cannot articulate: the fear of losing a parent and one's secure place in the world, the desire to exercise power over the darker elements of life, the need to explore the world beyond the boundaries of home while being reassured of a safe return when the exploration goes too far. The sacred stories of the ancient Hebrews in the Old Testament, the parables of Jesus in the New Testament, and the stories of the Qu'ran and other religious texts guide our spiritual and moral journey through life.

In ancient times, when literacy was rare, poets and storytellers, such as the Greek poet Homer and the griots of Africa, recited long and complex tales that recounted the stories and legends of their ancestors. Using rhyme, meter, repetitive verse, and recurring images to aid their memory as well as paint a vivid picture for their audiences, these early historians did more than tell riveting stories about their cultural heroes; they used their oral traditions to pass on the communal history of their people. As audiences listened to captivating tales of war and greed, friendship and heroism, they came to understand themselves as individuals with similar strengths and weaknesses, wants and needs, as well as members of a larger human community.

Those ancient stories continue to cast their spell, even in our technologically advanced twenty-first century world. In recent years, Homer's *The Odyssey* was a major television production, and the story Homer told in *The Iliad* was retold in the popular movie *Troy*. In the 1970s, writer Alex Haley introduced us to the African griots, whose stories, passed down orally to many generations, inspired his creation of *Roots,* an account of many generations of slaves traced into the twentieth century. Haley's book, and the television series it inspired, made "genealogy" a household word and sent millions of people of all backgrounds in search of their family stories. And consider for a moment the work of William Shakespeare. He may have been born in England in 1564 and died there in 1616, but it really isn't too much of a stretch to count him among the major screenwriters of modern day-Hollywood. Whether it's a traditional adaptation of one of his plays, such as Kenneth Branagh's *Hamlet,* or a humorous but fictional perspective of a love-struck Shakespeare with writer's block, as portrayed in the film *Shakespeare in Love,* or a modern-day reprise of the fiery Kate from *The Taming of the Shrew,* recast as the teenager Kate in the popular movie comedy *Ten Things I Hate About You,* Shakespeare's stories still captivate audiences. Classic authors such as Homer, Shakespeare, Jane Austen, Charles Dickens, and others live on in their books, and even more readily in our modern age in movies and television programs, because, regardless of the context of their settings, they tell stories that matter to us as human beings, stories about love and loss, about war and greed, about friendship and hero-ism, about joy and grief, and ultimately about the transitory nature of life.

Even as the ancients remain with us, their modern-day descendants con-tinue in their footsteps, creating new and clever ways of telling the stories that reflect the context of contemporary life. We find today's descendants of Homer and the African griots in blues, folk, and rap singers who use those same rhe-torical devices of meter, rhyme, and repetition to tell personal as well as com-munal stories. We find our continuing need for stories reflected in the rise and popularity of the novel, a story form which serves a literate and mobile society, and in the transference of many of those stories into movies and television programs.

Although the rise of literacy, the ease of printing, and the recent develop-ment of personal technologies such as DVD players allow us to read these stories, or increasingly to watch them, in isolation, the sharing of stories re-mains a fundamentally communal act. Book clubs of all varieties abound in communities across the nation and even on television. The book club spon-sored by talk show host Oprah Winfrey claims millions of viewers and un-precedented power to affect book sales. The technology of our age may be light years away from that of the ancient Greeks listening in the open air to a master storyteller, but the enduring need of the human spirit to share stories continues to shape our lives and help us understand who and where and what we are as individuals and as members of communities large and small, local and global.

What Literature Offers Adult Literacy Students

" . . . Coke bottles were the best because they had a shape like a body. You could tell the bottom from the top." That is how Hattie, a literacy student with whom I once worked, described the dolls she and her sister fashioned out of Coke bottles and whatever other bits of material they had available to them. Having grown up in the rural South, Hattie knew poverty, discrimination, and despair, as well as the hope born of close family and religious ties. In a small group tutoring session, I had read Cynthia Rylant's *When I Was Young in the Mountains* (see Sample Lesson 1 in this chapter) to the students and then asked them to write about a particular memory from their own childhoods. Hattie's vividly detailed and amusing story about making dolls out of Coke bottles delighted the other students, and it reminded me of the stories I had read in Maya Angelou's classic memoir of growing up black in the rural South, *I Know Why the Caged Bird Sings.* When I told Hattie my reaction, I was startled to realize that she had never heard of Maya Angelou. It seemed no less than a tragedy to me that Hattie—and so many others like her—might never enjoy the thrill of reading about experiences so similar to her own written by a writer whose language captivates readers and carries them along on a fascinating journey through the mind and heart of another human being.

It is the literature of any culture that tells its stories, and while it is true that selected stories are easily told to us as movies and television programs, it is equally true that the great wealth of stories exists in written form, waiting to be brought alive, time and time again, to individuals who relive them through the pleasure and power of reading. Whether they are fiction, folk tales, memoirs, biographies, or true-life accounts, they are the stories of our collective human family and the stories that we as librarians and literacy teachers want to make available to Hattie and all those other students who, for whatever reasons of birthplace, economic disadvantage, or family circumstance, have been denied access to them by their lack of literacy.

But how can we do this? Aren't most of the stories that we consider literature too difficult for literacy students to read? Certainly many are, but just as certainly many are not. Indeed, in most public libraries you will find a surprising number and variety of books that will be accessible to adult students with limited reading ability and even more books that can be made accessible to our students with the assistance of classroom teachers or individual tutors.

What the Library Offers: Literature for Adult Literacy Students
The public library is literally a house of stories, the preeminent keeper of the myriad manifestations of the human story. Looking at a typical library's extensive collection of stories with the varied audiences and ability ranges of literacy students in mind, we will find many books, both fiction and nonfiction, that are accessible or can be made accessible to our students. Let's look at a few examples.

Fiction
When we think of stories, we usually think of fiction, so let's begin by considering titles in that category. Although many works of fiction will be beyond the range of most adult literacy students, there are exceptions to this generali-

zation. Sandra Cisneros's *House on Mango Street,* with its short chapters and vivid images of a Latino family, is one example of a novel written for a general audience but well within the range of many intermediate and advanced level literacy students. Genre books, including romance novels and mystery stories, are often written to a formula that helps readers follow the thread of a story and maintain interest from one chapter to the next. Most public libraries have large collections of these books, and many will be within reach of some intermediate and most advanced new readers. Consider, too, the many book to movie combinations that may attract literacy students' interest in a particular book and offer them the opportunity to compare the visual representation with the original written version. A good example is Ernest Gaines's novel *A Lesson Before Dying,* a story which would be accessible to advanced new readers in its print form, but available to a wider audience in its movie version.

Although you might expect books labeled "young adult" or "juvenile" fiction to contain little of interest to adults, the fact is that many of these books present characters and situations that will appeal to adults. The term "juvenile" is a bit of library jargon used to designate fiction for elementary and middle grade students, thus distinguishing it from the young adult fiction that is geared toward students in high school. Obviously many of the books in these sections will focus on the particular problems of pre-teens and teens and thus will not interest adults. However, there are many titles within these categories that transcend age limitations and appeal to readers of all generations. These "crossover" titles feature strong adult characters in situations and contexts that adults will find familiar and intriguing. In Cynthia Voigt's *Dicey's Song,* for example, the narrator is a sixteen-year-old girl, but the story is about building a family where none had existed, and the central character is really the strong-willed and independent grandmother who comes to realize, in adopting her four orphaned grandchildren, that she has given herself a second chance at experiencing a family's love. Other books found in the children's section of the library examine the complexities of family life within a particular time in history, as does Mildred Taylor's *Roll of Thunder Hear My Cry,* the saga of a family of black farmers living through the trials of the Great Depression under the added burden of racial tension in rural Mississippi. This chronicle of the Logan family continues in *Let the Circle Be Unbroken,* where readers can follow the younger generation as they grow into adulthood. In yet another example, Karen Hesse's *Out of the Dust* presents a lyrical and poignant evocation in verse of living through the personal and economic hardships of losing a parent and surviving the Dust Bowl. Though the narrators in all three of these books are young persons, the stories told, the burdens borne, and the wisdom discovered are themes that will resonate with adult readers, sometimes even more so than with the young people to whom the books are marketed.

Fiction as Audio Books

The books mentioned above are also available as audio books, adding the dimension of listening to a well told story read by an accomplished actor and reader to the overall reading experience. Indeed, most libraries have large collections of audio books on tape and, increasingly, CD. Literacy teachers might consider bringing an audio book to class to play segments in each class session, with ongoing discussions about what was heard and what might be expected. Using audio books could be particularly helpful in ESOL classes as they offer the students opportunities to practice both listening and speaking skills. In addition, listening to books set in the context of important social movements, as *Roll of Thunder Hear My Cry* and *Out of the Dust* are, offers ESOL students a kind of story-window through which to view and perhaps better understand important aspects of American history and culture.

From a family literacy perspective, librarians can recommend many audio books with family themes that raise issues of importance to parents and their children. Some of these books might not appeal to adult students listening on their own; and some titles address difficult topics such as racist attitudes or the death of a parent that might be confusing or upsetting to children listening alone. As a shared, family reading experience, however, the characters and situations of these stories become part of a common reference that parents and children share, offering wonderful opportunities for discussing important issues that may be particularly relevant to a child's or family's own experience. Such discussions are often made easier when the context is moved outside immediate personal circumstances.

Biographies and Memoirs

Not all literature is fiction. As Anne Lundin says in her chapter advocating readers' advisory services for young adults, "Literature—whether fiction or fact—allows readers to try on alternative values, other ways of thinking, feeling and being in the world." (Lundin, 1993) Though Lundin was thinking of teenagers and their pressing need for self-identification, the fact remains that our search for ourselves continues throughout our lives and the stories told in works of nonfiction offer many opportunities for adults to experience "other ways of thinking, feeling and being in the world."

Biographies and memoirs tell stories from the lives of real people, famous and unknown, living and dead. We need only think of the popularity of TV talk shows and celebrity features on TV and in magazines to recognize how much we love to tell stories about our own lives as well as hear the stories about the lives of others. In the literary world, too, personal memoirs are a popular genre. While many of these books will be beyond most of our students, some are within range of advanced new readers and many are available in audio format and thus accessible to a wider audience. Some have even been made into movies, offering students opportunities to match the filmmaker's visual presentation with the author's verbal one. Frank McCourt's *Angela's Ashes,* an evocation of his desperately poor childhood in Limerick, Ireland, told through a series of often amusing and sometimes haunting stories, is one good example. McCourt reads the audio book himself, adding his accent and palpable emotional involvement with the characters and events, as well as a master storyteller's sense of timing, to the reader's experience of the story. Readers—or listeners—of his book will carry mental images from his stories long after they've read or heard the last page, so comparing their personal pictures of McCourt's Limerick family with the filmmaker's version could lead to a lively discussion.

Looking to the children's collection once again, you can find a wonderful source of biographies and memoirs that will appeal to adult new readers. Many books found there will be relatively brief and written in an informative, matter-of-fact tone of voice not obviously directed at children. Many such books emphasize the adult life of the subject and often contain photographs and other illustrations that add interest as well as information. An excellent example is *Through My Eyes,* Ruby Bridges's own account of her experience as a lone six-year-old black girl escorted to a previously all-white school in the company of federal marshals. In this book, Bridges recalls the events surrounding her entrance into her new school and discusses how that experience shaped her adult life. Biographies of historical figures, sports figures, and popular figures from contemporary culture abound in the children's collection, and many of them will appeal to adults. Two such books, Tonya Bolden's *The Champ: The Story of Muhammad Ali* and Sharon Bell Mathis's *Ray Charles,* explore the lives of two men whose importance to American cultural history was underscored by recent critically and popularly acclaimed movies.

Collections

A somewhat vaguely defined but important category of books that offer engaging stories that will appeal to adult new readers could be loosely labeled "collections." Collections may include short stories, letters, essays, newspaper columns, and poems among other kinds of writing. Most importantly from the perspective of teachers working with adult literacy students, these collections often include writings of varying length and difficulty from a short poem or song lyric to an extended oral history, thus offering selections that will appeal to and be within reach of students of widely varying ability. Consider, for example, *Listen Here: Women Writing in Appalachia,* Sandra Ballard and Patricia Hudson's collection of poems, memoirs, essays, and oral histories depicting real lives defined by the geography of hills and hollows as well as the rich tradition of music and oral history found in the often isolated region of Appalachia. Such a book can inspire students to mine the rich traditions of their own culture for topics to write about and share in their classes. A world away from the hills of Appalachia, an ever changing cast of characters is depicted in Randy Kennedy's book *Subwayland: Adventures in the World Beneath New York*. Kennedy traveled the more than 600 miles of New York City subway lines on assignment from the *New York Times,* and in his notes from the underground, which appeared as occasional columns in the newspaper, he gives readers snapshots of moments in ordinary lives that reveal some recognizable truth of our common human experience, whether we have ever been on a subway or not.

Collections Written for and by Adult New Readers
Although the bibliographies throughout the chapters focus on books available in the library's general collection, it is important to mention the many brief but topical and well written stories marketed particularly for the adult new reader audience. New Readers Press, a division of ProLiteracy Worldwide, is perhaps the preeminent publisher of materials for the ABLE and ESOL audiences. They produce practice books for the GED and for citizenship tests, books that address life skills and workplace issues, and a popular weekly newspaper, *News for You,* that covers current topics in the news. They also publish several story collections under the heading "Hi-Lo Readers," including series of Westerns, romance novels, and general fiction. Two other series published by New Readers Press are of particular note. The first is their Writers' Voices series which offers new readers a rich and varied introduction to the world of literature by featuring slim paperback books containing excerpted but unedited selections from the works of well known writers such as Maya Angelou, Rudolfo Anaya, and Stephen King. The second is their New Writers' Voices series which features the writings of adult literacy students themselves, and includes fiction, poetry, and real-life adventures. Globe Fearon is another publisher of numerous books written specifically for the new reader audience, including the works of Tana Reiff, perhaps the most prolific and well known author of novellas based on realistic life situations and aimed at adult learners and new

immigrants. Many public libraries will have books from New Readers Press, Globe Fearon, and other publishers shelved in special collections for adult literacy students. One other slightly different but intriguing venture in this publishing market that may be less available in local libraries but worth pursuing via the Internet is the Open Door series from New Island, an Irish publisher. For this series, the publisher has engaged popular and acclaimed authors from Ireland and England to write original stories for the new reader audience, using simplified sentence structure but language, setting, and plot that will appeal to adults. For American audiences, the settings and some vocabulary may be a bit unfamiliar, but given that the writers are masters of the storytelling art, the extra effort of obtaining and reading these stories promises to be well worth the effort.

There are also abridged and modified versions of many works of fiction which attempt to simplify the original and make the story available to a wider audience, but I would urge caution in using them. It is a rare feat when an abridged version of a book doesn't remove some sustaining essence of a story along with words and paragraphs. Better to find an audio version of the whole book than settle for a reduced version of the printed text.

Picture Books for All Ages

Returning once again to the children's collection, we find another important source of stories for adult new readers, an extraordinary collection of picture books that are truly "for all ages." Many of these books will appeal to adults of all reading levels as well as all ages, often even more than the children they are written for. I've often felt that people who have no particular reason to become familiar with books in the children's section of a library or bookstore are really missing out on some wonderful stories, not to mention extraordinary artwork. For example, many picture books published for children these days are actually brief but beautifully told and illustrated memoirs of the author's childhood, such as Louise Erdrich's recollection of life on the Turtle Mountain Reservation in North Dakota, *The Eternal Range.* Others are stories about famous people or incidents from history such as Nikki Giovanni's *Rosa,* a retelling of the day Rosa Parks decided to say "no" when asked to give up her seat on a bus to a white person. Still others present important concepts, such as racial tolerance, in the context of a simple but profound story, as bell hooks does in *Skin Again.*

Cynthia Rylant, a popular and prolific author of books for children and young adults, notes that many of her picture books are based on stories from her own life or the lives of people she has known. She says, further, that she chooses the picture book format "because that medium gives me a chance to capture in a brief space what I consider life's profound experiences." Although her books are written for the children's market, she says, "I write a picture book that speaks to any person, any age." (Rylant, 1988) The picture books suggested in the bibliography of this chapter give evidence to the truth of Rylant's words. For adult literacy students, moreover, these picture books offer something even more because they are models of brief but effective storytelling and good, concise writing that the students can learn from and emulate. See the sample lessons based on Cynthia Rylant's *When I Was Young in the Mountains* and Louise Erdrich's *The Range Eternal* suggested below.

Picture Books for Family Literacy

Of course picture books are essential to any family literacy program. Picture books delight young children as they introduce them to the magic of the written word and the pleasure of sharing stories in the comfort and security of a parent's lap. The bibliography at the end of this chapter includes a sampling from the thousands of picture books available at the local public library.

Using Literature in the Literacy Classroom

Once we begin to identify works of literature that will appeal to adult literacy students, how can we help the students read them? An answer lies in examining four practices found in elementary school reading programs and adapting them to adult literacy programs: reading aloud to students, assisted reading, literature-based approaches to reading instruction, and whole language.

Teaching Tips

Reading aloud to students.

Both research and common experience show that reading aloud to young children greatly enhances their initial reading success as well as the possibility they will grow into eager and mature readers. Reading aloud to children immerses them in the language of the written word and teaches them to use context, illustrations, and their own imaginations to understand the story even if they don't recognize all the words. Reading aloud also stimulates discussions about the events, characters, and language of the stories, as well as personal experiences, memories, and deeply rooted feelings that the story evokes. The same principles apply when reading aloud to adult literacy students. Listening to a story engages the students' intellects as well as their imaginations and frees them of the anxiety of figuring out words, enabling them to concentrate on characters, events, and meaning. Once a story has been shared between a tutor and student or within a class, there exists a common base of knowledge on which to build discussions, vocabulary lessons, writing lessons, and other activities that offer students opportunities to share their understanding of a story via the written word.

Assisted reading.

Assisted reading is an important and useful technique to help students advance beyond reading their own language experience stories or the simple sentences found in exercise books to reading more challenging materials. It also helps students develop fluency, an important factor in successful reading, as we discussed in Chapter 3. This method works best in a one-to-one tutoring situation, but can be used with small groups as well and perhaps even some classroom groupings. Choose a text of interest to your student and within range of, or even slightly above, his reading ability. With your student following along the page, read a passage aloud, emphasizing meaningful phrases and pointing to words as you go. When the student feels comfortable, ask him to join in by reading the words he knows and skipping over the ones he's not sure of. You keep reading at the pace and rhythm established. Like a partner following the lead of a more experienced dancer, the student will become more comfortable and more fluent with subsequent readings.

Literature-based reading programs.

In recent years, many elementary school reading programs have begun to incorporate works of children's literature into the curriculum, either as substitutes for traditional basal readers or as supplements to those readers and other skill-building aspects of the curriculum. Basal readers generally contain stories written with a strictly controlled vocabulary, intended to teach children to read certain words. In contrast, works of children's literature are written to tell a captivating story or convey information in a manner that makes the story or the information primary rather than the individual words used. With discussions before and after reading to review potentially difficult vocabulary or explain context, teachers guide students to look for meaningful elements of a story that are revealed in such things as details in a setting that set a mood, or descriptions of characters that indicate personality, or tone of voice in the dialogue that conveys something beyond the words.

Whole language.

The whole language concept of teaching reading recognizes that learning to read is just one aspect of learning to use language; it cannot be separated from the other language skills of listening, speaking, writing, and ultimately, thinking. In elementary classrooms where literature and whole language prevail, teachers not only engage the children in listening to an interesting story, they also create opportunities to involve them in the many language activities that connect the words on the page to the children's own attempts to express themselves. For example, a teacher might read Eric Carle's *The Hungry Caterpillar*, a picture book that lists all the foods a hungry caterpillar eats before turning into a butterfly, then ask students to create a class list of all the things they ate for breakfast that morning or have them cut out pictures of food items from newspapers or magazines to label and display around the classroom. Teachers employing a whole language approach use literature as the starting point, then involve the students in a variety of language-related activities: discussing the characters, events, and language of the stories; drawing pictures suggested by the story; imaging themselves in similar circumstances; writing sentences and stories of their own; creating language experience stories as a class; investigating the lives and other books of favorite authors; and acting out scenes from the stories. In other words, teachers involve students in the intellectual activities of discussing, analyzing, comparing, applying, and evaluating a story, skills they will eventually apply to words they read and write on their own.

Adult literacy teachers and tutors can easily adapt and incorporate these four practices into their classes and tutoring sessions. By introducing books from the public library that encourage and enhance the use of techniques such as reading aloud, assisted reading, literature-based curricula, and whole language, they will create opportunities for students to experience an inspired response to the written word and to learn to read from stories that teach more than words, stories that have something important to say about who we are and how we live our lives.

Sample Lessons

Sample Lesson 1: Using a Picture Book Memoir

The Audience
Beginning new readers; ABLE/ESOL

The Book

Rylant, Cynthia. *When I Was Young in the Mountains*. Illustrated by Diane Goode. New York: E.P. Dutton, 1992.
Introducing each memory with the rhythmic title phrase, Rylant recalls the days of her youth spent with her grandparents in Appalachian West

---

Virginia. It is a lyrical portrait of that life as seen through the eyes of a child and spoken through the experienced heart of an adult.

Suggestions for Teachers

If possible, have multiple copies of the book available so each student can follow along as you read the book aloud. Tell them that the book consists of a series of vignettes, or incidents, that the writer vividly recalls from her childhood. Show them the illustrations in the book to help them visualize the story. After you've read the story, begin a discussion by asking the students questions such as the following:

Sample Questions for Discussion

1. Describe your mental pictures of the events Rylant describes. What words and phrases help you "see" these events.
2. How does the author feel about the events and people she is describing? What words tell you this?
3. What do you think of the illustrations? Do they match the feelings conveyed by the words? What do they add to the story?

Suggestions for a Writing Exercise

Write the phrase "When I was young . . . " on paper or a classroom black- or whiteboard. Ask students to complete the phrase with words that describe their own childhoods such as "When I was young in the city," or "When I was young in Africa." Then have them write—or dictate if they are beginners—a list of sentences, all beginning with the same phrase and all describing a specific vignette or incidence from their childhoods. Encourage them to include details that will help readers of their stories picture the events they are describing.

Sample Lesson 2: Using a Picture Book Memoir.

The Audience

Intermediate new readers; ABLE/pre-GED/ESOL

The Book

Erdrich, Louise. *The Range Eternal.* Illustrated by Steve Johnson and Lou Fancher. New York: Hyperion, 2002.

Amid the efficiency and convenience of her modern kitchen, the narrator of this story recalls the old wood-burning stove that warmed her childhood home, cooked the food that nourished her body, and created the dreamy fires that fueled her imagination. Finding a similar stove in an antique shop, she brings it home to add that "center of true warmth" and continuity with the past that no modern appliance can provide. Erdrich based this story on her own memories of the wood-burning stove in her grandmother's house on the Turtle Mountain Reservation in North Dakota.

Suggestions for Teachers

If possible, have multiple copies of the book available. Read the book aloud to your student or a small group. After the initial reading and some discussion, read the book again with the students, using assisted reading if appropriate. Explain that the phrase "The Range Eternal" is actually the brand name of the stove. After you've read the story, begin a discussion by asking the students questions such as the following:

Sample Questions for Discussion

1. Thinking back on this story, are there particular words, phrases, or pictures that come immediately to mind?
2. Have you ever gotten rid of something you thought old or no longer important, then regretted doing so? Tell us about it.
3. If you had to define a "center of true warmth" in your home, either now or some time in the past, what would it be?
4. "The Range Eternal" is the name of the stove. What other meanings does the word "range" or the phrase "range eternal" have in this story?

Suggestions for a Writing Exercise

With your students, read the first paragraph of this story, using the assisted reading technique if appropriate:

"On cold winter days in the Turtle Mountains, I helped Mama cook soup on our woodstove, The Range Eternal. Bones went into the pot, for flavor, then potatoes and carrots. As I cut the onions, I held a kitchen match between my teeth. I still don't know why, but the match stopped my tears." (Erdich, 2002)

Ask students to note all the specific things mentioned in this paragraph: the season, the stove, the vegetables, etc. Discuss with them how these details make the paragraph easy to picture, even without the illustration from the book. Then ask them to think of a memory they would like to write about. Ask them to make a list of particular details of their memory, then write their story, using as many details as possible from their list. In a small group or class setting, have students share their writing so fellow students can respond to the specific details they heard or suggest details they would like to hear to help them "see" the memory being described.

Sample Lesson 3: Using a Picture Book Biography

The Audience

Intermediate new readers; ABLE/pre-GED/ESOL

The Book

Giovanni, Nikki. *Rosa.* Illustrated by Bryan Collier. New York: Henry Holt, 2005.

On a fateful day in December, 1955, a bus driver demanded that Rosa Parks give up her seat for a white person, and then threatened to call the police when she didn't. But Rosa stayed in her seat and said simpy, "Do what you must." Coinciding, as it happened, with the emerging leadership of a new minister in town named Martin Luther King, Jr., her simple act of civil disobedience led to a boycott by blacks of all the buses in Montgomery, Alabama, and a pivotal event in the burgeoning civil rights movement that would hasten the end of "separate but equal" laws began.

Suggestions for Teachers

1. This exercise would work best in a one-to-one or small group setting. If possible, have multiple copies of the book available so each student has a copy. First, ask students if they have heard of Rosa Parks. If they have not, briefly explain the situation that brought her to prominence. Then look through the book with the students. Ask them to comment on the illustrations. Encourage them to look at small details. What are people wearing? What are they doing? What do the students read in the people's facial expressions?

2. Depending on the number of students and their abilities, you can approach the reading in several ways. You might read the book aloud to them, stopping after each section to review what they've understood; you might use the assisted reading technique and have the students read along with you; or you might ask students to read each section silently, and then discuss what they've read. As you go through the book, make a list of vocabulary words students are unsure of or words they have difficulty reading.

3. Pick out some particular facts that are mentioned and ask students to find the text that explains them. For example, ask them why Rosa said, "those elves in the North Pole have nothing on us." Or ask them why Rosa paid her fare and then got off the bus.

4. Ask the students some questions that go deeper than the printed text. For example, How was Rosa treated by her supervisor and coworkers? How was she viewed by other blacks in her community?

5. Many other books have been written about Rosa Parks and the Montgomery bus boycott that resulted after she was arrested for refusing to relinquish her seat. Two in particular that would be interesting for students to compare with *Rosa* are *I Am Rosa Parks,* a simple telling of her story written by Parks herself and intended for elementary school children, and *Rosa Parks, My Story,* written by Parks in conjunction with author Jim Haskins and intended for middle and high school students. Ask students to compare the photographs in the Parks/Haskins book with the illustrations in Giovanni's book. Ask them to compare specific details such as Rosa Parks's own statement about why she decided not to leave her seat and the explanation given by author Giovanni in *Rosa.*

6. Giovanni mentions other events related to the struggle for civil rights, such as the murder of Emmett Till and the Brown vs. Board of Edu-

cation Supreme Court decision outlawing segregation in public schools. There will be many books in the library describing these events, as well as Internet sites that students could find. Depending on your students' abilities and interests, bring other books to the class or tutoring session which will provide some background information about the events mentioned in *Rosa,* or plan a field trip to the library so the librarian can help students find other sources of information, including Internet sites. Remember, too, that the library will have video and audio documentaries related to these events.

Suggestions for Writing Exercises

1. Ask students if they have ever made a decision that had unexpected repercussions, whether positive or negative. Ask them to write about the event and its aftermath or dictate the information for a language experience story.
2. Ask them to imagine that they were passengers on that bus. What would they have felt about Rosa Parks's act of disobedience, about the disruption it caused, about the bus driver's position? Would they have stayed on the bus or gotten off?

A Note to Librarians

Consider the many forms of literature in the library's collection that may be accessible to adult new readers: collections of short works such as letters, newspaper columns, and short stories; memoirs of people who are well known or who have prevailed over adversity and tell their story in a readable narrative style; biographies from the children's collection whose subjects and presentation will appeal to adults; picture books that tell stories and appeal to readers of all ages; young adult fiction that will appeal to adults; and adult fiction that is relatively easy to read, including genre fiction such as romance novels. Visit literacy programs to give book talks about titles you've selected. Work with literacy teachers to create local bibliographies of books of interest to literacy students. Ask the students to contribute reviews of books they've read either in class or on their own. When mounting displays to promote books on a particular topic or theme, include titles that will appeal to a range of patrons, including literacy students. Feature displays of audio books that tell family stories or books that have been made into popular movies. Sponsor author visits and invite students and teachers from the local literacy program. In conjunction with the local literacy program, organize book discussion groups for new readers. Sponsor oral history projects in your community and invite new readers as well as the general public to contribute interesting stories about the history of a neighborhood, a particular immigrant group, or any other appropriate topic. In these and other ways of your own creation, promote the public library as the preeminent keeper of the stories of the human family made available to all.

A Note to Literacy Teachers

Incorporate read-aloud segments into your class or tutoring sessions as much as possible, either by reading short pieces followed by discussion within class or by reading segments of larger works at the end of each session with ongoing discussions about reactions to what was read and expectations of what might be coming. Encourage your students to write about the stories of their own lives and the stories they see around them, including those they see on television. Consult with your local librarian to find titles from the young adult collection that would appeal to adult students. Invite librarians to give book talks to students in your literacy programs and ask them to suggest audio books that students might share with their families as well as books that the students themselves might want to read. Work with your local library and other community agencies to sponsor oral history projects encouraging residents to tell their stories. Together with the other agencies, collect the stories and create books that can be distributed to other literacy programs and libraries. In every way you can, remind students that books tell stories that enrich our lives and connect us to those who have gone before as well as to those who will follow in the paths we are creating.

Literature Books for Adult Literacy Students: A Bibliography

This bibliography is just a sampling of books containing stories that will be accessible to adult literacy students and available at the public library. Local librarians will be able to suggest many others. The bibliography is divided into five sections: fiction, biographies and memoirs, collections, picture books for all ages, and stories for family literacy programs. Titles listed under fiction that are also available as audio books will have the subject heading "audio book." As for books recommended for family literacy programs, there are obviously thousands of books appropriate for such a setting. The few titles listed here suggest some of the topics dealt with in picture books that adults will enjoy discussing with their children. Each annotation suggests subject headings, reading levels, and potential audiences and also indicates whether a book is most likely to be found in the children's or adult section of a typical library. Keep in mind that for fiction titles, some libraries separate books appropriate for young adults—usually labeled "YA"—from those books labeled "J" and suggested for younger readers. Since such designations may vary from one library to the next, I've indicated the location as the "children's collection" in all annotations for books not specifically adult books, even those that might be found in a "YA" section. Check with your local library to determine how they separate their fiction titles.

Fiction (Note: Titles available in audio format will have the subject heading "audio book.")

Cisneros, Sandra. *The House on Mango Street.* New York: Random House, 1989.
In a series of brief, imagistic vignettes, Cisneros tells the story of a young girl growing up in a Latino neighborhood in Chicago, facing the hard realities of life but maintaining an indomitable spirit. Each short chapter stands alone as a story and can be read aloud and discussed in one class session. (In fact one chapter of this book, *Hairs = Pelitos,* has been published separately as a children's picture book.) Although Cisneros's evocative, lyrical writing may present some difficulties to new readers, the literal meaning of her stories will be clear, and her poetic use of images and metaphors will stretch and challenge more able readers.
Intermediate-advanced new reader/ABLE/pre-GED/GED/ESOL/adult collection/ children's collection.
Subjects: audio book, fiction, Latinos.

Coman, Carolyn. *What Jamie Saw.* New York: Puffin, 1997.
What Jamie saw is something no one wants a child to see: his stepfather throwing his baby sister across a room. Luckily his mother catches the baby and in that moment understands what she must do to "catch" herself and her children before falling into the dark hole of an abusive relationship. Through Jamie's eyes, we watch as he and his mother find the courage, confidence, and help they need to escape the predictable dangers of the past for an uncertain, difficult but ultimately more hopeful future. Listening to the audio book as a family, adults will relate to the conflicts and decisions that Patty, Jamie's mother, must make. Children will recognize Jamie's fears and bewilderment, but also be inspired by his hope.
Intermediate-advanced new readers/pre-GED/GED/children's collection.
Subjects: audio book, families, fiction.

Curtis, Christopher Paul. *The Watsons Go To Birmingham—1963*. New York: Delacorte, 1996.

The "Weird Watsons" include Momma and Daddy, little sister Joetta, thirteen-year-old and almost an "official juvenile delinquent" Byron, and ten-year-old Kenny, the narrator. At first an affectionate and often humorous portrait of a closely knit black family, complete with incidents of sibling rivalry, bullying, and teenage rebelliousness, the story turns serious when Momma and Daddy decide that Byron needs to spend some time with his strict Southern grandmother who lives in Birmingham, Alabama. As the whole family prepares for the drive down south, they must consider the conditions that prevail in 1963, particularly the fact that restaurants, gas stations, and even bathrooms may not be available to them once they cross that invisible but consequential boundary into the American South of that era. The story takes an even more dramatic turn when this fictional family is placed in the vicinity of the real bombing of an Alabama church that killed four little girls. As young Kenny and Byron search for their sister, temporarily missing, readers know that their understanding of the world they live in has been forever changed.

LeVar Burton offers a masterful reading in the audio book.

Intermediate-advanced new reader/pre-GED/GED/children's collection.

Subjects: African American history and culture, the American South, audio book, families, fiction.

———————

Delacre, Lulu. *Salsa Stories*. New York: Scholastic, 2000.

At a New Year's holiday dinner, a friend gives young Carmen Teresa a blank notebook. As she considers what to put in her notebook, relatives around the table begin telling stories from their childhoods, memories all sparked by some kind of food. Carmen Teresa decides to use her notebook to collect the recipes for these dishes which come from several different locations throughout Latin America.

These simple stories are brief enough to be read aloud in one class or tutoring session and provide a good example to spark student writing about the foods—or anything else—of their childhood homes.

Intermediate-advanced new reader/pre-GED/GED/ESOL/children's collection.

Subjects: childhood memories, cultural traditions, family, fiction, food and cooking, Latin America and the Caribbean.

———————

DeSpain, Pleasant. *The Emerald Lizard: Fifteen Latin American Tales to Tell in English and Spanish.* Translated by Mario Lamo-Jimenez. Illustrated by Don Bell. Little Rock, Ark.: August House, 1999.

> For over 30 years, DeSpain has been collecting folk tales, myths, and legends representing the Native American, European, and African influences of Latin American culture. For this book he offers stories from fifteen countries and presents them in both English and Spanish versions. All are brief enough for reading aloud and discussing within one class session. Spanish-speaking students may enjoy discussing subtle differences in meaning or tone between the two language versions.

Intermediate-advanced new reader/pre-GED/GED/ESOL/adult collection.
Subjects: fiction, Latin America and the Caribbean, story collections.

Ellis, Deborah. *The Breadwinner.* New York: Scholastic, 2000.

> Ever since the Taliban hauled her father off to prison, eleven-year-old Parvana has been the family breadwinner, since she is the only member of her now all-female household old enough to go to the marketplace alone but young enough to disguise herself as a boy. In a society that forbids women to travel outside their homes unless accompanied by a male relative, Parvana finds the courage and the ingenuity to sustain life for herself and her family. Based on stories she heard from Afghan women in refugee camps, this novel contains references to horrific violence, yet speaks to the strength of the human spirit to overcome and survive.

Intermediate-advanced new reader/pre-GED/GED/ESOL/children's collection.
Subjects: Asia, audio book, family, fiction, political repression and resistance, women.

English, Karen. *Francie.* New York: Farrar, Straus & Giroux, 1999.

> Told in the voice of Francie, a quiet yet determined black girl living in Alabama in the 1930s, this story subtly conveys the complexity of life for African Americans in that time and place. Free and equal by law, but not by community standards, they worked hard to build opportunities for themselves and their children while being careful not to appear too ambitious in the eyes of the powers that wanted to keep them in their place.

Advanced new reader/pre-GED/GED/children's collection.
Subjects: African American history and culture, the American South, audio book, economic and social conditions, fiction.

Fleischman, Paul. *Seedfolks.* Illustrations by Judy Pedersen. New York: HarperCollins, 1997.

It begins with a young Vietnamese girl who decides to honor her dead father by planting bean seeds in a trash-filled vacant lot. Gradually, twelve others, some young and some old, some longtime residents and some newly arrived immigrants, all living in close proximity in this blighted Cleveland neighborhood but unknown to each other, begin to do the same thing. By the time harvest season comes around, something beautiful has happened to the lot and to a community of people who are no longer strangers. Each person is a chapter in this slim volume, telling his or her individual story, a story that becomes part of a modern American city's urban tapestry. For the audio book edition, different actors read each part, complete with accents, in this simple but profound statement about possibility and hope.
Intermediate new reader/ABLE/ESOL/pre-GED/children's collection.
Subjects: audio book, economic and social conditions, fiction, immigrants and immigration, inspirational stories or pictures, urban life.

Gaines, Ernest. *A Lesson Before Dying.* New York: Alfred A. Knopf, 1993.

When Jefferson, a young black youth, is wrongly accused of murder, a court-appointed lawyer defends him by claiming he was too dumb to have planned such a crime. Sentenced to die despite his innocence and the lawyer's misguided defense, the youth is befriended by a teacher who sets out to prove the lawyer wrong. As he endures imprisonment and impending death, Jefferson gains a measure of dignity and self-esteem denied him in freedom.
Advanced new reader/GED/adult collection.
Subjects: African Americans, audio book, fiction, political repression and resistance.

Giff, Patricia Reilly. *Pictures of Hollis Woods.* New York: Random House, 2002.

Abandoned as a baby, the now twelve-year-old Hollis has bounced from one foster home to another, hoping with each new placement that she will find a family, but ultimately running way. The one constant in her life is her art, her pictures of the people and places that have figured in her life-long search for stability. When she is placed with the Regans, she begins to believe that this time is for real, until an accident she thinks she caused sends her running away again. Finding shelter with an elderly woman, she slowly begins to understand that she is needed and that she is and has been loved. This heartwarming story of a young girl battling a well-meaning but overworked social service system as well as her own sense of failure offers hope not only in a reunion with the Regans but also in Hollis's own understanding that she is indeed worthy of a family of her own.

Intermediate-advanced new reader/pre-GED/GED/children's collection.

Subjects: audio book, families, fiction, loss.

Haddon Mark. *The Curious Incident of the Dog in the Night Time.* New York: Doubleday, 2003.

Mathematically gifted but socially inept, Christopher is an autistic fifteen-year-old boy struggling to make sense of a world he doesn't understand even as his beleaguered parents grapple with their ability to love and understand him. Determined to find out who has killed his neighbor's dog, he solves the mystery but also discovers some unhappy truths about his parents' failed marriage. This novel is an amazingly sensitive and perceptive look into the mind of a young boy who is decidedly different and the challenge that loving such a child presents.

Advanced new reader/pre-GED/GED/adult collection.

Subjects: audio book, families, fiction.

Hesse, Karen. *Out of the Dust.* New York: Scholastic, 1997.

In spare, lyrical verse, Hesse tells the story of fourteen-year-old Billie Jo, struggling to cope with the relentless dust of the Oklahoma prairie, the loss of her mother, and the silent brooding of her bereaved father. Desperate to find a way out of the dust and into a life filled with the music and beauty her mother taught her to love, Billie Jo discovers she must first recognize the deep attachments she will always feel to the land and the people that are seared into her sense of self.

Intermediate-advanced new reader/pre-GED/GED/children's collection.

Subjects: American history and culture, audio book, economic and social conditions, families, fiction.

Hiaasen, Carl. *Flush.* New York: Random House, 2005.

Families with teenagers will enjoy listening to this story, narrated by a young teenage boy whose father is in jail for sinking a gambling boat that was

spewing pollution directly into the ocean. The whodunit and adventure aspects of the book will amuse the teenagers, but the book raises many important questions that parents will want to discuss: questions about environmental responsibility, about speaking out against wrongdoing, and about the murky line that sometimes separates the righteous from the criminal.
Advanced new reader/pre-GED/GED/children's collection.
Subjects: audio book, families, fiction, nature and the universe.

Hobbs, Valerie. ***Letting Go of Bobby James or How I Found My Self of Steam.*** New York: Farrar, Straus & Giroux, 2004.
Jody Walker is only 16, but she is already married and has already experienced the physical anger of her husband. Determined not to follow her own mother down that path of enduring abuse, she leaves her husband, struggles on her own, then finds a few friends who help her and whom she can help in return. Readers of all ages, particularly women, will be rooting for Jody as she struggles to find the strength to create her own life.
Advanced new reader/pre-GED/GED/ESOL/children's collection.
Subjects: fiction, inspirational stories and pictures, women.

Hollander, John, ed. ***O. Henry.*** Illustrated by Miles Hyman. Series title: Stories for Young People. New York: Sterling, 2005.
The series title may be "stories for young people," but the vocabulary, use of language, and writing style of these stories are difficult and best suited for advanced students preparing for the GED and further education or advanced ESOL students wanting to increase their vocabulary and command of both spoken and written English. O. Henry's stories are classics in the canon of American literature, and with their vivid details, philosophical messages, and surprise endings, they provide an appealing vehicle to transport students to a deeper level of interaction with the written word and ultimately to a higher level of education. Whether teachers choose to read the stories aloud to promote listening comprehension, or have students read them on their own for silent reading comprehension practice, they will provide ample means for advanced oral and written language development.
Advanced new reader/ESOL/GED/children's collection.
Subjects: fiction, story collections.

Jimenez, Francisco. *Breaking Through.* Boston: Houghton Mifflin, 2001.
In this sequel to *The Circuit*, listed below, Jimenez again employs the tools
of fiction to recall his experiences as a teenage migrant worker struggling to
play his part in providing a family income yet fulfill his own dreams of a
university education.
Intermediate-advanced new reader/pre-GED/GED/ESOL/children's collection.
Subjects: audio book, fiction, immigrants and immigration, Latinos, rural life,
story collections, work.

Jimenez, Francisco. *The Circuit: Stories from the Life of a Migrant Child.*
Boston: Houghton Mifflin, 1999.
Looking back from his current life as a professor of language and literature
at an American university, Jimenez employs the emotional distance that
fiction imparts to write a series of interconnected stories based on his experiences as a child of migrant workers following the circuit of seasonal work.
Crossing the border from Mexico into California and then on through a
succession of labor camps, Jimenez watches his family and other workers
suffer hardships, humiliations, and disappointments and yet hold fast to
their enduring hope of providing a better life for the next generation.
Intermediate-advanced new reader/pre-GED/GED/ESOL/children's collection.
Subjects: audio book, fiction, immigrants and immigration, Latinos, rural life,
story collections, work.

Johnson, Angela. *The First Part Last.* New York: Simon & Schuster, 2003.
In alternating chapters of "then" when he was a carefree teenager in love
with Nia, and "now" when he is struggling to be a father to baby Feather
while also working and going to school, Bobby reveals both the great love
and attachment he feels for his baby daughter and the pull of the teenage
life he now needs to leave behind.
Intermediate-advanced new reader/pre-GED/GED/ESOL/children's collection.
Subjects: African Americans, audio book, families, fathers, fiction.

Joseph, Lynn. *The Color of My Words.* New York: HarperCollins, 2000.
In a time of poverty and political repression in the Dominican Republic, a
simple notebook can be both a luxury and a statement of defiance. Into
this notebook, twelve-year-old Ana Rosa pores her conflicting emotions

about living in a beautiful island home with a loving family but under a tyrannical regime that forces members of that family to make life-changing and life-threatening choices.

Intermediate-advanced new reader/pre-GED/GED/ESOL/children's collection.

Subjects: audio book, fiction, inspirational stories and pictures, political repression and resistance, Latin America and the Caribbean.

Lester, Julius. *Day of Tears: A Novel in Dialogue.* New York: Hyperion, 2005. Blending fact and fiction, many voices tell this story set in the context of the largest slave auction in America that took place in Savannah, Georgia, in 1859. Pierce Butler, owner of hundreds of slaves, has promised Emma, slave and loving caretaker of his two young daughters, that she will not be sold. But overwhelming gambling debts force his hand and he breaks his promise. The reactions of Emma, of the grieving daughters, of their estranged mother who opposes slavery, and of the owner himself as he confronts his own uncomfortable demons reveal the many ways in which slavery stained the lives of masters as well as the slaves they owned

Intermediate-advanced new reader/pre-GED/GED/children's collection.

Subjects: African American history and culture, audio book, fiction, slavery.

MacLachlan, Patricia. *Sarah Plain and Tall.* New York: Harper & Row, 1985. Amid the hardships of life on the Kansas prairie in the late nineteenth century, a widowed father of two young children advertises for a wife. When Sarah, self-described as plain and tall, arrives from Maine, everyone faces the challenges of adjustment. The children are drawn to their new mother but fear she misses her seacoast home too much and will leave them. In the end, Sarah explains that she will always miss the sound and smell of the sea, but she would miss her new family even more. This popular story of loss, love, and the power of family was followed by two sequels: *Skylark* (HarperCollins, 1994) and *Caleb's Story* (Joanna Cotler, 2001). All three have been recorded as audio books as well as made into movies. (Note: the movie version of *Caleb's Story* is called *Winter's End*).

Advanced new reader/pre-GED/GED/ESOL/children's collection.

Subjects: audio book, families, fiction, loss, love.

Matthews, L.S. *Fish*. New York: Delacorte, 2004.

In an unnamed country engaged in a civil war, a young child called Tiger and never identified by gender must flee to safer territory with his/her parents, aid workers in that country. Accompanied by a native guide, they set out on their perilous journey with a donkey carrying the only possessions they could gather together quickly. Just before leaving, Tiger rescues a little fish from a rare mud puddle in this drought-ridden land and begs to carry him along in a little jug. The fish becomes both symbol of hope and metaphor of the dangers they all face. The lack of particulars of place and character names make this a universal story of trust, family bonds, and survival in the face of great odds that refugees from any country or any tyranny will relate to.

Intermediate-advanced new reader/pre-GED/GED/ESOL/children's collection.
Subjects: audio book, families, fiction, political repression and resistance, refugees.

Mikaelsen, Ben. *Tree Girl*. New York: HarperCollins, 2004.

During his many travels to Central America, Mikaelsen met the real "tree girl" who told him the true story of her experience during the civil war in Guatemala that he recounts here in fictionalized form. Her family were "Indios," members of a tribe of original inhabitants of the land from which they eked out a subsistence living. Having attended a local school, "tree girl" had dreams of becoming a teacher. All dreams seemed lost, however, when soldiers killed most members of her family and village, a massacre she escaped by a twist of fate. Living in a refugee camp in Mexico, haunted by memories and guilt at her survival, she was moved to begin a school for the many children roaming the camp with little to do as they waited for deliverance. Although the "tree girl" described in the book is barely 15, her story reveals the extremes of human possibility, from cruelty and violence to courage and self-sacrifice.

Advanced new reader/GED/ESOL/children's collection.
Subjects: fiction, Latin America and the Caribbean, Native Americans, refugees, war.

Paterson, Katherine. *Lyddie.* New York: Lodestar, 1991.

In the mid-nineteenth century, the textile mills of Lowell, Massachusetts, employed and housed hundreds of young girls under near-slave labor-conditions, a situation vividly portrayed in this novel of a young girl's determination to help her family and improve herself. Forced to earn money after her father abandons their failing farm, Lyddie endures the hardships of factory life, but she also discovers the power of books to provide both escape from difficult surroundings and engagement with a wider world. Armed with that knowledge, she summons the courage to speak out on behalf of her fellow workers and to find a better life for herself and her family. Parallels to the difficult working environments many people, especially immigrants, face today offer opportunities for discussion, writing, and further research.

Advanced new reader/GED/ESOL/children's collection.

Subjects: American history and culture, audio book, fiction, women, work.

Paulsen, Gary. *Sarny: A Life Remembered.* New York: Delacorte, 1997.

Sarny was a young slave girl who learned to read in the secret school for slaves run by Nightjohn in Paulsen's earlier novel of that name. In this companion book, Sarny tells her own remarkable story as she sets out for New Orleans in the early and difficult days of freedom at the end of the Civil War to find her children, who have been sold away. Along the way, she meets the mysterious Miss Laura, who helps her find the children and also encourages her to establish a school to teach former slaves and their children to read.

Advanced new reader/pre-GED/GED/ESOL/children's collection.

Subjects: African Americans, the American South, audio book, fiction, slavery.

Rinaldi, Ann. *Hang a Thousand Trees with Ribbons: The Story of Phillis Wheatley.* San Diego: Harcourt Brace, 1996.

Rinaldi has written several books based on the lives of important figures from American history or set in times and circumstances of critical importance to an evolving American nation. In this novel, based on the known facts of the life of the poet Phillis Wheatley, she tells a poignant tale of a strong willed and intelligent slave girl who wrote poetry and was greatly admired by many friends of the Massachusetts family with whom she lived in the years prior to the American Revolution. But this is no simple tale of triumph in adverse circumstances, for although the family who owned her treated her kindly, recognized her intelligence, taught her to read, and encouraged her writing, they never understood her passionate yearning for freedom, and despite her acknowledged accomplishments, there was no place for her in the society of that day.

Advanced new reader/ESOL/pre-GED/GED/children's collection.

Subjects: African Americans, American history and culture, the arts and artists, fiction, slavery.

Ryan, Pam Munoz. *Esperanza Rising.* New York: Scholastic, 2000.

Ryan based this story on the life of her grandmother who was born into wealth and privilege in Mexico, but driven by political circumstances to flee her home as a child. She lived the rest of her life among the field workers and Mexican migrants of central California. This is a story of a young girl rising above adversity and learning to value the love of her family and the trust and companionship of her fellow workers over the physical comforts she once enjoyed. Set in the 1930s, it is also a history lesson about the immigrant workers who have been crossing the U.S. southern border for decades in search of a better life.

Advanced new reader/GED/ESOL/children's collection.

Subjects: audio book, families, fiction, Latin America and the Caribbean, political repression and resistance, refugees, work.

Taylor, Mildred D. *Roll of Thunder Hear My Cry.* New York: Dial, 1976.

First published to acclaim in 1976, *Roll of Thunder Hear My Cry* has been reissued in several editions and remains in print because it tells a timeless tale. The Logan family, black landowners in Mississippi, endure the hardships of the Great Depression amid the climate of racism and mistrust that characterized the American South in those days. Strong adult characters, the ever-present specter of bigotry and human weakness, the richly textured historical background, and the courage made possible by a family's love combine to make a compelling story that will captivate readers of all ages. Taylor published a sequel, *Let the Circle Be Unbroken* (Dial, 1981, and also an audio book narrated by Lynne Thigpen), and continues to write stories related to the Logan family, the latest of which is titled *The Land* (Phyllis Fogelman, 2001). Most of these stories are available as audio books; a video version of *Roll of Thunder Hear My Cry* has also been made.

Advanced new reader/pre-GED/GED/ESOL/children's collection.
Subjects: African American history and culture, American history and culture, the American South, audio books, families, fiction, rural life.

Testa, Maria. *Almost Forever.* Cambridge, Mass.: Candlewick, 2003.
In the voice of a child, the author looks back on the year her medical doctor father enlisted in the army and was sent to Vietnam. For a year, the family's life is disrupted as they move to a military base and live in a state of anxiety from letter to letter, until a happy reunion with an injured but alive father. The time and place are different, but the disruption and anxiety felt by the family of a soldier are forever the same.
Intermediate new reader/ABLE/pre-GED/children's collection.
Subjects: family, fathers, fiction, war.

Testa, Maria. *Becoming Joe DiMaggio.* Cambridge, Mass.: Candlewick, 2002.
Each chapter in this brief novel is a poem, spare and simple blank verse telling the story of a young boy, embarrassed by a father in jail, who seeks the wisdom and companionship of his Italian immigrant grandfather. It is the 1930s, and together they listen to baseball and the achievements of their Italian-American compatriot Joe DiMaggio. Uneducated but wise, the grandfather tells the young boy, when he declares he wants to grow up to be Joe DiMaggio, "That's wonderful . . . but someone else already is."
Intermediate new reader/ABLE/pre-GED/children's collection.
Subjects: family, fiction, grandparents, immigrants and immigrations, sports.

Voight, Cynthia. *Dicey's Song.* New York: Atheneum, 1982.
Abandoned by a mentally ill mother, Dicey and her three younger siblings arrive, unexpected, at the home of the grandmother they have never met. As they adjust to new lives and new relationships, they all learn to accept what can't be changed and embrace the opportunity to build a new family that fate has given them.
Advanced new reader/pre-GED/GED/children's collection.
Subjects: audio book, families, fiction, grandparents.

Biographies and Memoirs

Ada, Alma Flor. *Under the Royal Palms: A Childhood in Cuba.* New York: Atheneum, 1998.

In brief chapters, the author recalls the people of her extended family and their everyday activities in the small town in which they lived in pre-revolutionary Cuba. Family photographs add the feeling of a kind of scrapbook to the lively and lovingly told stories.

Intermediate-advanced new reader/pre-GED/GED/ESOL/children's collection.
Subjects: biography and memoirs, Latin America and the Caribbean, memories of childhood.

Bolden, Tonya. *The Champ: The Story of Muhammad Ali.* Illustrated by R. Gregory Christie. New York: Alfred A. Knopf, 2004.

From Cassius Clay, a little boy whose favorite game was dodging the rocks he asked his brother to throw at him, to Muhammad Ali, boxing champion, political dissident, and larger-than-life character on the American cultural stage, this biography presents the many facets of Ali's remarkable life.

Intermediate new reader/ABLE/pre-GED/ESOL/children's collection.
Subjects: African Americans, American history and culture, biography and memoirs, sports.

Bolden, Tonya. *Maritcha: A Nineteenth-Century American Girl.* New York: Harry N. Abrams, 2005.

Bolden's book is based on the memoir of Maritcha Rémond Lyons, entitled *Memories of Yesterdays: All of Which I Saw and Part of Which I Was.* Although born of educated parents at a time when slavery had been abolished in New York State, Maritcha and her family had to flee New York City during the draft riots of 1863. She eventually returned to the city and became a teacher in the school system, and then an assistant principal, a position she held for almost fifty years. More than a story of one woman's remarkable life, this book tells the story of a whole class of educated and upwardly mobile blacks and the obstacles they faced in the late nineteenth and early twentieth centuries. Illustrations from the period add documentary authority to a fascinating life story.

Intermediate-advanced new reader/pre-GED/GED/ESOL/children's collection.
Subjects: African American history and culture, biography and memoirs.

Bridges, Ruby. *Through My Eyes.* New York: Scholastic, 1999.

In the autumn of 1960, six-year-old Ruby Bridges became an unwitting symbol of an extraordinary change in American history. As the lone black girl surrounded by federal marshals walking into a formerly all-white school, an event immortalized in a painting by Norman Rockwell, Ruby became a symbol of courage and hope to some and of unwanted government intrusion to others. In this book, her recollections of that day and the effect it had on the rest of her life are augmented by photographs and news clippings from that time and an interview with the white teacher who accepted and befriended the young black girl.

Intermediate new reader/ABLE/ESOL/pre-GED/children's collection.

Subjects: African American history and culture, American history and culture, the American South, biography and memoir, inspirational stories and pictures.

Duggleby, John. *Story Painter: The Life of Jacob Lawrence.* San Francisco: Chronicle, 1998.

The text tells the story of Lawrence's life as an African American painter who first came to prominence in the days of the Harlem Renaissance but whose lasting fame came from his work as a "story painter." The paintings reproduced in the book are series of images from African American history, including the story of Harriet Tubman and the underground railroad, of Toussaint L'Ouverture and the liberation of Haiti, and of the great migration of blacks from the rural South to the urban North in the years between the wars of the twentieth century. Although the text alone will be beyond beginners, the pictures offer many opportunities for discussion and language experience stories. This book would also be a good choice for listening comprehension exercises as students can examine the pictures while listening to the narrative read aloud.

All three of the series of paintings mentioned above have been reproduced as children's books which will have wide appeal among adults and will be available at many public libraries. (See entry below under Myers for *Toussaint L'Ouverture: The Fight for Haiti's Freedom*).

Beginning-intermediate new reader/ABLE/ESOL/pre-GED/children's collection.

Subjects: African Americans, the arts and artists, biography and memoir.

Ehrlich, Amy. *When I Was Your Age: Original Stories About Growing Up.* Volume 2. Cambridge, Mass.: Candlewick, 1999.

Ehrlich invited ten authors of popular novels for young adults to write a story about their own childhood experiences. Although intended for the young readers of these authors, all the pieces in this collection are in essence wonderful responses to the age-old child-to-parent question, "What was it like when you were young?" Written with the clarity and attention to detail that spark a reader's imagination and convey the sometimes conflicting feelings of the author, these stories serve as excellent examples of memoir writing that may inspire literacy students to produce some stories of their own. For those students with children in their lives, this book offers opportunities for an intergenerational discussion comparing an author's personal experiences with her fictional creations.

Volume 1 of the same title was published in 1996 and offers the same quality and usefulness.

Intermediate-advanced new reader/ABLE/ESOL/pre-GED/children's collection.
Subjects: childhood memories, biography and memoirs, family, story collections, writing.

Greenberg, Jan. *Romare Bearden: Collage of Memories.* New York: Harry N. Abrams, 2003.

Greenberg tells the facts of artist Romare Bearden's life in this biography, but the reproductions of his work add nuance and texture. Living much of his adult life in Harlem, a world filled with jazz, the blues, and a vibrant, almost palpable aura of artistic creativity, Bearden translated his memories and experiences into crazy-quiltlike collages of painted paper, photographs, scraps of fabric, and odd bits of stuff that seem to expose all the complex layers of human life and activity at once. Although Bearden transformed his memories into pictures, his work suggests possibilities for writing. Teachers might suggest that students describe an incident from their own experience from several points of view—perhaps with a varying cast of characters or perhaps first describing the incident in one setting, then imaging the same incident in a different setting.

Intermediate-advanced new reader/ABLE/ESOL/preGED/GED/children's collection.
Subjects: African Americans, the arts and artists, biography and memoir, urban life.

Kirkpatrick, Patricia. *Maya Angelou.* Illustrations by John Thompson. Mankato, Minn.: Creative Education, 2004.

An actress, a singer, a dancer, and ultimately a writer of memoirs, poetry, and children's books, Maya Angelou has led a truly extraordinary life. Raped at the age of eight, she fell silent for many months, believing her voice had caused her assailant's death. But a kind and wise teacher helped her discover the power and solace of words in literature, a lesson she has clearly taken to heart as she has used her words to share the varied and intriguing chapters of her life as she rose from the poverty and racism of Stamps, Arkansas, in the 1930s to her place as one of the preeminent writers of our time. In this book, excerpts from her memoirs and poetry and photographs from various parts of her life are interspersed with Kirk's narrative presentation of Angelou's life story. Teachers will want to have copies of her poetry and, for advanced classes, her memoirs on hand to share with students.

Intermediate-advanced new reader/pre-GED/GED/ESOL/children's collection.
Subjects: African American history and culture, African Americans, the arts and artists, biography and memoir.

Krinitz, Esther Nisenthal, and Bernice Steinhardt. *Memories of Survival.* New York: Hyperion, 2005.

Growing up in Brooklyn, New York, in the 1950s, Bernice Steinhardt heard many harrowing tales of her mother's experiences when hiding from Nazi soldiers in the woods of Poland during World War II. She encouraged her mother to write these stories down, but writing was difficult for Esther, so she used her skills with a needle and thread to tell her story. Thirty-six of her fabric art pictures illustrate this book, with additional commentary from her daughter. It is a remarkable story and a remarkable work of art that will resonate with all readers, especially those who carry their own memories of family and a way of life lost to war.

Intermediate-advanced new reader/pre-GED/GED/ESOL/children's collection.
Subjects: arts and crafts, inspirational stories and pictures, mothers, war.

Lowry, Lois. *Looking Back: A Book of Memories.* Boston: Houghton Mifflin, 1998.

In this memoir, award-winning children's author Lowry recounts brief vignettes from her life, all of which are preceded by brief quotes from her many books which reflect, to a greater or lesser extent, her experience. She recalls memories from both her childhood and her adult life, most poignantly the death of her son. The translation of her life experiences into the related yet original scenes and characters in her fiction presents interesting writing lessons for any level of students needing inspiration and encouragement to write.

Intermediate new reader/ABLE/pre-GED/children's collection.

Subjects: biography and memoir, childhood memories, writing.

McCourt, Frank. *Angela's Ashes.* New York: Scribner's, 1996.

Although born in Brooklyn, New York, to immigrant Irish parents, Frank McCourt grew up in the impoverished lanes of Limerick, Ireland, to which his parents returned, distraught after the death of their baby girl in America. But "home" doesn't treat the returning family kindly, as McCourt recalls in this poignant yet wryly funny memoir. Despite poverty, despair, and his father's alcoholism and chronic unemployment, young Frank holds onto his boy's dream of returning to America.

Advanced new reader/GED/ESOL/adult collection.

Subjects: audio book, biography and memoir, families, fathers, immigrants and immigration, mothers.

Mathis, Sharon Bell. *Ray Charles.* Illustrated by George Ford. New York: Lee and Low, 1973, 2001.

Updated and reissued, this biography of musician Ray Charles tells a remarkable story of one man's rise above the seemingly overwhelming burdens of poverty, racism, and blindness. Sent away from home at the age of seven to attend a school for the blind, young Ray Charles Robinson discovered solace in music, and the music he would write and perform throughout his long life and career would forever reflect the pain and promise of his life. Reading this book and then viewing the recent movie *Ray* offers students an opportunity to compare both the facts of his life and the character of his person as portrayed in the book and in the movie.

Intermediate new reader/ABLE/pre-GED/children's collection.

Subjects: African Americans, the arts and artists, biography and memoir, loss, music.

Myers, Walter Dean. *Toussaint L'Ouverture: The Fight for Haiti's Freedom.* Paintings by Jacob Lawrence. New York: Simon & Schuster, 1996.

In his brief introduction to this book, painter Jacob Lawrence explains that when he first moved to Harlem in 1930, at the age of thirteen, he would

walk through the neighborhood and listen to street orators tell stories about famous blacks who had accomplished extraordinary deeds, people like Harriet Tubman, Frederick Douglass, and Toussaint L'Ouverture. Those stories inspired him as a young man and again later when he became a painter and decided to tell those stories on canvas. The story of Toussaint L'Ouverture, the liberator of Haiti, became the first subject of the series paintings that would become the hallmark of Lawrence's artistic career. Myers, a prolific author of books for children, has written a text to accompany the pictures. Together, words and pictures tell a stirring tale, one that is all the more poignant given the state of affairs in Haiti today.
Intermediate new reader/ABLE/pre-GED/ESOL/children's collection.
Subjects: African Americans, the arts and artists, biography and memoirs, inspirational stories or pictures, Latin America and the Caribbean, political repression and resistance.

Stone, Miriam. *At the End of Words: A Daughter's Memoir.* Cambridge, Mass.: Candlewick, 2003.

As a senior in high school looking forward to college, Stone had to abruptly put aside her plans for her own future and confront the fact that her mother was dying of cancer. In spare and simple language, these essays and poems reveal the many facets of grief she experienced as she cared for and comforted her mother while struggling with the vagaries of fate that had changed her life forever.
Intermediate-advanced new reader/pre-GED/GED/children's collection.
Subjects: biography and memoirs, mothers, loss.

Warren, Andrea. *Escape from Saigon: How a Vietnam War Orphan Became an American Boy.* New York: Farrar, Straus & Giroux, 2004.

With only vague memories of his American father and deeply saddened by the suicide of his Vietnamese mother, eight-year-old Long faced yet another heartbreaking loss as his grandmother gave him up to an adoptive American family during Operation Babylift, a desperate attempt to remove orphaned and mixed-race children from the ravages of war when American soldiers left Vietnam in 1975. Based on many personal interviews, Warren tells Long's story: how he survived a refugee camp, met his new brothers and parents, and became Matt Steiner, an American boy who learned to honor those he left behind while creating a promising future for himself. As an adult and a practicing physician, Steiner returned to Vietnam to make his peace with the grandmother who had sacrificed so much so that he could live a life she could never have imagined.

Warren herself is the mother of a child of Operation Babylift, and she weaves some of the history of that effort into Matt Steiner's story, including stories that didn't end quite so happily, reminding us once again that children are always the unintended victims of war.

Advanced new reader/pre-GED/GED/ESOL/adult collection.

Subjects: Asia, biography and memoirs, families, war.

Collections

Baer, Ulrich, ed. *110 Stories: New York Writers After September 11.* New York: New York University Press, 2002.

The date September 11, 2001 has been seared into the collective memory of all Americans alive and old enough at the time to understand the horror and sense the implications of that tragic event. Many newspaper and magazine stories have been written and television programs presented that relive the events preceding, during, and after that fateful morning. What this book adds to our understanding are the personal reactions and reflections of people living within physical proximity to the towers. All the contributors are professional writers who turned to words, the tools of their trade, to confront the anger, fear, bewilderment, and despair they faced in the days and months after that beautiful blue September sky turned black.

Intermediate-advanced new reader/ESOL/pre-GED/GED/adult collection.

Subjects: American history and culture, disasters, loss, personal reflections, story collections.

Ballard, Sandra L., and Patricia Hudson. *Listen Here: Women Writing in Appalachia.* Lexington, Ky.: University of Kentucky Press, 2003.

In their poems, stories, and memoirs, the writers whose work is collected in this book address what the book's jacket refers to as "the fundamental truths in the hills and hollows and rivers, the communities and traditions of their homeland." The setting may be unique to them, but the issues they raise will resonate with all people who share a strong attachment to the land and customs of their homeland. A few of the writers, such as Barbara Kingsolver and George Ella Lyon, are known beyond Appalachia, but most are not. All

write vividly of the stuff of everyday life, transcending barriers of time, place, and culture, and in the process, offer inspiration to fledgling writers everywhere to recall and preserve the stories of their own homeland
Intermediate-advanced new reader/ABLE/pre-GED/GED/adult collection.
Subjects: Appalachia, cultural traditions, story collections, women.

Berry, Cecelie S., ed. ***Rise Up Singing: Black Women Writers on Motherhood.***
New York: Doubleday, 2004.
In a rich chorus of voices, an intergenerational gathering of black mothers describe their experiences, express their feelings, and reflect on the results of their parental efforts in stories, poems, and essays. Anyone who has been a mother or had a mother will find some resonance in the many shades of love, commitment, anxiety, joy, disappointment, and loss reflected in these recollections of women recalling what all would agree was the most important role of their lives.
Intermediate-advanced new reader/pre-GED/GED/ESOL/adult collection.
Subjects: African Americans, inspirational stories and pictures, mothers, story collections, women.

Bolden, Tonya, ed. ***33 Things Every Girl Should Know About Women's History.*** New York: Crown, 2002.
Offering poems, essays, letters, photos, a time line of significant events, and a roll call of significant women, Bolden has gathered together a veritable encyclopedia of facts and stories to inform and inspire readers. Topics range from changes in fashion to changes in laws to changes in cultural perspectives, and the variety of formats makes the book accessible to students from a range of reading levels and with varying levels of knowledge about the women's movement as it has evolved over the last century and a half.
Intermediate-advanced new reader/pre-GED/GED/children's collection.
Subjects: American history and culture, story collections, women.

Carroll, Andrew, ed. ***Behind the Lines: Powerful and Revealing American and Foreign War Letters—And One Man's Search to Find Them.*** New York: Scribner's, 2005.
For three years, editor Carroll traveled around the globe seeking letters from families, former soldiers, and those still on the battlefield that told

true stories of being at war. From the American Revolution to Afghanistan and Iraq, from handwritten notes to rambling e-mails, Carroll's extraordinary collection of letters tell stories that are riveting, funny, angry, inspiring, and heartbreaking.
Intermediate-advanced new reader/ABLE/pre-GED/GED/ESOL/adult collection.
Subjects: American history and culture, story collections, war.

Coles, Robert, and Randy Testa, eds. *Growing Up Poor: A Literary Anthology.* New York: New Press, 2001.
As a "literary" anthology, this book would serve as an excellent introduction to some of the writers and styles of writing that students aspiring to community college or beyond might encounter. The stories, poems, and essays of Raymond Carver, Ralph Ellison, Richard Ford, Zora Neale Hurston and others, all reflecting on childhood experiences of physical or emotional want, will offer advanced new readers, both native English speakers and ESOL students, ample opportunities for vocabulary development, discussion of ideas, and perhaps even added research into an author's other work or into the places and events described.
Advanced new reader/ESOL/pre-GED/GED/adult collection.
Subjects: childhood memories, economic and social conditions, family, story collections.

Giovanni, Nikki, ed. *Grand Fathers: Reminiscences, Poems, Recipes, and Photos of the Keepers of Our Traditions.* New York: Henry Holt, 1999.
Following a similar collection titled *Grand Mothers,* Giovanni gathered pictures, poems, and family stories from a multicultural and intergenerational group of writers who offer moving tributes to or recall complicated memories of grandfathers they respected, feared, loved, and lost.
Intermediate-advanced new reader/ABLE/ESOL/pre-GED/adult collection
Subjects: African Americans, childhood memories, grandparents, story collections.

Kennedy, Caroline, ed. *A Patriot's Handbook: Songs, Poems, Stories, and Speeches Celebrating the Land We Love.* New York: Hyperion, 2003.
From the text of the Pledge of Allegiance to the songs of Bob Dylan; from the letters of the second president, John Adams, to the inaugural address of the thirty-fifth, her father, John F. Kennedy; from the lyrics of George M.

Cohan's "You're a Grand Old Flag" to the poetry of Paul Laurence Dunbar, Caroline Kennedy has gathered a stunning array of materials that present a panoramic perspective on the values inherent in the idea of American patriotism. Part history lesson and part reflection on the diverse range of events, people, and opinions that have shaped and continue to shape the United States, this book offers many opportunities for native-born Americans and newcomers alike to consider their own response to the question of what it means to be a patriotic American.

Intermediate-advanced new reader/pre-GED/GED/ESOL/adult collection.
Subjects: American history and culture, civil rights.

Kennedy, Randy. *Subwayland: Adventures in the World Beneath New York.* New York: St. Martin's, 2003.

In large cities like New York, the subway is an instrument of democracy as well as a means of transportation. Bankers, construction workers, actors, students, mothers with their children, homeless people, and even the mayor ride the trains. As Kennedy says in his introduction to this collection of his columns for the *New York Times,* the subway makes us sit with people we'd rarely meet otherwise and often wouldn't want to. In depicting an ever evolving cast of characters and their stories in these sometimes funny, sometimes poignant notes from the underground, Kennedy reminds us of the rich diversity of life that lives and works in the modern American city.

Intermediate new reader/ABLE/ESOL/pre-GED/adult collection.
Subjects: story collections, urban life.

Knepper, Cathy D., ed. *Dear Mrs. Roosevelt: Letters to Eleanor Roosevelt through Depression and War.* New York: Carroll & Graf, 2004.

Eleanor Roosevelt was the First Lady of the United States during the Depression and World War II, among the most turbulent times the nation and its people ever faced, and she was determined to reach out to the ordinary Americans who were suffering the consequences of those events. That she succeeded in connecting with the people is obvious in the hundreds of letters collected here from farmers losing their land, elderly people with little means of support, and mothers worried about sons at war. As the book jacket says, these letters are "history from the grassroots." They also paint a telling portrait of the woman so many Americans turned to in their time of need.

Intermediate-advanced new reader/ABLE/pre-GED/ESOL/adult collection.
Subjects: American history and culture, economic and social conditions, story collections, war.

Kurtz, Jane, ed. *Memories of Sun: Stories of Africa and America.* New York: HarperCollins, 2004.

The child of American parents who lived in Africa, editor Kurtz calls several places home, but Africa first among them. For this collection, she has gathered short stories and poems by African writers in both Africa and in America, and by American writers in Africa, all exploring their personal and communal relationship with that vast and varied continent.
Intermediate-advanced new reader/pre-GED/GED/ESOL/children's collection.
Subjects: Africa, African American history and culture, story collections.

Lyon, George Ella. ed. *A Kentucky Christmas.* Lexington, Ky.: University of Kentucky Press, 2003.

The warmth of family gatherings, the smells of home-cooked food, the surprises beneath all the wrappings, and all the other sensory memories of Christmas are vividly depicted in these poems, stories, and memoirs, but so, too, are the unhappy memories, the loneliness, and the wistfulness that comes with confronting the inevitability of change. As in Ballard's collection of women's writing described above, the details are regional, but the feelings and experiences are universal.
Intermediate-advanced new reader/ABLE/ESOL/pre-GED/GED/adult collection.
Subjects: Appalachia, cultural traditions, story collections.

Martz, Sandra Haldeman, ed. *Grow Old Along with Me the Best Is Yet to Be.* Watsonville, Calif.: Papier-Mache, 1996.

As with several other collections from this publisher, this book includes work gathered from nonprofessional writers participating in various writing groups across the country. In stories, essays, and poems, the voices of these men and women are reflective, defiant, wistful, playful, grateful for what they've had and hopeful for more to come. Not for senior citizens only, though, as the wisdom and insight they offer can benefit readers—and aspiring writers—of any age.

Intermediate-advanced new reader/ABLE/ESOL/pre-GED/adult collection.
Subjects: inspirational stories and pictures, story collections.

My Hero Project, ed. *My Hero: Extraordinary People on the Heroes Who Inspire Them.* Introduction by Earvin "Magic" Johnson. New York: Free Press, 2005.

Congressmen, sports stars, artists, as well as others whose names will not be so familiar contribute brief essays describing a person who inspired them. The My Hero Project was started by Karen Pritzker and a few friends who wanted to create a bank of uplifting stories to share with the young people in their lives. The book offers an interesting model for a class writing project.

Intermediate-advanced new reader/ABLE/ESOL/pre-GED/GED/adult collection.
Subjects: inspirational stories and pictures.

No More Strangers: Young Voices from a New South Africa. Foreword by Archbishop Desmond Tutu. Interviews by Tim McKee. Photographs by Anne Blackshaw. New York: DK, 1998.

The voices are those of teenagers, but the experiences they describe and the wisdom they display belie their ages. Born into the strict and brutal system of apartheid but coming of age in a newly liberated South Africa, what one refers to as "the joyous yet challenging years of freedom," these young people, black and white, tell their stories of before and after, of fear and despair giving way to possibility and hope. As Archbishop Tutu says in his foreword, "We are learning to heal through the telling of stories like these."

Intermediate-advanced new reader/pre-GED/GED/ESOL/children's collection.
Subjects: Africa, civil rights, economics and social conditions, political repression and resistance, story collections.

Out on the Porch: An Evocation in Words and Pictures. Chapel Hill, N.C.: Algonquin, 1992.

Brief excerpts from the works of William Faulkner, Eudora Welty, Mark Twain, and many other writers of the American South evoke the mystique and recall many a treasured moment passed on a front porch. Accompanied by photographs of porches big and small, ornate and simple, this marriage of words and pictures will evoke memories of special places in the hearts of all readers, regardless of physical locale.

Intermediate new reader/ABLE/pre-GED/GED/adult collection.

Subjects: the American South; art and literature collections; general photography collections; writing.

———————————

Philip, Neil, ed. *In a Sacred Manner I Live: Native American Wisdom.* New York: Clarion, 1996.

As editor Philip says in his introduction, to live in a sacred manner is "to live with respect for the environment, for the community, and for oneself." The writings he has collected here, from many tribes and from as early as 1609, all reflect that desire to live in harmony with one's surroundings. Photographs and brief descriptions of the various tribes and the geographical areas they called home give historical texture as well as philosophical substance to this small but inspiring collection.

Intermediate new reader/ABLE/pre-GED/ESOL/children's collection.

Subjects: inspirational stories and pictures, Native Americans, story collections.

———————————

White, Bailey. *Sleeping at the Starlight Hotel: And Other Adventures on the Way Back Home.* New York: Vintage, 1996.

Bailey White says that she knows the people of her small Georgia town so well she can "call every old lady's cat by name." She obviously knows their hearts as well as is evident in this collection of funny, touching, and true stories about the people who share her attachment to the place she calls home.

Intermediate-advanced new reader/ABLE/pre-GED/adult collection.

Subjects: the American South, rural life, story collections.

———————————

Picture Books for All Ages

Agee, Jon. *Terrific.* New York: Hyperion, 2005.

It's all in your attitude. That's the moral of this quirky and amusing tale of Eugene, a classic sourpuss, whose unlikely friend, a parrot, saves his life and helps him learn that anyone can find happiness if he looks around and makes the best of a given situation. This is a story that could spark an interesting discussion about the varying ways in which individuals and cultures respond to circumstance and experience.

Beginning new reader/ABLE/ESOL/children's collection.

Subjects: inspirational stories and pictures, picture books for all ages.

———————————

Erdrich, Louise. *The Range Eternal.* Illustrated by Steve Johnson and Lou Fancher. New York: Hyperion, 2002.

> Amid the efficiency and convenience of her modern kitchen, the narrator of this story recalls the old wood-burning stove that warmed her childhood home, cooked the food that nourished her body, and created the dreamy fires that fueled her imagination. Finding a similar stove in an antique shop, she brings it home to add that "center of true warmth" and continuity with the past that no modern appliance can provide. Erdrich based this story on her own memories of the wood-burning stove in her grandmother's house on the Turtle Mountain Reservation in North Dakota, and it is an excellent example of memory recalled and shared through a story.
>
> The title of the book is the name of the old stove, but the phrase offers an opportunity to discuss multiple meanings of words, especially with ESOL students, since the word range is used not only as a synonym for stove, but also to describe the mountain ranges of Erdrich's ancestral lands and the stretches of land that the buffalo and elk roamed before the great ranges of the Dakotas were settled.

Intermediate new reader/ABLE/ESOL/pre-GED/children's collection.
Subjects: American history and culture, family, Native Americans, picture books for all ages.

Giovanni, Nikki. *Rosa.* Illustrated by Bryan Collier. New York: Henry Holt, 2005.

> It started as an ordinary bus ride like all the others she had taken after an ordinary day working at the department store, but when the bus driver demanded that Rosa Parks give up her seat for a white person, and then threatened to call the police when she didn't, she simply stayed in her seat and said, "Do what you must." Coinciding, as it happened, with the emerging leadership of a new minister in town named Martin Luther King, Jr., her simple act of civil disobedience led to a boycott by blacks of all the buses in Montgomery, Alabama, and a pivotal event in the burgeoning civil rights movement that would hasten the end of "separate but equal" laws began. As she relates the details of that particular event, Giovanni also describes the cultural climate in which Rosa Parks had lived for some forty years before that fateful day when she decided that the time had come to say, "No."

Intermediate new reader/ABLE/pre-GED/children's collection.

Subjects: African American history and culture, American history and culture, the American South, civil rights, picture books for all ages.

Hall, Donald. *Lucy's Summer.* Illustrated by Michael McCurdy. San Diego: Harcourt Brace, 1995.

Set in rural New England in the early twentieth century, this book presents an intriguing look at a way of life that has all but disappeared from the modern American scene. Lucy and her family support themselves mostly from the products of their small farm, but Lucy's mother also runs a successful milliner's business from their home. Acclaimed poet Hall has turned many stories from his mother's rural New Hampshire childhood into picture books that adults will savor, whether they share them with children or not. His books also serve as lovely examples of family stories turned into works of art.

Intermediate new reader/ABLE/ESOL/children's collection.
Subjects: childhood memories, families, picture books for all ages, rural life.

Hesse, Karen. *The Cats in Krasinski Square.* Illustrated by Wendy Watson. New York: Scholastic, 2004.

Based on actual accounts of survivors of the Warsaw Ghetto of Poland during World War II, this story of creative and determined opposition to the forces of oppression will unfortunately have many echoes in the contemporary world. A young Jewish girl escapes the ghetto, passes as a non-Jew, and works with others to smuggle bread and supplies to those still trapped inside. In the process she befriends the many cats who are also displaced from their homes and devises an ingenious plan to use the cats to confuse the dogs trained by the soldiers to hunt down the bread smugglers.

Intermediate new reader/ABLE/ESOL/pre-GED/children's collection.
Subjects: inspirational stories and pictures, picture books for all ages, political repression and resistance, war.

---

hooks, bell. *Skin Again.* Illustrated by Chris Raschka. New York: Hyperion, 2004.

The simple text offers lots of repetition to aid reading. The endearing, childlike illustrations add a whimsical note. Yet this book sends a powerful and profound message: if you want to know someone well, you have to let go of preconceptions, including those based on skin color, before you can "come inside and let me be real and you become real to me." Teachers and tutors could ask the question, "tell me something about the 'real' you I might not know or guess."

Beginning new reader/ABLE/ESOL/children's collection.

Subjects: inspirational text and pictures, picture books for all ages.

Rylant, Cynthia. ***When I Was Young in the Mountains.*** Illustrated by Diane Goode. New York: E.P. Dutton, 1982.

Introducing each memory with the rhythmic title phrase, Rylant recalls the days of her youth spent with her grandparents in Appalachian West Virginia. It is a lyrical portrait of that life as seen through the eyes of a child and spoken through the experienced heart of an adult.

Beginning new reader/ABLE/pre-GED/ESOL/children's collection.

Subjects: Appalachia, childhood memories, grandparents, picture books for all ages.

Russo, Marisabina. ***Always Remember Me: How One Family Survived World War II.*** New York: Atheneum, 2005.

In a story based on her own experience, Russo explains how her grandmother used two photo albums to tell stories from her family's past. At first she showed the young child only pictures of the happy times, but eventually she shared photos from another album, one that told of the atrocities and deprivations endured by her family during World War II. The grandmother and her three daughters, separated during the war, were eventually reunited in the United States. In addition to photographs, the illustrations for this book show items like passports, tickets for boat passage, and newspaper clippings in a scrapbook-like fashion that students might imitate as they recreate a story from their own family history.

Intermediate new reader/ABLE/ESOL/pre-GED/children's collection.

Subjects: childhood memories, families, picture books for all ages, war.

Say, Allen. ***Tea with Milk.*** Boston: Houghton Mifflin, 1999.

Say has written and illustrated many picture books based on his own and family member's experiences living between two cultures, sometimes in Japan and sometimes in America. This story recalls the experience of his mother, who, like the character in the book, was born and raised in America, but returned to Japan with her parents just when she was ready to go to college. Resentful of the confinement and formality of traditional Japanese

society, she left home and found a job in a big city department store, where she met a young Japanese man who was raised, as an orphan, by an English family. Their preference for "tea with milk" becomes symbolic of their shared experience and love for things English, even though when they marry, they choose to live in Japan because, as the young man says, "home is where you make it." A beautifully illustrated story suggestive of many issues relevant to adults, including tensions between generations and cultures, traditional marriage customs, and the elusive concept of "home."
Intermediate new reader/ABLE/ESOL/pre-GED/children's collection.
Subjects: Asia, cultural traditions, families, love, picture books for all ages.

Shea, Pegi Deitz. *The Whispering Cloth: A Refugee's Story.* Illustrated by Anita Riggio. Stitching by You Yang. Honesdale Pa.: Boyds Mills, 1995.
Waiting in a refugee camp for a trip to a better life, a Hmong grandmother teachers her granddaughter how to stitch traditional Hmong story cloths. At first, the little girl just stitches borders on her grandmother's cloths, but as her needle skills grow, she finds in that craft the means to tell the horrific story of events she witnessed but could never find words to describe: the massacre in her Laotian village which killed her parents. A story cloth picturing their eventual resettlement in the United States ends the book on a hopeful note.
Beginning-intermediate new reader/ABLE/ESOL/pre-GED/children's collection.
Subjects: arts and crafts, Asia, cultural traditions, immigrants and immigration, picture books for all ages, refugees.

Siebert, Diane. *Rhyolite: The True Story of a Ghost Town.* Illustrated by David Frampton. New York: Clarion, 2003.
Named for an abundant local mineral, Rhyolite was a real Nevada town that grew and prospered with lightning speed when gold was discovered in the land nearby but returned to barren desert almost as quickly when rich financial backers panicked and withdrew support. Siebert tells this story in rhythmical rhyming verse filled with vivid details of the dusty landscape, the scheming speculators, the hoards of fortune seekers rushing to this new-found wealth, and the laughing coyotes, always in the distance, watching as if they knew the land would return to them one day, as it did. Frampton's richly detailed and golden-hued woodcuts add texture to Siebert's clever yet haunting narrative. Echoes of modern instances of human folly, both personal and corporate, offer many opportunities for discussion.

Intermediate new reader/ABLE/ESOL/pre-GED/children's collection.
Subjects: American West, economic and social conditions, loss, picture books
for all ages.

Steig, William. ***When Everybody Wore a Hat.*** New York: HarperCollins, 2003.
The drawings are childlike and slightly off-beat. The text is a straightforward account of what he and his family had—a wind-up phonograph, colorful neighbors—or didn't have—cars, telephones, TV—in the years of his
youth in the immigrant neighborhoods of the Bronx, New York, in the
early twentieth century. Yet in this simple evocation of his childhood, Steig
manages to convey some sense of the hardships he and his family experienced, as when he says, in describing their small apartment, "It was impossible to be alone." This book is an excellent example of how recalling simple
memories can lead to a deeper understanding or appreciation of what is
remembered.
Beginning new reader/ABLE/ESOL/children's collection.
Subjects: childhood memories, immigrants and immigration, picture books
for all ages.

Weatherford, Carole Boston. ***Freedom on the Menu: The Greensboro Sit-ins.***
Illustrated by Jerome Lagarrigue. New York: Dial, 2005.
From the perspective of a young black girl living in Greensboro, North
Carolina, in 1960, we watch as first a few, then several black students "sit-
in" at a segregated lunch counter, thus breaking the "whites only" law. Gradually, others in the town begin to picket shops that refuse to serve blacks, and
a crucial event in the civil rights movement of the 1960s begins. Somber
illustrations convey a sense of the moral darkness of the time.

The characters created for this book are fictional, but the historical events
that form the context of the story are true, as a brief explanation and chro-
nology of events at the end of the book explains. This is one example of
many picture books which illuminate particular events in history, keeping
the stories alive for generations to come.
Intermediate new reader/ABLE/ESOL/pre-GED/children's collection.
Subjects: African Americans, American history and culture, the American South,
civil rights, picture books for all ages.

Weatherford, Carole Boston. *The Sound that Jazz Makes.* Illustrated by Eric Velasquez. New York: Walker, 2000.

In a rhyming, rhythmical poem that echoes the musical history she is describing, Weatherford pays homage to the many roots of jazz: the drumbeats of Africa, the laments and work songs of slaves, the soothing balm of spirituals and the blues, the syncopation of ragtime. From Armstrong In New Orleans to Ellington in Harlem to the hip hop culture of today, Weatherford explores the musical connections of this uniquely American art form.

Intermediate new reader/ABLE/ESOL/pre-GED/children's collection.

Subjects: African American history and culture, the arts and artists, music, picture books for all ages.

Whelan, Gloria. *Friend on Freedom River.* Illustrated by Gijsbertvan Frankenhuyzen. Chelsea, Mich.: Sleeping Bear, 2004.

The setting is December, 1850, in a small town along the Detroit River in Michigan. A father, who must leave his family to work in the logging camps for the winter, places his son in charge with the words, "If you don't know what to do, just do what you think I would have done." The young boy is soon put to the test when a slave woman and her two children ask him to row them across the river to Canada and freedom. Deciding that his father would have ignored the danger and the cold to help a family, he agrees. The profound message of this simple story is conveyed as much in the illustrations as in the words, as the dark and brooding background of night and the river are contrasted against the warm glow of hope and human kindness displayed by the boy and his passengers.

Intermediate-advanced new reader/ABLE//pre-GED/children's collection.

Subjects: African American history and culture, inspirational stories and pictures, picture books for all ages, slavery.

Wood, Michele. *Going Back Home: An Artist Returns to the South.* Story interpreted and written by Toyomi Igus. San Francisco: Children's Book, 1996.

Remembering the family stories she heard while growing up, Wood, an accomplished artist, traveled to the Mississippi Delta to see and feel the land where her ancestors had lived as slaves and sharecroppers. Inspired by her journey, she created the pictures which illustrate this book, then collaborated with Igus to create a narrative to tell the stories behind each picture. The recurring motifs and quilt-like patterns of the pictures show, in Igus's words, "how pieces of a life can fit together." American and ESOL students alike will be intrigued by this extraordinary combination of art and words that conveys a depth of complexity neither could accomplish alone.

Intermediate new reader/ABLE/pre-GED/children's collection.

Subjects: African American history and culture, the arts and artists, arts and crafts, picture books for all ages, slavery.

Stories for Family Literacy Programs

Anaya, Rudolfo. *Farolitos for Abuelo.* Illustrated by Edward Gonzales. New York: Hyperion, 1998.

> When a young girl's abuelo, or grandfather, dies, she finds ways to keep his memory alive. Her practice of placing farolitos, or little candle lights, around his graveside every Christmas becomes a family tradition. Several Spanish words are used in the story, and all are explained in the glossary.

Intermediate new readers/ABLE/ESOL/children's collection.

Subjects: cultural traditions, family literacy, grandparents, Latinos.

Borden, Louise. *The A+ Custodian.* Illustrated by Adam Gustavson. New York: Simon & Schuster, 2004.

> Children and teachers work together to hang a banner as well as individual notes thanking Mr. Carillo, the school custodian, for his dedication to his job. Several vocabulary words related to schools and to handyman chores will be a boon to ESOL parents.

Intermediate new reader/ABLE/pre-GED/ESOL/children's collection.

Subjects: family literacy, work.

Carling, Amelia Lau. *Mama and Papa Have a Store.* New York: Dial, 1998.

> Author and illustrator Carling was born in Guatemala, the daughter of Chinese immigrants who operated a store in their adopted home. In that store, young Carling heard stories about China from her parents and their friends and stories about the Spanish and Mayan cultures from their customers, a multicultural learning experience that she revisits in this charming picture book.

Intermediate new reader/ABLE/pre-GED/ESOL/children's collection.
Subjects: Asia, cultural traditions, family literacy, Latin America and the Caribbean.

English, Karen. *Just Right Stew.* Illustrated by Anna Rich. Honesdale, Pa.: Boyds Mills, 1998.

Mama and Aunt Rose are trying to make Big Mama's (their mother's) favorite oxtail stew, but they can't figure out the secret ingredient. So little Victoria goes from one relative to the next to find the secret, but only Big Mama knows for sure. Sibling rivalry knows no age limit.
Intermediate new reader/ABLE/pre-GED/ESOL/children's collection.
Subjects: families, family literacy.

English, Karen. *Speak English for Us, Marisol!* Illustrated by Enrique O. Sanchez. Morton Grove, Il.: Albert Whitman, 2000.

Marisol is rushing home from school to see if her cat has had her kittens, but on the way she is asked by an uncle, an auntie, a neighbor, and finally her Mama to help them communicate in English with various merchants. As the story ends, we see Mama studying English and Marisol fondling the kittens.
Beginning-intermediate new reader/ABLE/pre-GED/ESOL/children's collection.
Subjects: families, family literacy, language, Latinos.

Frazee, Marla. *Roller Coaster.* San Diego: Harcourt, 2003.

Who looks eager? Who's not so sure? Who's terrified? Who could be twins? These are some of the language-generating questions that could be asked just looking at the first few pages of this delightful ride of a book in which a young girl summons up the courage to ride the roller coaster.
Beginning new reader/ABLE/ESOL/children's collection.
Subjects: family literacy, language.

Hesse, Karen. *Come On, Rain.* Illustrated by Jon J. Muth. New York: Scholastic, 1999.

In rhythmic, poetic text, a young girl yearns for rain to break the hot dry spell that has hovered over the city for three weeks. When she sees a cloud formation in the distant sky, she runs to gather her friends together to dance in the welcome rain. Even the mothers join in.

This book is also available with an accompanying CD.
Beginning-intermediate new reader/ABLE/pre-GED/ESOL/children's collection.
Subjects: family literacy, nature and the universe.

Isadora, Rachel. ***Caribbean Dream***. New York: Putnam, 1998.
"When morning meets light, we rise." In lilting, repetitive verse that echoes that pattern, two children go through a Caribbean day.
Beginning new reader/ABLE/ESOL/children's collection.
Subjects: family literacy, Latin America and the Caribbean.

James, Simon. ***Little One Step***. Cambridge, Mass.: Candlewick, 2003.
Just one more step, then one more, and before you know it, the tired little one is home. A parenting technique within a charming story.
Beginning new reader/ABLE/ESOL/children's collection.
Subjects: families, family literacy.

Khan, Rukhsana. ***The Roses in My Carpets***. Illustrated by Ronald Himler. New York: Holiday House, 1998.
There has been a war. The young Afghan boy is in a refugee camp with his mother and sister. The father was killed by a bomb. There is mud and dirt and fear. But the boy is determined to carry on. He goes to school and continues to learn to make beautiful carpets, into which he weaves his dreams for peace and a life where roses are real, not just patterns in a carpet. The war is not named, but the sentiments apply to all conflicts, past and present.
Intermediate new reader/ABLE/pre-GED/ESOL/children's collection.
Subjects: families, family literacy, refugees, war.

Kushkin, Karla. ***Under My Hood I Have a Hat***. Illustrated by Fumi Kosaka. New York: HarperCollins, 2004.
As the little girl dons her layers of winter clothing, she gives a vocabulary lesson for ESOL students, especially those unfamiliar with the many garments of winter.
Beginning new reader/ABLE/ESOL/children's collection.
Subjects: family literacy, language.

Lauture, Denize. ***Running the Road to ABC***. Illustrated by Reynold Ruffins. New York: Simon & Schuster, 1996.
The children rise before dawn and run, barefoot, over steep hills, past working peasants, and a market coming to life. They run "six days each week,

forty weeks each year, for seven years of their short lives." Haitian-born author Lauture never mentions words like poverty, hardship, or determination, but they are there in the action of these children determined to get whatever education is available to them. The text is simple and flows with the rhythm of the children as they run, but the story is profound.
Beginning new reader/ABLE/ESOL/children's collection.
Subjects: family literacy, inspirational stories, Latin America and the Caribbean.

Markes, Julie. *Shhhhh! Everybody's Sleeping.* Illustrated by David Parkins. New York: HarperCollins, 2005.
Everybody in the town—the teacher, the librarian, the policeman, the grocer, etc.—is asleep, whimsically so, as the illustrations show the teacher in her classroom and everyone else in their everyday environment, not in their beds. The rhyming verse is simple, the illustrations amusingly detailed, and, for ESOL students, the labeling of all the actors and their places of work presents a kind of fun vocabulary lesson.
Beginning new reader/ABLE/ESOL/children's collection.
Subjects: family literacy, language.

Reid, Barbara. *The Subway Mouse.* New York: Scholastic, 2003.
By day, Nib, a little mouse, learns the skills of living in his community in the subway tunnel. By night, he hears stories of a land called Tunnel's End that is mysterious, beautiful, and dangerous. Unable to resist the lure, he leaves his familiar world and heads for that magical-sounding Tunnel's End. He manages to return safely, but parents will take advantage of the opportunity to discuss the importance of staying close to home. Reid incorporated many fun objects into the plasticine models she created for her illustrations. Parents and children will have fun looking for recognizable objects.
Intermediate new reader/ABLE/pre-GED/ESOL/children's collection.
Subjects: family literacy, subways, urban life.

Shulevitz, Uri. *Snow.* New York: Farrar, Straus & Giroux, 1998.
In an old-fashioned city, in the company of pessimistic adults, one enthusiastic little boy and his dog believe that one snowflake will soon become a snow storm that will turn the gray city white. And it does!
Beginning new reader/ABLE/ESOL/children's collection.
Subjects: family literacy, nature and the universe.

Spinelli, Eileen. *Night Shift Daddy*. Illustrated by Melissa Iwai. New York: Hyperion, 2000.

> In a clearly urban setting, a father who works the night shift reads to his daughter and tucks her into bed before leaving for work. When Daddy comes home in the morning, he shares breakfast with the little girl, then *she* tucks *him* into bed. The simple rhyming text and softly hued illustrations set a gentle tone to this bedtime companion.
>
> *Beginning-intermediate new reader/ABLE/pre-GED/ESOL/children's collection.*
> *Subjects:* family literacy, fathers.

Weatherford, Carol Boston. *Grandma and Me*. Illustrated by Michelle Mills. New York: Black Butterfly Children's Books, 2004.

> This is one of a series of board books portraying black families in a variety of familiar and homey settings. The text is simple but engaging.
>
> *Beginning new reader/ABLE/ESOL/children's collection.*
> *Subjects:* African Americans, family literacy.

Williams, Sam. *Talk Peace*. Illustrated by Mique Moriuchi. New York: Holiday House, 2005.

> In simple, rhyming, rhythmic verse, parents and children talk about what to do when conflicts arise. The childlike drawings might inspire children to draw some of their own conflicting situations.
>
> *Beginning new reader/ABLE/ESOL/children's collection.*
> *Subjects:* families, family literacy.

Yolen, Jane. *Baby Bear's Chairs*. Illustrated by Melissa Sweet. Orlando, Fla.: Gulliver Books, Harcourt, 2005.

> In a bear family, mama and papa have the big chairs, older brother has "middling chairs," and baby bear has a high chair and his very special chair: his daddy's lap. Playful illustrations will amuse all.
>
> *Beginning-intermediate new reader/ABLE/ESOL/children's collection.*
> *Subjects:* families, family literacy.

Chapter 7

Nonfiction: Seeking Information, Exploring Interests

Lessons for the Literacy Classroom

A World of Information

Hardly a day goes by without some reminder that we live in the Information Age and that a mind-numbing cornucopia of facts and opportunities that could affect every aspect of our lives exists just beyond our fingertips. These are indeed exciting times, but they are daunting as well. We must keep up not only with what it is possible to know but also with the constantly changing technology that allows us access to all this information.

If an entire society, including the most educated among us, is challenged by the extraordinary quantity of information that is available as well as the fundamental and profound changes in the way we learn and receive it, where does this leave adult literacy students? They still lack mastery of the most basic information retrieval skill, the ability to read effectively. What is perhaps even more problematic, literacy students, because of their poor reading skills, missed much of the content that is generally presented through the printed word in history, social studies, science, civics, and other classes at the elementary and high school levels. As a result, they lack much of the background knowledge in which current information is rooted, as well as the habit of referring to and applying that knowledge to the problems and situations of their everyday lives. Adult literacy students are thus among the most vulnerable in this Information Age, surrounded by an ever-increasing flood of information, but increasingly limited in their ability to understand and apply it.

What Nonfiction Offers Adult Literacy Students

Many literacy students are motivated to enter reading programs at least in part because they need help acquiring information to improve various aspects of their lives. They need to be able to read the directions on the asthma medication they must give their child or read the schedule for the bus that will take them to their new job. They want to be able to read the newspaper and discuss the issues of the day with their friends and coworkers. Immigrants need to read the government papers that explain their rights and responsibilities and tell them how to become citizens.

From the very beginning of their literacy classes, no matter the level they start at, teachers can use readily available informational materials to help ABLE and ESOL students develop the basic skills of reading while they are also learning about things they want and need to know. For example, teachers can generate vocabulary lessons using grocery store flyers or articles from the sports pages of the local newspaper. They can have students write language experience stories that are reactions to the messages—direct and indirect—they find in advertisements on local billboards and in newspapers and magazines. In a class situation, they can help students compile recipes for favorite dishes to create a class cookbook. Learning to read information that matters in their everyday lives helps students recognize the link between their ability to read and their ability to function in their roles as parents, workers, and community members, thus encouraging them to stay in the literacy program, even when difficult circumstances—whether at home or in the classroom—tempt them to give up their efforts. Using such "real life" materials that are familiar and important in their everyday lives, tutors and teachers will be helping students make the crucial leap from learning to read to reading to learn. Taking the next step in that process, teachers can introduce their students to the world of information available to them in the nonfiction books in the public library.

What the Library Offers

Every public library offers books that can help adult literacy students become more skilled workers, wiser consumers, better parents, and more informed citizens. Some of these books will be in the adult section of the library, but many will come from the children's collection, which contains numerous non-fiction books appealing to adults, whether they are new readers or highly proficient readers new to a topic and looking for a basic but clear and informative presentation. These books address their subjects in a direct narrative style intended to convey information simply but accurately. They are well researched and make extensive and appealing use of photographs, illustrations, and graphic displays of facts and figures. They are not condescending to readers and they don't identify children as the intended audience. These books are written at varying levels of depth and complexity and so will be accessible to students at a range of reading levels. Some will be accessible to students reading on their own, others can be made accessible through the use of the information reading technique (explained in Chapter 3). Many will be appropriate for use in family literacy programs.

The nonfiction collection of the public library offers books on virtually every conceivable topic. The bibliography at the end of this chapter groups books into seven rather broad and somewhat arbitrary categories that suggest kinds of books as well as specific titles. Inevitably there is some overlap among the categories, but the purpose is to help librarians and teachers look at the library's nonfiction collection with a new audience in mind: adult literacy and ESOL students. Let's consider a few examples from each of those categories.

Arts, Crafts, Music

Some books in the arts and crafts category introduce readers to a particular kind of art as in Carol Finley's discussion of the making and displaying of masks by various African tribes in her book, *The Art of African Masks.* Other books focus more on the artist than the art as in Tonya Bolden's profiles of thirty-two African American artists in *Wake Up Our Souls: A Celebration of Black American Artists.* Then there are books that defy classification, such as Wynton Marsalis's *Jazz ABZ: An A to Z Collection of Jazz Portraits,* which is an alphabet book, a biography of jazz greats, a collection of stunning portraits of the musicians, and an anthology of poems that spans the genre from list poems to odes to sonnets to hip hop. *Jazz ABZ* is one of those children's books that will delight any adult lucky enough to discover it.

In a family literacy program, books about the arts offer adults and children numerous opportunities to look at and talk about pictures. Looking at the pictures in Lucy Micklethwaite's *I Spy: An Alphabet in Art,* for example, readers can find the objects that represent the letters, but then go on to talk about other elements of the picture that attract their attention such as the colors or the clothes or the way the people seem to be relating to each other.

Geography, History, Social Issues

The bibliography could have hundreds of books in this category. Publishers produce many books, often in series, that supplement and extend the curricula of elementary, middle school, and even high schools. Although marketed for children, many of these books will be appropriate for adults. For example, the National Geographic Society publishes a series titled American Documents, which includes books such as *The Constitution, The Bill of Rights,* and *The Declaration of Independence.* These books will be of particular help to ESOL students preparing for citizenship. Another series from National Geographic, Crossroads America, examines issues that transformed the history of a growing country such as the movement for women's suffrage and the building of the transcontinental railroad.

Beyond these series, there are certain authors who are truly masters of the genre of nonfiction books for children, producing numerous titles that reflect not only their extensive research but also their obvious engagement with the subject. Raymond Bial, for example, is both author and photographer of books about the Underground Railroad, the immigrant tenements of New York City, and the art of quilting, among other subjects. Lynn Curlee, as both artist and writer, has explored the history of topics as diverse as the Statue of Liberty,

Mt. Rushmore, and America's baseball parks. Newbery Medal winner Russell Freedman's books range from a photo biography of Abraham Lincoln to several profiles of American Indian tribes. Important chapters in the history of African Americans are examined in the numerous books of writers Jim Haskins and Walter Dean Myers. In all their books, these authors—and there are others whom librarians will be able to recommend—offer a depth of information and a quality of writing that readers of all ages and levels of ability will appreciate.

In the family literacy category, there are books from various publishers written about historical persons or events and designated by a phrase such as "easy readers" that indicates they are easy enough for children in grades one through three to read with minimal assistance. Rosa Parks's book *I Am Rosa Parks*, written with Jim Haskins, is one such example. Although picture books are not generally considered as sources of information, many tell stories that reveal facts and something beyond facts about individuals or events important to our nation's history. Ann Turner's *When Mr. Jefferson Came to Philadelphia*, for example, weaves the events surrounding Jefferson's writing of the Declaration of Independence into a story about a young boy fascinated by the redheaded stranger renting a room in his mother's boardinghouse.

Health and the Human Body

Several publishing companies produce series of books about health topics and particular diseases intended for middle and high school students but appealing and useful to adults. These books provide factual information with relevant vocabulary and lists of additional resources, especially online resources. Lucent Books's series Diseases and Disorders is accessible to advanced new readers, while Heinemann's series Just the Facts offers numerous pictures and text that is less dense, making the books accessible to intermediate level readers and even some more advanced beginners who have the help of a tutor or teacher. Librarians in a children's department could suggest many other series.

Although not published as a series in the strict sense, several books created by writer and photographer Seymour Simon combine extraordinary photographs with text that reveal facts as well as wonder at the workings of the human body. Some of his titles are *Eyes and Ears*, *The Brain*, and *Guts*.

Some health series are clearly written for an audience of children and would be appropriate for a family literacy setting. KidHaven's *Diabetes*, for example, part of their series KidHaven Science Library, introduces several young adults who talk about their reaction to learning they had diabetes and describe how they control their disease through diet, exercise, and a positive attitude. Picture books, too, offer opportunities to examine health issues from the perspective of story. Jamee Heelan's *Rolling Along: The Story of Taylor and His Wheelchair*, for example, presents the real life story of a set of twins, one with cerebral palsy and one without.

Language

Alphabet books are associated with children, yet many of them are quite sophisticated in concept and design. We mentioned Wynton Marsalis's *Jazz ABZ* above, a book that will delight and challenge literacy students who share the author's love of jazz. Books that explain idioms, proverbs, and other usages that native English speakers take for granted can be particularly helpful to ESOL students. Many are a bit offbeat as well, such as Loreen Leedy's *There's a Frog in My Throat: 440 Animal Sayings a Little Bird Told Me*, turning a language lesson into a humorous discussion of the vagaries and contradictions inherent in language.

Of course, alphabet books have an obvious appeal in a family literacy setting. Joanne Dugan's *ABC NYC* offers both an entertaining book based on photographs she took at various locations in New York City and a model that groups of adults and children might follow, taking photographs of their own neighborhood or city and compiling them into an alphabet book. In many libraries, alphabet books are shelved together as a group, so teachers can browse the collection looking for books that will appeal to their students. Picture books can also spark many a language lesson. Tana Hoban's numerous picture books, for example, are all simple collections of her photographs with descriptive titles such as *Cubes, Cones, Cylinders, and Spheres; 26 Letters and 99 Cents; Colors Everywhere* and *Push Pull Empty Full*.

Nature, Science, Technology

If you've ever helped a child find materials for a school science project, you've probably discovered books in the children's section of the library that intrigued you and taught you things you never knew. Books about the weather such as Patricia Lauber's *Hurricanes: Earth's Mightiest Storms*, or books about space such as Alvin Jenkins's *Next Stop Neptune: Experiencing the Solar System* are just two examples of books that seek to explain our world in ways that reveal the author's continuing wonder at its majesty and mystery.

Sharing that discovery of majesty and mystery in our world with the children in our lives is one of the best ways of keeping it alive for ourselves. Picture books like Molly Bang's *My Light,* which speaks in the voice of the sun explaining how sunlight becomes electricity, help us do just that. Many nonfiction books can also suggest projects for adults and children in a family literacy program. George Levenson's *Bread Comes to Life: A Garden of Wheat to Eat,* a rhyming romp through the process of growing wheat and making bread, would be the perfect introduction to a bread baking session for family groups.

Religion, Folklore, Cultural Traditions
With a growing population of immigrants in our country, even literacy programs in rural areas are becoming multicultural. In the public library, students will find books that represent their own religious or cultural backgrounds as well as books that will help them understand the religious and cultural backgrounds of their classmates. Anita Ganeri's book *Religions Explained: A Beginner's Guide to World Faiths,* for example, uses photographs, symbols, and excerpts from holy books to discuss the origins and current practices of religions from all over the world. Books explaining specific traditions abound as well. Azra Kidwai's *Islam,* a survey of the customs, beliefs, and writings of that faith, and Leo and Diane Dillon's picture book *To Everything There is a Season,* illustrating the text of the verse from the Book of Ecclesiastes, are two good examples.

For family literacy programs, there are many books that discuss various festivals and cultural traditions in bright and bold color. Elisa Amado's *Barrilete: A Kite for the Day of the Dead* is but one example. Picture books also help explain traditional customs. In Karen English's *Nadia's Hands,* for example, a young Pakistani-American girl learns the custom of decorating her hands with henna before she can be a flower girl in her aunt's wedding.

Sports, Leisure
DK Publishing is a company noted for its presentation of a multitude of facts and figures in a visually appealing way. Sports is one topic they cover extensively. Ivor Baddiel's *Ultimate Soccer* is one example of a book packed with photographs, diagrams, and a number of fun facts and statistical charts that will appeal to any sports fan. Baseball is a sport famous for its appeal to writers and artists, and there are numerous collections of such work. Lynn Curlee's *Ballpark: The Story of America's Baseball Fields* is perhaps unique, however. The illustrations are not photographs of the parks, but Curlee's paintings, and his verbal descriptions place these parks in the cultural setting of their time and their neighborhoods.

Biographies of sports figures abound and many fascinating and accessible ones will be found in the children's section. Sharon Robinson's tribute to her father, *Promises to Keep: How Jackie Robinson Changed America,* is one example of a sports biography that recognizes the profound influence of certain players on their country as well as their sport.

Many biographies of sports figures will appeal to children in a family literacy setting as well. Noted illustrator Floyd Cooper's *Jump! From the Life of Michael Jordan,* for example, describes the early life of disappointment and determination of the basketball legend. Publishing companies that produce "easy reading" books for elementary schoolchildren offer many titles in the sports arena. PowerKids Press, for example, offers a series titled Sports Training that features books on many sports.

Using Nonfiction Books in the Literacy Classroom
Here are a few sample lessons based on the books listed in the bibliography at the end of the chapter.

Sample Lessons

Sample Lesson 1: Finding Information in Prose

Potential Audience

- Intermediate new readers
- ABLE, pre-GED, GED

Procedure

- Give students a list of questions to review.
- Give them the text containing the information that answers those questions.
- Have them answer the questions by referring back to the text.

Questions

1. What group of people are most likely to develop type 1 diabetes?
2. What is the name of the substance that the pancreas does not make in a person with type 1 diabetes?

---

3. Why is type 2 diabetes becoming more common?

4. What appears to be a good way to avoid getting type 2 diabetes?

Text

From Bryan, Jenny. *Diabetes*. Series title: Just the Facts. Chicago: Heinemann, 2004, pp. 4–5.

Types of diabetes

There are two main types of diabetes: type 1 and type 2. Type 1 diabetes is most common in young people. At an early age, their pancreas stops making insulin.

Type 2 diabetes used to occur only in middle-aged and elderly people. But it is now starting to affect people in their 20s and 30s, and even some teenagers. The pancreas still makes some insulin, but the body does not use it properly. Glucose levels build up in the blood instead of being broken down and turned into energy.

The main reason that type 2 diabetes is growing more common is that many people are becoming overweight. A big effort is needed to change the way people take care of themselves.

Now go back and answer the questions, using the information from these three paragraphs.

Note to Teachers

With beginning level students, read the material to them first, then, using the information reading technique, have them create paragraphs stating the information in their own words. Read the questions to the students, then have them find the answers in the text they have created.

Sample Lesson 2: Finding Information in Charts

Potential Audience

- Intermediate—advanced new readers
- Pre-GED, GED, ESOL

Procedure

- Give students the following chart and the list of questions.
- Ask them to find the answers to the questions by reading the chart.

Questions

1. How many soccer World Cup events occurred from 1930 to 1994?
2. What is the usual interval between World Cup events?
3. How many teams have won more than one championship? Make a list.
4. What country has won the most championships?
5. How many different countries have appeared in a championship game?
6. Why do you think there were no World Cup events between 1938 and 1950?
7. What were or will be the four World Cup events after 1994?
8. What continents are represented by the teams on this list?
9. Are there any countries on the list that no longer exist as named?

Text

Baddiel, Ivor. *Soccer.* New York: DK Publishing, 1998.

World Cup Championship Games

1930	Uruguay 4	Argentina 2	
1934	Italy 2	Czechoslovakia 1	(after overtime)
1938	Italy 4	Hungary 2	
1950	Uruguay 2	Brazil 1	
1954	West Germany 3	Hungary 2	
1958	Brazil 5	Sweden 2	
1962	Brazil 3	Czechoslovakia 1	

1966	England 4	West Germany 2	(after overtime)
1970	Brazil 4	Italy 1	
1974	West Germany 2	Holland 1	
1978	Argentina 3	Holland 1	
1982	Italy 3	West Germany 1	
1986	Argentina 3	West Germany 2	
1990	West Germany 1	Argentina 0	
1994	Brazil 0	Italy 0	
	(Brazil won 3–2 on penalties)		

Sample Lesson 3: Creating an Alphabet Book

Potential Audience

• Family Literacy Programs.

Procedure:

1. Librarians: Gather a collection of several alphabet books that show the range of topics and creativity they represent. Joanne Dugan's *ABC NYC,* Mike Ulmer's *J is for Jump Shot: A Basketball Alphabet,* and Jennifer Belle's *Animal Stackers* are three that are mentioned in the bibliography for this chapter, but there are numerous others.
2. Teachers: Have families work in groups. Review the books with them, pointing out elements that seem important to you and asking the students to respond to the books. Encourage comments from both children and adults. Then ask each group to decide on a theme for an alphabet book they will create. Help them find pictures they can use. Make several dictionaries available to help them find words.
3. Librarians and teachers: Discuss ways to display the books in the library.

Sample Lesson 4: Gathering Facts

Potential Audience:

• ABLE, pre-GED, ESOL students
• Family literacy programs

Source of Information

Hopkins, Lee Bennett. *Days to Celebrate: A Full Year of Poetry, People, Holidays, History, Fascinating Facts, and More.* Illustrated by Stephen Alcorn. New York: Greenwillow, 2005.

Procedure

1. This book provides a calendar for each month that is full of information about events that happened on each day of the year.
2. Pick a day. Talk with students about the events mentioned and discuss possible projects related to the events.
3. This example is based on March 1. Two things that happened on that date:
   a) 1803—Ohio became the seventeenth state to enter the Union.
   b) 1867—Nebraska became the thirty-seventh state to enter the Union.
4. Suggested activities:
   Librarians: Help teachers identify books and Web sites that will provide information for this project.
   Teachers: Discuss possible projects such as the following:
   a) Make a list of the states that entered the Union between Ohio and Nebraska.
   b) Create lists of facts about Ohio and facts about Nebraska.
   c) Make a list of sports teams from each state.
   d) List the capital and other major cities for each state.
   e) Make a list of important people born in each state.
   f) Make a fabric or paper collage of items related to each state, such their flags, state flowers, state birds, etc. (See Adrienne Yorinks *Quilt of States: Piecing Together America,* listed in the bibliography, for inspiration.)

Nonfiction Books for Adult Literacy Students: A Bibliography

This bibliography is a sampling of the many books covering a wide array of subjects that will help adult literacy students obtain the information they need and pursue interests new and old. Books listed here come from both the adult and children's sections of the library. Each annotation suggests reading levels and potential audiences, notes the section of the library where the title is likely to be found, and indicates subjects covered. If specific titles are not available in your local library, ask your librarian to help you find similar books. The titles in this bibliography are organized by the categories discussed in the chapter, and each subject area includes books for adult new readers and books for family literacy.

Arts, Crafts, Music

Amistad: "Give Us Free": A Celebration of the Film by Steven Spielberg. Paintings by Kadir Nelson. Photographs by Andrew Cooper. New York: Newmarket, 1998.

> Steven Spielberg's movie *Amistad* chronicled a little-known episode in the story of slavery in the United States. African captives on the Spanish slave ship *Amistad* revolted, but were then captured by the American Navy and put on trial in Connecticut. An aging former president, John Quincy Adams, argued and won the case for their freedom. With still photographs from the movie and from activity on the set, paintings depicting the time and circumstances of the actual events, maps showing areas of activity in the slave trade, and excerpts from John Quincy Adams's diary of the events of the trial, this book offers a plentitude of historical background, Hollywood trivia, and visual engagement to appeal to a range of readers, especially if reviewed in conjunction with veiwing the movie.
> *Intermediate-advanced new reader/ABLE/pre-GED/GED/ESOL/adult collection.*
> *Subjects:* African American history and culture, American history and culture, the arts and artists, slavery.

Bial, Raymond. ***With Needle and Thread: A Book About Quilts.*** Boston: Houghton Mifflin, 1996.

> More than just "a book about quilts," this is a book about families and their connections through generations, about stories of the past retold in remembered patterns and scraps of worn clothing, about history and tradition, but also about creativity. As he describes the process of making quilts and explains some of the patterns, Bial also discusses how quilts helped runaway slaves find the path to freedom, how supporters of temperance and of women's suffrage created quilts that illustrated their beliefs, how the AIDS Memorial Quilt brought the nation's attention to the personal suffering of thousands affected by that disease, how Hmong refugees from

Asia have integrated their story cloths into the American art of quilt making, and how a new generation of quilt makers are using fabrics to create abstract and expressive works of art. Bial's own photographs illustrate the range of quilts beautifully.

Intermediate new reader/ABLE/pre-GED/ESOL/children's collection.

Subjects: arts and crafts, women.

Bingham, Jane. *Aboriginal Art and Culture*. Chicago: Raintree, 2005.

The aboriginal art of Australia is discussed in the context of the land and history of the aboriginal people who created it as well as of the European settlers who created the country that now dominates that land. This book offers pre-GED and GED students opportunities to practice the skills of finding specific facts and discerning relationships within a given text as well as in the pictorial and symbolic representations of that text.

Advanced new reader/pre-GED/GED/children's collection.

Subjects: art, art collections, the arts and artists.

Bolden, Tonya. *Wake Up Our Souls: A Celebration of Black American Artists*. New York: Harry N. Abrams, in association with the National Museum of American Art, Smithsonian Institution, 2004.

In chronological order, Bolden reviews the historical context of the works of thirty-two African American artists, including Romare Bearden, Jacob Lawrence, Gordon Parks, and Faith Ringgold, among others. Several works of each artist are displayed, along with brief but enlightening descriptions. A work of art history and art appreciation, this book also serves to remind readers that all great works of art fit into a larger picture of social history and personal achievement.

Intermediate-advance new reader/ABLE/pre-GED/GED/children's collection.

Subjects: African American history and culture, the arts and artists.

Finley, Carol. *The Art of African Masks*. Series title: Exploring Cultural Traditions. Minneapolis: Lerner, 1999.

Finley first explains how these elaborate masks are made and then explores specific masks and their uses in particular ceremonies of several African tribes. Detailed and brightly colored photographs convey the importance, drama, and beauty of these intriguing cultural artifacts.

Intermediate new reader/ABLE/pre-GED/ESOL/children's collection.
Subjects: Africa, arts and crafts, cultural traditions.

Igus, Toyomi. *I See the Rhythm.* Illustrated by Michele Wood. San Francisco: Children's Book Press,1998.

This book is hard to classify, but equally hard to resist. Michele Wood, an artist known for her paintings of musicians and singers, studied the history of African American music from slave songs through jazz and gospel all the way to hip hop. The paintings she created as a result of her study convey a sense of both the history and the emotional impact of those musical movements. Writer Igus listened to these styles of music while looking at Wood's pictures and wrote poems to express her own emotional reactions. The resulting book is a bold, colorful, and unique blending of history, art, and poetry.

Intermediate new reader/ABLE/pre-GED/ESOL/children's collection.
Subjects: African American history and culture, the arts and artists, music, collections, art and literature collections.

Marsalis, Wynton. *Jazz ABZ: An A to Z Collection of Jazz Portraits.* Illustrated by Paul Rogers. Cambridge, Mass.: Candlewick, 2005.

As descriptive adjectives go, extraordinary hardly covers it for this book. An alphabet book, an introduction to the great jazz artists of the twentieth century in words and in stunning portraits, a collection of poems that is also a review of several different kinds of poetry, this book is all these things, and still more than the sum of its parts. For each letter of the alphabet, Marsalis has written a poem in praise of a jazz musician, from Louis Armstrong to Count Basie all the way to DiZZy Gillespie. Written in a variety of forms, these poems fit the artist they describe: a beat poem, a blues poem, a limerick, a haiku, and so on. Some are easy to read, others quite difficult. Explanations of the forms appear at the end of the book, as do biographical summaries of each musician that will give readers basic facts to help them decipher some of the more obscure meanings or references in the poems. Originating from the desire of artist and illustrator Paul Rogers to celebrate the jazz musicians he's admired all his life, this book is a fittingly creative tribute to those musicians and the creative art form that is jazz.

Beginning-advanced new reader/ABLE/pre-GED/GED/children's collection.
Subjects: African American history and culture, African Americans, language, music.

Mason, Antony. *In the Time of Warhol.* Series title: Art Around the World. Brookfield, Conn.: Copper Beech, 2002.

The various art movements that followed World War II—abstract expressionism, surrealism, and pop art, for example—produced the kind of art that leaves many viewers wondering who decided such works were "great art," or indeed "art" at all. This book helps to answer that question. Reproductions of such iconic works as Roy Lichtenstein's "comic strip" paintings and Andy Warhol's Campbell's soup cans are discussed briefly but within the context of social movements and attitudes of the time, helping us see some connection between the art and the society that produced it. Readers may still shake their heads, but they will also have some idea of what the artist was trying to do.

Intermediate-advanced new reader, pre-GED/GED/children's collection.
Subjects: art collections, the arts and artists.

Sola, Michele. *Angela Weaves a Dream.* Photographs by Jeffrey Jay Foxx. New York: Hyperion, 1997.

Angela, a young Mayan girl living in southern Mexico, is learning to weave as she prepares to enter a contest for the "best first weaving." Photographs show Angela and her friends weaving out-of-doors, with their work tethered to a tree, in the manner such weaving has been done for generations. The patterns are traditional as well, each telling a different story or representing a different belief or custom. Close-up shots of the designs show the intricacy of the pattern.

Intermediate new reader/ABLE/pre-GED/ESOL/children's collection.
Subjects: arts and crafts, cultural traditions, Latin America and the Caribbean.

Arts, Crafts, Music—Family Literacy

Angelou, Maya. *Kofi and His Magic.* Photographs by Margaret Courtney-Clarke. New York: Clarkson Potter, 1996.

In a West African country, Kofi weaves Kente cloth to help earn money for his family. Despite the hardships of his life, Kofi is a dreamer and as he weaves his cloth, he imagines himself living in places he's heard about but never been to. Colorful photographs of Kofi, his family, and the surrounding villages and countryside give readers a sense of the larger context of Kofi's life.

Beginning-intermediate new reader/ABLE/pre-GED/ESOL/children's collection.

Subjects: Africa, arts and crafts, economic and social conditions, family literacy.

Casteñeda, Omar. S. ***Abuela's Weave****.* Illustrated by Enrique O. Sanchez. New York: Lee & Lothrop, 1993.

Although she is known as one of the most talented weavers in the village, the *abuela* (grandmother) of this story shuns the crowds of the open market of her village because of a disfiguring birthmark covering her face. But when she teaches her young granddaughter how to weave, they go to the market together and the young girl learns a lesson about the many kinds of beauty.

Intermediate new reader/ABLE/pre-GED/ESOL/children's collection.

Subjects: arts and crafts, families, family literacy, Latin America and the Caribbean.

Chocolate, Debbie. ***Kente Colors****.* Illustrations by John Ward. New York: Walker, 1996.

In simple rhyming verse, Chocolate shows how the bright and bold colors of African Kente cloth are used for certain ceremonies and seasons. An author's note at the end offers a brief description of the making of this fabric which has long been an important part of the traditions and rituals of particular African tribes and is now popular among African Americans as well.

Though an excellent choice for beginning new readers in a family literacy programs, the descriptive verse and boldly colored illustrations will appeal to readers of all ages.

Beginning new reader/ABLE/ESOL/children's collection.

Subjects: Africa, arts and crafts, cultural traditions, picture books for all ages.

---

de Brunhoff, Laurent. ***Babar's Musuem of Art****.* New York: Harry N. Abrams, 2003.

With all the quirky humor of the Babar stories, this book offers a distinctly exploratory approach to looking at art with young children. As Queen Celeste says to Cornelius, who tries to *explain* the art to the children, "Hush Cornelius . . . Let them have fun. They'll have plenty of lectures later." The setting is an abandoned train station that Babar and Celeste save from the wrecking ball by turning it into an art museum. (Visitors to Paris will recognize the Musée D'Orsay.) The paintings are whimsical take-offs of famous works of art, with elephants as the major characters. Beyond encouraging the children to express their reactions to the "elephant" pictures, it would be a fascinating exercise for children and adults alike to compare them to the originals (all of which are identified at the back of the book). Reproductions of the originals would also be easy to find in library collections or among postcard collections of art works found in many museum gift shops.

Beginning-intermediate new reader/ABLE/pre-GED/children's collection.
Subjects: the arts and artists, family literacy.

Lyon, George Ella. *Weaving the Rainbow.* Illustrations by Stephanie Anderson. New York: Atheneum, 2004.

A young girl watches over a flock of sheep as they grow their coats. Then in spring, she helps to shear the sheep, spin the wool, dye the yarn with herbs and flowers, and then weave the yarn from the white sheep into a rainbow of colors.

Beginning-intermediate new reader/ABLE/ESOL/children's collection.
Subjects: arts and crafts, family literacy, nature and the universe.

Micklethwait, Lucy. *I Spy: An Alphabet in Art.* New York: Greenwillow, 1999.

Within twenty-six great works of art from a wide variety of traditions, viewers must find the object beginning with "a," "b," etc. Great fun for adults and children alike, this exercise also leads viewers to look more carefully at each picture. Micklethwait has also produced *I Spy Two Eyes: Numbers in Art* and *I Spy a Lion: Animals in Art,* both from Greenwillow, and *A Child's Book of Art* from Dorling Kindersley, which organizes great works of art according to subjects such as boats, playing games, opposites, and more.

Beginning new reader/ABLE/ESOL/children's collection.
Subjects: the arts and artists, family literacy, language.

Museum Shapes. New York: Metropolitan Museum of Art, 2005.

First comes the question: "What shape is . . . " followed by the several reproductions from the Museum's collection in which that shape appears, and then the answer: circle or square or arch, and so on. A simple book with an extraordinary collection of art work that offers adults and children many opportunities to talk about what is in a picture, and perhaps what is just beyond that picture.

In a similar style, the Museum has also produced *Museum ABC* and *Museum 123.*

Beginning new reader/ABLE/ESOL/children's collection.

Subjects: the art and artists, family literacy, language.

Wolfe, Gillian. ***Look! Body Language in Art.*** London: Frances Lincoln Children's Books, 2004.

With directions to look at the hands or the face or for a particular message, this book helps readers look at pictures, all reproductions from several museums, to find the story behind the surface, in effect, to "read behind the lines."

Beginning-intermediate new reader/ABLE/pre-GED/ESOL/children's collection.

Subjects: the arts and artists, family literacy.

Geography, History, Social Issues

The American Immigrant. New York: Time-Life, 2004.

Starting with the Asian peoples who crossed the land bridge over the Pacific Ocean into what is now Alaska and covering every major immigration movement into the twenty-first century, this book offers a broad overview that clearly establishes immigration as a multifaceted topic that is fundamental to an understanding of the history and culture of the United States. Both negative and positive effects are discussed, from the diseases brought by early settlers that devastated native populations to the injustice and cruelty rendered to those brought here against their will to the heroic struggles of so many immigrants and refugees whose ultimate success contributed so much to the prosperity of the growing nation. Numerous photographs and illustrations add both information and texture to this fascinating and ongoing story.

Intermediate-advanced new reader/pre-GED/GED/ESOL/adult collection.

Subjects: American history and culture, immigrants and immigration.

Bartoletti, Susan Campbell. *Growing Up in Coal Country*. Boston: Houghton Mifflin, 1996.

Child labor, immigrant labor, the tyranny of the company town, the lack of opportunity for young people in rural America, these issues are all part of the history of coal mining, particularly in Appalachia. Using historical documents, quotations from letters and diaries, and many archival photographs, Bartoletti describes the long and dangerous hours that coal workers, many of whom were children, endured. The story may seem old and far removed from our modern-day world, but recent newspaper headlines remind us that men and women still descend underground everyday to dig the coal that powers that modern world we so easily take for granted.

Intermediate-advanced new reader/pre-GED/GED/children's collection.

Subjects: American history and culture, Appalachia, rural life, work.

Bial, Raymond. *Tenement: Immigrant Life on the Lower East Side*. Boston: Houghton Mifflin, 2002.

As the arrival point for so many immigrants, especially in the late nineteenth and early twentieth centuries, New York City played a large role in the history of immigration. In this book, Bial offers a vivid and informative portrait of life for many of those immigrants who clustered together in the tenements of the Lower East Side neighborhoods of New York. Using documents and photographs from the Lower East Side Tenement Museum, a museum housed in a former tenement building, Bial takes readers on a virtual tour through the hallways and apartments of these tenements, showing how the new arrivals lived, worked, raised families, made friends, and struggled to fulfill their personal version of the American dream.

As both writer and photographer, Raymond Bial has produced several books about various aspects of American history for juvenile and young adult audiences that will be appealing and informative for adults. Among the topics he has covered are rural life, the Shakers, several different Indian tribes, and the underground railroad. See also the annotation for *With Needle and Thread: A Book About Quilts* above.

Intermediate new reader/ABLE/pre-GED/ESOL/children's collection.

Subjects: American history and culture, immigrants and immigration, urban life.

Bodnarchuk, Kari J. *Kurdistan: Region Under Siege*. Series title: World in Conflict. Minneapolis: Lerner, 2000.

This book predates the American invasion of Iraq, but it describes the roots of the long-standing conflict between the Kurdish people and their neighbors, particular Turkey and Iraq, which continues to affect political developments throughout the region. The discussions from all perspectives of this complex situation will help advanced new readers interested in following current events understand the ongoing conflict.

Other titles in the World in Conflict series include *Rwanda: Country Torn Apart, Haiti: Land of Inequality,* and *Sudan: North Against South.*
Advanced new reader/pre-GED/GED/ESOL/children's collection.
Subjects: the Middle East, political repression and resistance, war.

Caputo, Philip. ***10,000 Days of Thunder: A History of the Vietnam War.*** New York: Atheneum, 2005.
Caputo's memoir of his own experience as a marine lieutenant in the Vietnam War, *A Rumor of War,* has become a classic in the annals of war stories. In this book, he introduces new generations of readers to the history of that most controversial of American wars. In brief but informative chapters, Caputo reviews the origins of the war, discusses some of the major battles and battle strategies, and profiles many of the leaders, American and Vietnamese, who made the decisions that determined the war's course and ultimate outcome. He also looks beyond the battlefield to discuss the draft, the antiwar movement, and the music that became forever linked with the turmoil of that time, and he examines the aftermath of the war, both in the United States and in Vietnam.
Intermediate-advanced new reader/pre-GED/GED/ESOL/children's collection.
Subjects: American history and culture, war.

Curlee, Lynn. ***Liberty.*** New York: Atheneum, 2000.
That quintessential emblem of America, the Statue of Liberty, was conceived of, built, and, to a large extent, paid for by the people of France. In this stunning picture book, Curlee gives readers a detailed account of one Frenchman's dream to build a statue in honor of the idea of liberty, and his illustrations convey the monumental size, not only of the statue, but of the seemingly impossible task that resulted in the creation of this world-renowned symbol of freedom.
Intermediate-advanced new reader/pre-GED/GED/ESOL/children's collection.

Subjects: American history and culture, the arts and artists, immigrants and immigration, international perspectives, picture book for all ages.

Ferroa, Peggy, and Elaine Chan. *China*. Series title: Cultures of the World. New York: Marshall Cavendish, 2002.

Covering the basic issues of history, geography, and government and the lifestyle issues of food, the arts, festivals, and leisure activities, the books in this series present a well rounded view of life in the country under discussion. Numerous photographs as well as maps, a time line, a glossary, and other features add to the content and the appeal of these titles. Among the many other countries studied are Colombia, Indonesia, Iran, Mexico and the Philippines.

Intermediate-advanced new reader/pre-GED/GED/ESOL/children's collection.
Subjects: Asia, cultural traditions, geography, international perspectives.

Finkelman, Paul. *The Constitution*. Series title: American Documents. Washington, D.C.: National Geographic, 2004.

As noted in this book, the United States Constitution is the oldest and shortest written constitution of any government functioning today, but its development was a process of debate, trial and error. The book briefly reviews the weaknesses of the original Articles of Confederation and the compromises reached by the men who gathered in Philadelphia in 1787 to write the document that has governed the United States for more than 200 years. A discussion of how some provisions of the Constitution and its twenty-seven amendments affect issues in the news of the twenty-first century indicates that the debates begun by the Founding Fathers continue. The full text of the Constitution and its Amendments and a glossary of related terms are included. A reproduction of a sculpture that spells out the Preamble in license plates would make the once required school practice of memorizing the Preamble an entertaining exercise.

Other books in the National Geographic's series American Documents include *The Bill of Rights* and *The Declaration of Independence*.

Intermediate new reader/ABLE/pre-GED/ESOL/children's collection.
Subjects: American history and culture.

Freedman, Russell. *In Defense of Liberty: The Story of America's Bill of Rights*. New York: Holiday House, 2003.

Freedman begins with a list of questions that reflect issues in the news today: Do minors have the same constitutional rights as adults? Does the Bill of Rights guarantee a right to personal privacy? He then goes on to review each of the ten amendments to the U.S. Constitution that are known collectively as the Bill of Rights, describing the issues that led to the adoption of the amendments and discussing sample cases argued on their basic principles, including many currently under discussion.

Freedman is an award-winning author of several books of history written for young readers but appealing and informative for adults. Among them are biographies of Abraham Lincoln and Eleanor Roosevelt and several books about the American West and the life and culture of Native Americans.

Intermediate-advanced new reader/pre-GED/GED/ESOL/children's collection.
Subjects: American history and culture.

Freedman, Russell. *The Voice that Challenged a Nation: Marian Anderson and the Struggle for Equal Rights*. New York: Clarion, 2004.

The name Marian Anderson may not be well known, especially among younger generations of Americans, but she figured in one of those transforming events on the road to equal rights for black Americans that we all need to be reminded of. Although acknowledged as a singer of immense talent, in 1939 she was denied the right to perform in Constitution Hall in Washington, D.C., because the owners of that building, an organization of descendants of early settlers called the Daughters of the American Revolution, forbade performances by blacks. Numerous people spoke out in protest, including then First Lady Eleanor Roosevelt, who withdrew her own membership in the D.A.R. and arranged for Anderson to sing in front of the Lincoln Memorial, which she did to an audience of more than 75,000 people. Freedman recalls this event in some detail, but also describes Anderson's subsequent career in which she broke other color lines in the world of classical music, just as Jackie Robinson did in the world of baseball.

Recordings of Marian Anderson singing, including archival recordings of her concert on the Mall, will be available in many libraries and will add the beauty and richness of her voice to a discussion of her contribution to civil rights.

Intermediate-advanced new reader/pre-GED/GED/children's collection.
Subjects: African American history and culture, American history and culture, the arts and artists, civil rights.

Granfield, Linda. *97 Orchard Street, New York: Stories of Immigrant Life*. Photographs by Arlene Alda. Toronto: Tundra, 2001.

Once a tenement home to numerous immigrant families, 97 Orchard Street in New York City is now the site of the Lower East Side Tenement Museum. For this book, Granfield and Alda have used photographs and stories from the museum to tell the story of those early immigrants, a story that many of today's immigrants would find familiar, no matter where they've landed in their search for a better life.

Intermediate new reader/ABLE/pre-GED/GED/ESOL/children's collection.
Subjects: American history and culture, immigrants and immigration, urban life.

Hopkinson, Deborah. *Shutting Out the Sky: Life in the Tenements of New York 1880–1924*. New York: Orchard, 2003.

Focusing on the experiences of five immigrants who came to the United States as children but grew and prospered here in a variety of ways, Hopkinson gives names and faces to the story of massive immigration in the days before the 1924 law establishing immigration quotas was enacted. Longer and more detailed than the Bial and Granfield books mentioned above, this book fills in the details of particular lives, giving dimension and texture to a story that continues to shape life in the United States.

Intermediate-advanced new reader/pre-GED/GED/ESOL/children's collection.
Subjects: American history and culture, immigrants and immigration, urban life.

Little, Charles E. *Discover America: The Smithsonian Book of the National Parks*. Photographs by David Muench. Washington, D.C.: Smithsonian, 1995.

Both the natural history of the American continent and the human history of the people who established a country on this land are preserved by the National Park Service. From the stunning beauty of the Grand Canyon to the soul-stirring sight of the Statue of Liberty, from our democracy's birthplace in Independence Hall in Philadelphia to the childhood home of Abraham Lincoln, from the battlefields of the bloody Civil War to the memorial to Nobel Peace Prize winner Dr. Martin Luther King, Jr., the Park Service takes care of it all. In words and pictures, this book takes readers of all levels, and Americans new and old, on a virtual tour of the geological wonders and historical landmarks that tell America's story. In addition, the substantive content of the text offers GED students opportunities to practice the skill of reading historical and scientific material to identify specific details and concepts.

Beginning-advanced new reader/ABLE/pre-GED/GED/ESOL/adult collection.

Subjects: American history and culture, geography, nature and the universe.

Lyons, Mary E., ed. *Feed the Children First: Irish Memories of the Great Hunger.* New York: Atheneum, 2002.

At a time when the victims of famine and brutal political feuds stare out at us from our television screens and newsmagazines, a book such as this reminds many of the prosperous and comfortable among us that we are but a few generations removed from immigrant ancestors who fled desperate conditions brought on by nature or politics or both. In her introduction to this book, editor Lyons gives a brief explanation of the natural disaster that spoiled the potato crop most poor Irish people depended on for sustenance and the political cruelty that compounded nature's blow. She then lets the victims and their descendants tell the rest of the story, as she presents excerpts from the accounts of survivors and their children that have been collected by the Irish Folklore Commission. A compelling example of collected folklore, this book reminds us of the importance of telling our stories to preserve them for future generations.

Intermediate new reader/ABLE/pre-GED/ESOL/children's collection.

Subjects: disasters, economic and social conditions, immigrants and immigration.

McWhorter, Diane. *A Dream of Freedom: The Civil Rights Movement from 1954 to 1968.* New York: Scholastic, 2004.

Although McWhorter addresses an audience of young people in her Introduction, this book is included in this bibliography because it is such a well documented, well written, and thorough review of the major events of the civil rights movement, and because, beyond the Introduction, its language and visual clarity will appeal to readers of all ages. The book is also unusual because it is written by a white woman who grew up in Birmingham, Alabama, amid all the privilege and opportunity that her race afforded her. But the events that unfolded in that city forever changed her understanding of her world as much as they did for Birmingham's black citizens, and she has spent much of her professional life studying and writing about race relations in America. Each section of the book covers one year and describes the pivotal events that advanced the movement. Numerous photographs and quotations from leaders and participants add to the documentary quality of the book.

Advanced new reader/pre-GED/GED/children's collection.

Subjects: African American history and culture, American history and culture, political repression and resistance.

Myers, Walter Dean. ***Antarctica: Journeys to the South***. New York: Scholastic, 2004.

As a young soldier on a mission bringing supplies to a military base in the Arctic, Myers became fascinated by the geology of the polar regions and curious about the men who were adventurous—or foolish—enough to explore them. In this book, he presents portraits of those men and their difficult missions to Antarctica, a place most of us would consider an extremely inhospitable landscape, but one we also now know plays a major role in determining the climate, water supply, and air quality of those places on earth that we choose to inhabit.

Advanced new reader/pre-GED/GED/children's collection.

Subjects: geography, nature and the universe.

Rossi, Ann. ***Created Equal: Women Campaign for the Right to Vote 1840–1920***. Series title: Crossroads America. Washington, D.C.: National Geographic, 2003.

An engaging mix of text, drawings, editorial cartoons, and a few photographs combine to tell the story of the suffragist movement in support of women's right to vote. Quotations from women of the time as well as brief profiles of some of the leaders of the movement, women like Susan B. Anthony and Elizabeth Cady Stanton, help set the context of the times for a modern audience.

Other titles in the series include *Cultures Collide: Native Americans and Europeans* and *Railroad Fever: Building the Transcontinental Railroad.*

Intermediate new reader/ABLE/pre-GED/ESOL/children's collection.

Subjects: American history and culture, women.

Rubin, Susan Goldman. ***The Flag with Fifty-Six Stars: A Gift from the Survivors of Mauthausen***. Illustrations by Bill Farnsworth. New York: Holiday House, 2005.

Having heard, on their jury-rigged radios, of the advancing American army, and having watched their German captors flee, the prisoners in the Austrian concentration camp of Mauthausen decided to welcome their liberators with an American flag made from whatever scraps of material they had at hand. Not knowing the number of stars to put on the flag, they guessed 56. When the Americans arrived, the prisoners gave the astonished commander a gift of the flag, which the prisoners and soldiers together raised over the camp. That flag now resides in the Simon Wiesenthal Museum in Los Angeles.

This is but one example of a multitude of picture books that tell personal and deeply moving stories from the annals of World War II that reveal both the depths of cruelty and the heights of courage that humans are capable of.

Intermediate-advanced new reader/pre-GED/GED/ESOL/children's collection.
Subjects: American history and culture, inspirational stories and pictures, picture books for all ages, war.

Sandler, Martin W. *America Through the Lens: Photographers Who Changed the Nation.* New York: Henry Holt, 2005.

Sandler highlights the work of eleven photographers and two government agencies whose photographs do what photographer Lewis Hine regarded as the mandate of the profession: "show the things that need to be appreciated; show the things that need to be changed." Mathew Brady's photographs from the Civil War, Hine's exposition of conditions of child labor, and James Van Der Zee's portraits of middle-class life in Harlem are here. So are NASA's (National Aeronautics and Space Administration) photographs from outer space and NOAA's (National Oceanic and Atmospheric Administration) explorations of life under water. For beginning new readers, the photographs alone offer a panoramic view of the major events that have shaped our history over the last century and a half. For intermediate and advanced readers, the clearly written and informative text offers depth and detail to help Americans long established and newly arrived understand what has brought us to the life we know today.

Sandler has published other books exploring aspects of American history that will appeal to new readers. Two examples are *Island of Hope: The Story of Ellis Island and the Journey to America* (Scholastic, 2004) and *Vaqueros: America's First Cowmen* (Henry Holt, 2001).

Beginning-advanced new reader/ABLE/pre-GED/ESOL/children's collection.
Subjects: American history and culture; photography, thematic collections.

Thomson, Sarah L. *Stars and Stripes: The Story of the American Flag*. Illustrated by Bob Davey and Debra Bandelin. New York: HarperCollins, 2003.

The American flag we are all familiar with has undergone many changes in its lifetime, from the discussion about whether or not to keep the number of stripes at thirteen to the numbers and arrangements of the stars in the field of blue. This book reviews that history, including some conflicting stories about who made the first flag, and also discusses changes in the frequency and manner in which the flag is displayed, particularly after the events of September 11, 2001.

Intermediate new reader/ABLE/pre-GED/ESOL/children's collection.
Subjects: American history and culture.

Vieira, Linda. *The Mighty Mississippi: The Life and Times of America's Greatest River*. Illustrations by Higgins Bond. New York: Walker, 2005.

Among the repercussions of the devastation that Hurricane Katrina brought to the Gulf Coast of the United States is a renewed understanding of the vital role that the Mississippi River plays in the history, agriculture, commerce, transportation, and ecological stability of so much of the country. Originating in the mammoth glaciers that created much of the geography of North America, the Mississippi runs through the very heart of the continent from Minnesota to the Louisiana delta. As a pictorial time line running across the top of each page graphically reminds us, this river has affected many aspects of life along its path from long before the days when European settlers traversed its length and many tributaries in their explorations of what they called The New World.

Intermediate-advanced new reader/ABLE/pre-GED/GED/ESOL/children's collection.
Subjects: American history and culture, geography.

Waterlow, Julia. *A Family from Ethiopia*. Series title: Families Around the World. Austin, Tex.: Raintree Steck-Vaughn, 1998.

By focusing on one particular family and their everyday way of life, the books in this series invite readers to imagine themselves in the situations described, making the people and their land less foreign, no matter how different or far away they may be. Other countries profiled in the series include Bosnia, Guatemala, and Vietnam.

Intermediate new reader/ABLE/pre-GED/ESOL/children's collection.
Subjects: Africa, geography, international perspectives.

Geography, History, Social Issues—Family Literacy

Burgan, Michael. ***The Declaration of Independence***. Series title: We the People. Minneapolis: Compass Point, 2001.

In simple text that will be accessible even to some beginning new readers, this book discusses the roots of the struggle for independence and introduces the major figures gathered in Philadelphia to produce a document that continues to influence democratic movements around the world. With a glossary, time line, index, and list of sources for additional information, this book, and others in this series, also introduces literacy students as well as school-aged children to the variety of ways in which information is presented in nonfiction books.

Other titles in the series include *The Jamestown Colony, The California Gold Rush, and The Santa Fe Trail.*

Beginning-intermediate new reader/ABLE/pre-GED/ESOL/children's collection.
Subjects: American history and culture, family literacy, political repression and resistance.

Carlson, Laurie. ***Boss of the Plains: The Hat that Won the West***. Illustrated by Holly Meade. New York: DK, 1998.

The son of a hat maker who became bored with the family business, John Batterson Stetson decided to seek his fortune with the cowboys and gold seekers heading west. He never succeeded with horses or gold, but he made a hat that shielded the cowboys and gold seekers from sun and rain and could fan the flames of a campfire to boot, and so the name Stetson lives on. The dusty-colored illustrations add a rollicking, Wild West flair to this amusing but insightful biography of a hat.

Intermediate new reader/ABLE/pre-GED/children's collection.
Subjects: the American West, family literacy.

Chin-Lee, Cynthia, and Terri de la Pena. ***A is for the Americas***. Illustrated by Enrique O. Sanchez. New York: Orchard, 1999.

Although written in the form of an alphabet book, the primary message here is that the term "America" can refer to any country in North, Central, or South America. The objects that represent each of the letters come from those various countries. The text of the book is English, but the entries include both English words, as "I" is for igloo, and Spanish words, as "F" is for futbol (or soccer as it is known in the United States).

Beginning-intermediate new reader/ABLE/ESOL/children's collection.
Subjects: family literacy, geography, Latin America and the Caribbean.

Martin, Bill, Jr. and Michael Sampson. *I Pledge Allegiance.* Illustrated by Chris Raschka. Cambridge, Mass.: Candlewick, 2002.

The words of the Pledge of Allegiance are the text, with some explanatory notes provided along the way, such as explaining the numbers of stars and stripes and what a republic is. The childlike illustrations are playful, but the overall message conveys the fundamental principles upon which the United States stands.

Beginning new reader/ABLE/ESOL/children's collection.
Subjects: American history and culture, family literacy.

Parks, Rosa. *I Am Rosa Parks.* With Jim Haskins. Illustrated by Wil Clay. New York: Dial, 1997.

In her own words, Parks talks a little about her background but mostly about the day she refused to relinquish her seat on a bus to a white man and the Montgomery Bus Boycott that followed her courageous decision.

Beginning new reader/ABLE/pre-GED/ESOL/children's collection.
Subjects: African American history and culture, civil rights, family literacy.

Rappaport, Doreen. *Martin's Big Words: The Life of Dr. Martin Luther King, Jr.* Illustrated by Bryan Collier. New York: Hyperion, 2001.

Rappaport inserts quotes from Martin Luther King into this brief overview of his life. Dramatic illustrations help convey a sense of the magnitude of purpose that characterized his time as a leader in the civil rights movement. This book can introduce young readers to one of the most important figures in American history in the twentieth century. For adults and children who wish to pursue more information, a list of additional books and web sites is given at the end.

Beginning new reader/ABLE/ESOL/children's collection.
Subjects: African American history and culture, civil rights, family literacy.

Raschka, Chris. *New York is English, Chattanooga is Creek.* New York: Atheneum, 2005.

Clever, informative, even a bit wacky, this amazing and amusing book conveys a serious message: America has always been a multicultural country.

Raschka personifies places, so New York, who is English, decides to have a party, and in the course of introducing his guest list, explains the origin of all their names. So we learn, for example, that El Paso is Spanish, Minneapolis is part Sioux and part Greek, Brooklyn is Dutch, Chicago is Algonquin, and so on. Raschka's quirky and colorful illustrations add to the party atmosphere and will delight the children. Adults will be fascinated by the polyglot nature of American place-names and may be inspired to investigate the origin of names in their local areas.

Intermediate new reader/ABLE/pre-GED/ESOL/children's collection.

Subjects: American history and culture, family literacy, geography, language, picture book for all ages.

Turner, Ann. *When Mr. Jefferson Came to Philadelphia: What I Learned of Freedom, 1776*. Illustrated by Mark Hess. New York: HarperCollins, 2003.

Weaving the fictional story of a young boy who helps his mother run a boardinghouse into the true story of Thomas Jefferson's writing of the Declaration of Independence, this picture book introduces young readers to the man, the circumstances, and the words that set the course for the founding of the United States.

Beginning-intermediate new reader/ABLE/pre-GED/ESOL/children's collections.

Subjects: American history and culture, family literacy.

Yorinks, Adrienne. *Quilt of States: Piecing Together America.* Quilts by Adrienne Yorinks. Written by Yorinks and 50 librarians from across the nation. Washington, D.C.: National Geographic Society, 2005.

A unique and imaginative approach to geography, and a boon to learners with good visual memory, this book represents each state by a quilt cut in the state's shape and decorated with symbols of significance to that state, such as a trumpet for Louisiana and snow-covered trees for New Hampshire. The states are presented in their order of entrance into the Union, from the first, Delaware, to the latest, Hawaii, adding yet another piece of information beyond the lists of fun facts and claims to fame that are included in this visually fascinating book.

Intermediate new reader/ABLE/pre-GED/ESOL/children's collection.

Subjects: American history and culture, arts and crafts, family literacy, geography.

Health and the Human Body

Barnard, Bryn. ***Outbreak: Plagues that Changed History***. New York: Crown, 2005.

At a time when discussions of "bird flu" and "pandemic" are frequently heard on radio and television, this book offers a timely reminder of the power of nature to affect the lives of individuals and of societies. In a kind of witty, offbeat tone, Barnard explains the devastating and far-reaching impact of various disease outbreaks on the course of human history. Informative yet lively and engaging, sections of this book would provide excellent practice for the science reading section of the GED.

Advanced new reader/pre-GED/GED/children's collection.

Subjects: international perspectives, nature and the universe, science and technology.

Bryan, Jenny. ***Diabetes***. Series title: Just the Facts. Chicago: Heinemann Library, 2004.

With illustrations—many featuring adults—and text organized in clearly labeled segments, this book will be accessible even to some upper beginning level students, with the help of a tutor or teacher using an information reading technique. The book discusses both type 1 and type 2 diabetes, the importance of diet, and cultural aspects of the increase in this disease. It also offers suggestions for adopting a lifestyle compatible with the disease as well as additional sources for information.

Intermediate-advanced/ABLE/pre-GED/GED/ESOL/children's collection.

Subjects: health and the human body, science and technology.

Jackson, Donna M. ***In Your Face: The Facts About Your Features***. New York: Viking, 2004.

From our evolutionary origins in sea creatures to the modern technology of face recognition as a means of identification, this book examines many aspects of the human face, our first encounter with another person. Rich in fascinating facts, this book also provides several possibilities for language lessons. There is a wealth of vocabulary for ESOL students in the names of all the parts of, for example, the eye: iris, pupil, cornea, eyelash, etc. There are cultural discussions as, for example, when is it proper to make eye contact with another person, or how do various cultures adorn faces with make-up or tattoos? And there are idioms associated with just about every part of the face: "all ears," "won by a nose," "face the music," and the title itself, "in your face."

Advanced new reader/pre-GED/GED/ESOL/children's collection.

Subjects: health and the human body, language, science and technology.

Sheen, Barbara. *Hepatitis*. Series title: Diseases and Disorders. Farmington Hill, Mich.: Lucent, 2003.

This series offers individual books discussing a range of diseases and disorders including Alzheimer's disease, breast cancer, epilepsy, autism, and dyslexia. The chapters in each of the books discuss the nature of the disease or disorder, how it is diagnosed, what the standard treatments are, some possible alternative treatments, and day-to-day problems. They also offer an overview of potential research developments as well as a list of organizations to contact for additional information.

Advanced new reader/pre-GED/GED/children's collection.

Subjects: health and the human body, science and technology.

Silverstein, Alvin, Silverstein, Virginia and Laura Silverstein Nunn. *Polio*. Series title: *Diseases and People*. Berkeley Heights, N.J.: Enslow, 2001.

The Silversteins have written many books explaining various diseases intended for young people but informative and appealing to adults. In their books, they describe symptoms, causes, and treatments of the particular disease. For this book on polio, they also discuss its history in connection to President Roosevelt, the founding of the March of Dimes, and the development of the vaccines that drastically reduced the number of people affected by this disease.

Intermediate-advanced new reader/pre-GED/GED/children's collection.

Subjects: health and the human body, science and technology.

Simon, Seymour. *Eyes and Ears*. New York: HarperCollins, 2003.

With astonishing photographs of the inside of the eye and the ear, diagrams to explain such conditions as nearsightedness, and clear, engaging, and informative text, Simon shares his understanding as well as his awe of the workings of the human body. He has produced a series of similar picture books about the body, including *The Brain, Bones, The Heart,* and *Guts*.

Intermediate new reader/ABLE/pre-GED/GED/children's collection.
Subjects: health and the human body, nature and the universe, science and technology, picture books for all ages.

Viegas, Jennifer. ***The Heart: Learning How Our Blood Circulates***. Series title: The 3-D Library of the Human Body. New York: Rosen, 2002.

The 3-D Library series is an excellent example of scientific information presented in the correct vocabulary but well explained in declarative sentences and enhanced by clearly labeled digital images. This book discusses the anatomy of the human heart and the functions of the cardiovascular system. Other titles in the series include *The Brain and Spinal Cord: Learning How We Think, Feel, and Move; The Ear: Learning How We Hear;* and *The Head and Neck: Learning How We Use Our Muscles.*
Intermediate-advanced new reader/pre-GED/GED/children's collection.
Subjects: health and human body, nature and the universe, science and technology.

Williams, Frances. ***Human Body: An Extraordinary Look from the Inside Out***. Series title: *Inside Guides*. New York: DK, 1997.

In this comprehensive yet very accessible atlas of the human body, all the body systems are represented by handcrafted models and plastic skeletons in extraordinary detail and many shades of color. Microscopic photographs offer a look at the cellular level and clear text explains the function of each body section. Although marketed to children, many libraries will have additional copies in the adult collection.
Beginning-advanced new reader/ABLE/pre-GED/GED/ESOL/children's collection.
Subjects: health and the human body, science and technology.

Health and the Human Body—Family Literacy

Bee, Peta. ***Living with Asthma***. Austin, Tex.: Raintree Steck-Vaughn, 2000.

Following the daily routines of three children, this book discusses the various ways that asthma affects their lives. It is a hopeful book, however, as we see the children learn how to control their environment so as to minimize the effects of the disease. Color photographs and an uncluttered layout make this book particularly appealing to new readers.

Beginning-intermediate new reader/ABLE/pre-GED/ESOL/children's collection.
Subjects: family literacy, health and the human body.

First Human Body Encyclopedia. Series title: First Reference for Young Readers and Writers. New York: DK Publishers, 2005.

Chock-full is the term that comes to mind browsing through this book. Pictures, diagrams, charts, fun facts, and a curiosity quiz are all features designed to attract the attention of media-savvy young readers. Browsing with them, adults will learn many facts as well as find opportunities to share some of their own knowledge and experiences.

Beginning-intermediate new reader/ABLE/pre-GED/ESOL/children's collection.
Subjects: family literacy, health and the human body.

Heelan, Jamee Riggio. *Rolling Along: The Story of Taylor and His WheelChair.* Illustrated by Nicola Simmonds. Atlanta: Peachtree, 2000.

Taylor and Tyler are twin brothers and best friends, but Taylor has cerebral palsy and Tyler does not. This inspiring book follows Taylor through his normal activities, sometimes with Tyler, but sometimes on his own meeting with his therapist and maneuvering in his wheelchair. Most children encounter other children with disabilities in these days of mainstreaming, and with a book such as this, adults can help them know how best to interact with those children.

Beginning-intermediate new reader/ABLE/pre-GED/children's collection.
Subjects: families, family literacy, health and the human body.

O'Donnell, Kerri. *Inhalants and Your Nasal Passages: The Incredibly Disgusting Story.* Series title: Incredibly Disgusting Drugs. New York: Rosen, 2001.

"Inhalants are the fourth most abused substance among young people ages seven to seventeen" according to O'Donnell. Their ready availability—under the sink, in the refrigerator, in the bathroom cabinet—makes them easy to obtain and to hide. Aimed at young people who often start such use innocently enough—what harm can hairspray cause, after all—this book describes the many unappealing and possibly deadly effects of the use of different kinds of inhalants. Adults will be surprised by many of the potentially dangerous products in their cupboards.

Other titles in this series look at the potential dangers of crack, ecstasy, and steroids, among others.

Intermediate new reader/ABLE/pre-GED/ESOL/children's collection.

Subjects: family literacy, health and the human body.

Rabe, Tish. ***Inside Your Outside: All About the Human Body***. Series title: The Cat in the Hat's Learning Library. Illustrated by Aristides Ruiz. New York: Random House, 2002.

Dr. Seuss's Cat in the Hat takes some children on a tour of the "inside your outside machine," that is, the human body. In whimsical, rhyming verse, the tour begins in the brain and visits the bones, the senses, the heart, and on through to the exit. Along the way, readers are introduced to lots of vocabulary as well as many bits of information such as the difference between the right and left brain and the size of the bones in your ear. Children and adults will laugh at the antics of The Cat, but they will learn a lot as well.

Beginning-intermediate new reader/ABLE/pre-GED/ESOL/children's collection.

Subjects: family literacy, health and the human body.

Silverstein, Alvin, Silverstein, Virginia, and Laura Silverstein Nunn. ***Dyslexia***. Series title: *My Health*. New York: Franklin Watts, 2001.

For parents whose children are having difficulty learning to read, this book can help them understand that the problem may arise from a neurological difficulty, not a behavioral one. It also offers hope by suggesting several techniques that parents can use to help their children and listing organizations and web sites that may offer additional assistance.

Intermediate new reader/ABLE/pre-GED/children's collection.

Subjects: family literacy, language, health and the human body.

Stewart, Gail B. ***Diabetes***. Series title: The KidHaven Science Library. Farmington Hills, Mich.: KidHaven, 2003.

This book is written for children who are diagnosed with diabetes and thus face a lifetime of coping with the disease. Several young adults who were diagnosed as children tell stories about learning to watch their diets and even give themselves injections. Photographs and diagrams help convey the message of taking control of your disease by maintaining a healthy lifestyle.

Beginning-intermediate new reader/ABLE/pre-GED/ESOL/children's collection.
Subjects: family literacy, health and the human body, science and technology.

Language

Browne, Philippa-Alys. *A Gaggle of Geese: The Collective Names of the Animal Kingdom.* New York: Atheneum, 1996.

With just one simple phrase per page—"a gaggle of geese gathering," "a knot of toads scrambling"—illustrated in bold colors, this picture book offers an unusual vocabulary lesson for more advanced students, both ESOL and English-speaking. Some of the collective nouns are commonly used in other contexts, as in "a cluster of cats;" others are unfamiliar and strange-sounding to our modern ears. But Browne explains the origin of all the terms in the back of the book, and even provides information about the animals themselves. For students aiming for higher education, this book offers an entertaining introductory exercise into the practice of researching the origins of words.

Intermediate-advanced new readers/pre-GED/GED/ESOL/children's collection.
Subjects: animals, language, picture book for all ages.

Bryan, Ashley. *The Night Has Ears: African Proverbs.* New York: Atheneum, 1999.

Each page presents one brief proverb boldly illustrated in a style reminiscent of multicolored African shirts. Though attributed to particular tribes or cultures, the proverbs express universally recognizable sentiments. Some will have a familiar ring to American ears, while others will sound familiar to students from Africa or other cultures. Numerous lessons can be developed from a book of this kind. Beginning ABLE students might develop a language experience story based on a personal experience that illustrates one of the proverbs. In an ESOL or joint ABLE/ESOL class, students can share proverbs from their countries that convey similar ideas. For more advanced students, teachers might consider reading a few entries from *Aesop's Fables* to demonstrate a story that illustrates a proverb, then ask the students to reverse the process by choosing a proverb from this book and creating a story to illustrate its meaning.

This book would also work well in a family literacy setting.

Beginning-intermediate new reader/ABLE/ESOL/children's collection.
Subjects: Africa, family literacy, language, picture book for all ages.

Collis, Harry. *101 American English Riddles: Understanding Language and Culture Through Humor*. Illustrated by Joe Kohl. Lincolnwood, Ill.: Passport, 1996.

"What kind of pool can't you swim in?" The answer is: a carpool. This question and answer format, accompanied by a humorous illustration and a straightforward explanation of the various meanings of the word "pool," will help to explain some of the many and confusing idioms that are part of the English we speak every day. Although primarily aimed at the ESOL population, this book will be both amusing and helpful to American students as well.

Intermediate new reader/pre-GED/ESOL/adult collection.
Subjects: language.

Hoban, Tana. *Animal, Vegetable, or Mineral?* New York: Greenwillow, 1995.

Tana Hoban has produced more than twenty books, all with a similar pattern, all marketed to children, and all extremely useful to adult literacy students. Each book presents one photograph per page. Sometimes a few words accompany the photograph, sometimes not, but the pictures are always intriguing. In this title, for example, the vegetables include gourds and the animals include flamingos. And where shall we put those seashells? Beyond naming and categorizing the item, each picture offers opportunities for describing surface shapes, shadings of color, and relationships within the picture. ABLE and ESOL students alike will find much to talk about and wonder about in this and all Hoban's books.

Beginning new reader/ABLE/ESOL/children's collection.
Subjects: animals; family literacy; nature and the universe; photography, thematic collections; language; picture books for all ages.

Hoban, Tana. *Exactly the Opposite*. New York: Greenwillow, 1990.

These are not just ordinary opposites. There is an open fist and a closed fist, for example. Are the opposites "open" and "closed" or "friendly" and "angry" or "possibility" and "despair"? There is no right answer—only much opportunity for discussion and language building. A glass of ice and a fire can represent "cold" and "hot," but the pictures suggest more, a list of synonyms, for example: icy, frosty, chilly and blazing, roasting, scorching.

And what about metaphorical meanings? Cold can mean temperature, but it can also describe a temperament, as can the word "hot." So, are these things *exactly* opposite?
Beginning-intermediate new reader/ABLE/ESOL/children's collection.
Subjects: language, photography, picture books for all ages, thematic collections.

Jenkins, Jessica. ***Thinking About Colors***. New York: Dutton, 1992.
Possibilities for vocabulary and language lessons abound in this picture book. Looking at the double page presenting the color green, for example, we find *things* that are green like leaves and frogs, *metaphorical uses* of green such as being environmentally responsible, *proverbs* using the word green such as "the grass is always greener," and even *shades* of green as you might find them named on a paint company's color wheel: sap green, lime green, apple green.

This book would also be suitable in a family literacy setting.
Beginning-intermediate new reader/ABLE/ESOL/children's collection.
Subjects: language, picture books for all ages.

Leedy, Loreen and Pat Street. ***There's a Frog in My Throat: 440 Animal Sayings a Little Bird Told Me***. New York: Holiday House, 2003.
Inventive, whimsical drawings show the improbable but literal meaning of many common sayings and proverbs, while an explanation of the metaphorical meaning is printed below the illustration in plain-face type. The groupings of the sayings add to both the enjoyment and the instruction as, for example, the many uses of "eggs"—don't put all your eggs in one basket, you can't unscramble eggs, etc.—all appear on the same page, joined not only by the words but by amusingly interlocking pictures. For some beginners, the amount of information on any one page may be overwhelming, but the overall effect is so engaging that teachers and students should find a way around that problem should it arise.
Beginning-intermediate new reader/ABLE/ESOL/children's collection.
Subjects: animals, language, picture books for all ages.

Samoyault, Tiphaine. ***Alphabetical Order: How the Alphabet Began***. New York: Viking, 1998.
Translated from the original French, this book first discusses how the con-

cept of an alphabet developed and grew, then offers numerous examples from the hieroglyphics of Egypt to the ideographs of Asian alphabets to the sound-symbol alphabets such as the Roman, Greek, Arabic, and Cyrillic. She also discusses such specialized alphabets as the Sign Language alphabet, the Braille alphabet, Morse Code, and even the varied colored flags that are the "code of the high seas" used by navies and boatmen. Chapters on calligraphy, typography, and the use of various fonts in advertisements add social and artistic dimensions to this discussion of an ingenious system of communication we mostly take for granted. Many ESOL students will find something familiar in this book to share with other students; ESOL teachers will discover similarities and differences among various alphabets that will inform their understanding of the English alphabet they are teaching.

Intermediate-advanced new reader/ABLE/pre-GED/ESOL/children's collection.
Subjects: international perspectives, language.

Language—Family Literacy

Ada, Alma Flor. *Gathering the Sun: An Alphabet in Spanish and English.* Illustrated by Simon Silva. English translation by Rosa Zubizarreta. New York: Lothrop, Lee & Shepard, 1997.

In simple poems celebrating farm workers and the bounty of the fields they pick, Ada reviews not only the twenty-eight letters of the Spanish alphabet but also the lives and long struggles of all those families who have made their living putting food on America's dinner tables. Each verse is also translated into English.

Beginning-intermediate new reader/ABLE-pre-GED/ESOL/children's collection.
Subjects: family literacy, language, Latinos, rural life.

Belle, Jennifer. *Animal Stackers.* Illustrated by David McPhail. New York: Hyperion, 2005.

This book is both an alphabet book and a book of simple rhymes introducing animals from A to Z. The names of one animal for each letter are spelled out vertically (that is, *stacked).* Each letter in the animal's name thus becomes the first letter of a line of clever and whimsical verse describing that animal. Adults and children will enjoy reading these amusing verses together.

Beginning-intermediate new reader/ABLE/pre-GED/ESOL/children's collection.
Subjects: animals, family literacy, language.

Brennan-Nelson, Denise. *My Momma Likes to Say*. Illustrated by Jan Monroe
Donovan. Chelsea, Mich.: Sleeping Bear, 2003.

Each page features a commonly used maxim or idiom, introduced by an
amusing illustration and a brief verse in the repeating formula: "Time flies
when you're having fun/my momma likes to say./I'm not sure what she
means/but I like it anyway." This is followed by four more lines imagining
the saying literally, followed by an explanation of the metaphorical meaning and some speculation on its origin.

This same author-illustrator pair have also created *My Teacher Likes to
Say*, published by Sleeping Bear Press.

Beginning-intermediate new reader/ABLE/pre-GED/ESOL/children's collection.
Subjects: families, family literacy, language.

Cleary, Brian. *Hairy, Scary, Ordinary: What is an Adjective*. Illustrated by
Jenya Prosmitsky. Minneapolis: Carolrhoda, 2000.

As the title might suggest, this book takes a humorous approach to teaching the not so humorous topic of grammar. With simple easy rhymes such
as "Adjectives tell us more, like *narrow* street or *favorite* store," this books
doesn't explain adjectives, it *shows* what adjectives are by giving examples,
and then illustrates those examples with goofy but amusing drawings.

Cleary and Prosmitsky have also collaborated on *A Mink, a Fink, a Skat-
ing Rink: What is a Noun*, and with illustrator Brian Gable, Cleary has
produced *Under, Over, By the Clover: What is a Preposition* and *Dearly, Nearly,
Insincerely: What is an Adverb*. All are published by Carolrhoda.

Beginning-intermediate new reader/ABLE/pre-GED/ESOL/children's collection.
Subjects: family literacy, language.

Dugan, Joanne. *ABC NYC*. New York: Harry N. Abrams, 2005.

"B is for Bagel. M is for Manhole Cover." It's a good bet that such a combination is unique in the genre of alphabet books, which was photographer
Dugan's goal. Traveling the city with her young son, she wanted to create
an alphabet book that used letters and objects familiar to kids growing up
in an urban environment. Subway stations, department stores, billboards,

and even graffiti on walls provide the letters in a fascinating variety of fonts, locations, and writing styles. But you don't have to live in New York City to appreciate the whimsy and creativity of this book. In fact, it could inspire a class project to create an alphabet book based on any geographical location.
Beginning new reader/ABLE/ESOL/children's collection.
Subjects: geography, language, urban life.

Fraser, Betty. ***First Things First: An Illustrated Collection of Sayings Useful and Familiar for Children***. New York: Harper & Row, 1990.
Each page asks a question. For example, "What do you say when you are late?" Then a series of illustrations presents scenes showing the problem and the solution: "Better late than never." The repeated format assists even beginning new adult or child readers. The serial pictures also offer lots of conversation opportunities between parent and child. ESOL students might offer examples of similar proverbs from their own situations.
Beginning-intermediate new reader/ABLE/pre-GED/ESOL/children's collection.
Subjects: family literacy, language.

Greenway, Shirley. ***Two's Company***. Photographs by Oxford Scientific Films. Watertown, Mass.: Charlesbridge, 1997.
"One sheep alone, two sheep together, a flock of sheep grazing in the snow." And so it goes as each collective noun for a group of a particular animal is introduced. The simple and appealing layout is complemented by lovely, almost calming photographs. The repetitive text is easy, but still offers much in the way of vocabulary for children and ESOL students learning the names of animals and ABLE students learning to read those names.
Beginning new reader/ABLE/ESOL/children's collection.
Subjects: animals, family literacy, language.

Gritz, Ona. ***Tangerines and Tea: My Grandparents and Me***. Illustrated by Yumi Heo. New York: Harry N. Abrams, 2005.
With cozy illustrations befitting the setting of a visit to the grandparents' house, each letter in this alphabet book is introduced by a sentence with several words beginning with that letter, as in "a farm where we're free to pick fruit off a tree."
Intermediate new reader/ABLE/ESOL/children's collections.
Subjects: family literacy, grandparents, language, rural life.

Hoban, Tana. *Cubes, Cones, Cylinders, and Spheres*. New York: Greenwillow, 2000.

Alphabet blocks, ice cream cones, and drums are among the familiar objects that will help children and adults learn some less familiar words. As always, Hoban's photographs are clear, colorful, appealing, and suggestive of questions and discussions.

As mentioned in the annotation for Hoban's *Animal, Vegetable, or Mineral?* above, she has produced over twenty titles of books in which her photographs are labeled with names or concepts. They offer many possibilities for sharing in a family literacy setting.

Beginning new reader/ABLE/ESOL/children's collection.
Subjects: family literacy, language.

"Too Many Cooks . . . " and Other Proverbs. Illustrated by Maggie Keen. New York: Green Tiger, 1992.

Children will need some help understanding proverbs such as "Don't put the cart before the horse," but the whimsical illustrations will help adults explain the meaning. This book provides lots of opportunities for adults and children to discuss and laugh together.

Beginning new reader/ABLE/ESOL/children's collection.
Subjects: family literacy, language.

Nature, Science, Technology

Busby, Peter. *First to Fly: How Wilbur and Orville Wright Invented the Airplane*. Illustrated by David Craig. New York: Crown, 2002.

From their earliest days, the Wright brothers were fascinated by anything mechanical, especially things that moved, such as bicycles, newly invented automobiles, and their dream machine, the airplane. This book recounts the events leading up to their famous first flight at Kitty Hawk, North Carolina, in 1903. Several insets also explain the mechanics of flight as the brothers were learning them. For example, one describes how they watched bicycle riders and birds turn not just by turning a handlebar or a head but by actually leaning or rolling the whole body. Both text and diagrams show how they tried to apply this principle to a flying machine, providing excellent practice for students gleaning information from a combination of words and text.

Intermediate-advanced new reader/pre-GED/GED/children's collection.
Subjects: American history and culture, science and technology.

The Environment: Atlases of the Earth and Its Resources. Milwaukee, Wis.: World Almanac Library, 2004.

> For students preparing for the GED or for admission to community college, this book provides many opportunities to practice reading from maps, graphs, charts, and other kinds of graphic presentations of information, what the National Assessment of Adult Literacy calls "document literacy." From an environmental perspective, it discusses issues such as population growth and the effect of natural forces such as hurricanes and soil erosion. Though dense with information, the presentation is appealing and appendices, such as a glossary of environmental terms, provide additional help to readers.

Advanced new reader/pre-GED/GED/children's collection.
Subjects: geography, nature and the universe, science and technology.

Jackson, Donna M. **In Your Face: The Facts About Your Features.** New York: Viking, 2004.

> From our evolutionary origins in sea creatures to the modern technology of face recognition as a means of identification, this book examines many aspects of the human face, our first encounter with another person. Rich in fascinating facts, this book also provides several possibilities for language lessons. There is a wealth of vocabulary for ESOL students in the names of all the parts—for example, iris, pupil, cornea, eyelash, etc., for the eye. There are cultural discussions as, for example, when is it proper to make eye contact with another person, or how do various cultures adorn faces with makeup or tattoos? And there are idioms associated with just about every part of the face: "all ears," "won by a nose," "face the music," and the title itself, "in your face."

Advanced new reader/pre-GED/GED/ESOL/children's collection.
Subjects: health and the human body, science and technology.

Jenkins, Alvin. **Next Stop Neptune: Experiencing the Solar System.** Illustrated by Steve Jenkins. Boston: Houghton Mifflin, 2004.

> Author Jenkins is an astronomer and physicist; his artist son is the illustrator. Together they have created a display of the solar system that tells many

facts but preserves the wonder as well. Each page features an illustration of a planet, moon, comet, or asteroid, along with several insets offering pertinent facts and figures. Students can peruse one page to find the answers to specific questions—for example, how far is the earth from the sun. Or they can extrapolate from the given information—how much would you weigh on the moon?

Intermediate-advanced new reader/pre-GED/GED/children's collection.

Subjects: nature and the universe, science and technology.

Kerrod, Robin. ***Hubble: the Mirror on the Universe.*** Buffalo, N.Y.: Firefly, 2003.

From the spectacular photographs sent back to earth from the Hubble Space Telescope, we can witness stars being born and dying, planets in the making, and galaxies colliding. Hundreds of these photographs are reproduced in this book, providing an almost unimaginable window on the universe. The text provides many opportunities for science reading for students preparing for the GED or community college, but the photos alone will inspire any student to marvel not only at the vast mystery of space but also at the accomplishment of the men and women whose creativity and knowledge created this telescope and the means to send it on its mission of discovery.

Intermediate-advanced new reader/pre-GED/GED/adult collection.

Subjects: nature and the universe; photography, thematic collections; science and technology.

Kramer, Stephen. ***Eye of the Storm: Chasing Storms with Warren Faidley.*** Photographs by Warren Faidley. New York: G.P. Putnam's, 1997.

Everybody talks about the weather. For Warren Faidley, weather is both hobby and occupation. He has traveled the country in search of opportunities to photograph tornadoes, hurricanes, dust storms and lightning strikes. The spectacular drama of the storms pictured in this book reveal the power and majesty of nature, as well as the heartrending devastation that follows in the aftermath of major storms.

Intermediate new reader/ABLE/pre-GED/ESOL/children's collection.

Subjects: disasters, nature and the universe.

Lauber, Patricia. *Hurricanes: Earth's Mightiest Storms*. New York: Scholastic, 1996.

With their ferocious winds pushing huge surges of water that can topple trees, buildings, and virtually anything in their path, hurricanes are among the most destructive forces of nature. Using photographs, charts, maps, diagrams and clear descriptive text, award-winning science writer Lauber describes some of the twentieth century's fiercest storms and the toll they took on human life. She also explains how hurricanes are formed—and named—and discusses how population shifts and environmental factors have affected both the number of these storms and their power to effect profound change in many lives.

Intermediate-advanced new reader/pre-GED/GED/ESOL/children's collection.
Subjects: disasters, nature and the universe.

Lauber, Patricia. *Painters of the Caves*. Washington, D.C.: National Geographic Society, 1998.

Much of what we know of our earliest human ancestors comes from archeological finds of bones, tools, and other remnants of human activity and from the drawings that have been discovered on the walls of caves hidden from the elements and preserved for future generations—if we are lucky enough to find them. In this book, Lauber tells the story of just such a lucky discovery made in 1994 by three friends pursuing their favorite outdoor activity: climbing in the limestone hills and exploring the caves of southeastern France. It turned out to be a remarkable adventure, as the three climbers discovered a cave dated to 32,000 years ago and containing over 300 drawings created by people living in what we refer to as the Stone Age. Numerous photographs and drawings depict other cave paintings that give us a picture of how these distant ancestors lived and died long before writing had been invented. An appendix explains how scientists who study the past date these ancient sites and artifacts.

Intermediate-advanced new reader/pre-GED/GED/children's collection.
Subjects: the arts and artists, nature and the universe.

Sullivan, George. *Built to Last: Building America's Amazing Bridges, Dams, Tunnels, and Skyscrapers*. New York: Scholastic, 2005.

The design and construction of seventeen engineering marvels that exhibit "American ingenuity and determination" and "thinking on a grand scale" also reflect the technological, social, and cultural changes inherent in the country's progress. The Erie Canal, the Brooklyn Bridge, the U.S. Interstate Highway System, and the Jefferson National Expansion Memorial Arch are a few of the projects that are featured in wonderful photographs and graphic illustrations from initial stages to finished product. Many of these buildings are icons of the American landscape that should become familiar at least in name to all ESOL students.

Intermediate—advanced new reader/ABLE/pre-GED/GED/ESOL/children's collection.

Subjects: American history and culture, science and technology.

Nature, Science, and Technology—Family Literacy

Bang, Molly. *My Light*. New York: Scholastic, 2004.

Speaking in the voice of the sun, Bang explains how the light from the sun is turned into the energy of water, wind, and coal to create our light—the light of electricity. Her clear prose and brightly colored illustrations make the details of science both fascinating and understandable.

Beginning-intermediate new reader/ABLE/pre-GED/children's collection.

Subjects: family literacy, nature and the universe, science and technology.

High, Linda Oatman. *Under New York*. Illustrated by Robert Rayevsky. New York: Holiday House, 2001.

With their keen sense of curiosity and imagination, children love discovering "hidden" worlds, such as the one depicted in this book. Each illustration is divided horizontally into what is going on above the street—shopping, working, playing—and what is going on below the street—subways, waterworks, electrical lines, rocky foundations, and more shopping.

Beginning new reader/ABLE/ESOL/children's collection.

Subjects: family literacy, science and technology, urban life.

Krensky, Stephen. *Taking Flight: The Story of the Wright Brothers*. Series title: Ready to Read. Illustrated by Larry Day. New York: Simon & Schuster, 2000.

From a printing press to bicycles to an airplane, the Wright brothers were always tinkering with mechanical devices. As this book explains, their skill coupled with their fascination for flight and their determination to see their dream come to reality resulted in their invention of the first airplane to fly in the United States.

The Ready to Read series offers books at 4 levels, from recognizing words to reading alone, so they offer adult students and their children participating in family literacy programs a range of opportunities to share books about a wide variety of subjects.

Intermediate new reader/ABLE/pre-GED/ESOL/children's collection.
Subjects: family literacy, science and technology.

Levenson, George. ***Bread Comes to Life: A Garden of Wheat to Eat.*** Photography by Shmuel Thaler. Berkeley, Calif.: Tricycle, 2004.

In rhythmic, appealing verse, this book describes the process of making bread from planting the wheat seeds to grinding, mixing, kneading and baking. Brightly colored photographs display all the steps from the grain of wheat growing in the field to the mouth-watering loaves on the table. The repetitive language, "white bread/black bread/small bread/tall bread" invites beginning ABLE students to read aloud while all the vocabulary associated with bread making offers many words for ABLE and ESOL students alike to say and read.

Beginning-intermediate new reader/ABLE/pre-GED/ESOL/children's collection.
Subjects: family literacy, nature and the universe.

Lyon, George Ella. ***Weaving the Rainbow.*** Illustrations by Stephanie Anderson. New York: Atheneum, 2004.

A young girl watches over a flock of sheep as they grow their coats. Then in spring, she helps to shear the sheep, spin the wool, dye the yarn with herbs and flowers, and then weave the yarn into a rainbow of colors from the white sheep.

Beginning-intermediate new reader/ABLE/ESOL/children's collection.
Subjects: arts and crafts, family literacy, nature and the universe.

Pinczes. Elinor J. ***Inchworm and a Half.*** Illustrated by Randall Enos. Boston: Houghton Mifflin, 2001.

The inchworm measures everything in the garden, until he comes upon an item that, as he measures it, leaves some left over that is too small for his inch length. Then along comes the one-half inchworm, and the problem is solved—that is, until they need a one-third inchworm and a one-fourth inchworm. With rhyming rhythmic language, the concept of fractions is delightfully presented. Reading this book with children could lead to all kinds of activities involving measuring things.

With illustrator Bobbie MacKain, author Pinczes also writes about math concepts in *One Hundred Hungry Ants* and *A Remainder of One,* both from Houghton Mifflin.

Beginning new reader/ABLE/ESOL/children's collection.

Subjects: family literacy, science and technology.

Rylant, Cynthia. *In November.* Illustrated by Jill Kastner. San Diego: Harcourt, 2000.

Each vignette about the approaching winter begins, "In November" as people, animals, and all of nature ready for the coming cold and dark of a long winter. But the preparations for a feast of the harvest convey a sense of comfort.

Beginning-intermediate new reader/ABLE/pre-GED/ESOL/children's collection.

Subjects: family literacy, nature and the universe.

Rylant, Cynthia. *Long Night Moon.* Illustrated by Mark Siegal. New York: Simon & Schuster, 2004.

Rylant revives and celebrates a tradition of Native Americans to name the full moons of each month. In her brief, poetic descriptions of each moon, she captures many moods of the night, moods that are beautifully reflected and illuminated in the velvety charcoal drawings of Siegal, who spent many nights outdoors observing the moon's traverse across a year of night skies.

Intermediate new reader/ABLE/pre-GED/ESOL/children's collection.

Subjects: family literacy, nature and the universe.

Scieszka, John. *Math Curse.* Illustrated by Lane Smith. New York: Viking, 1995.

In this clever, funny, and fascinating book, a young girl finds math problems everywhere—at the breakfast table, on the school bus, in the candy store. Working through the problems with children would be a fun and instructive way to review basic math principles and, for ESOL students, a way to talk about math in English. The children may well lead the parents in solving the problems in this book and finding additional ones in the world at their fingertips.

Even without the children, this book could offer both instruction as well as amusing diversion for students reviewing math for the GED or other exams.

Advanced new reader/pre-GED/GED/ESOL/children's collection.
Subjects: family literacy, science and technology.

Williams, Karen Lynn. *Circles of Hope*. Illustrated by Linda Saport. Grand Rapids, Mich.: Eerdman's, 2005.

Facile, a young Haitian boy, wants to plant a tree for his baby sister, just like his father did for him when he was born. But several attempts fail because so many trees have been cut down in the area where he lives that the soil is vulnerable to erosion. Finally, he realizes he needs to build a small, circular stone wall around his seedling to help protect it. This simple story conveys an important ecological lesson. Williams has lived and worked in Haiti and is familiar with a project to build these "circles of hope" around fledgling trees to help rebuild the forest destroyed by overdevelopment.

Intermediate new reader/ABLE/pre-GED/ESOL/children's collection.
Subjects: family literacy, nature and the universe.

Religion, Folklore, Cultural Traditions

Avery, Byllye. *An Altar of Words: Wisdom, Comfort and Inspiration for African-American Women*. New York: Broadway, 1998.

Brief meditations on topics such as courage, love, power, and activism offer a kind of verbal sacred place where readers can strengthen their inner spirit. Quotations from writers including Alice Walker and Sonya Sanchez echo Avery's sentiments.

Intermediate new reader/ABLE/pre-GED/adult collection.
Subjects: African Americans, religious and spiritual themes, women.

Behnke, Alison with Vartkes Ehramjian. *Cooking the Middle Eastern Way*. Series title: Easy Menu Ethnic Cookbooks. Minneapolis: Lerner Publications, 2005.

Behnke first reviews a little history of the region known as the Middle East, describing its land, its food, its holidays and festivals. She then offers several recipes for every part of a meal, the results of which are beautifully photographed.

There are more than twenty books from this publisher in the series: Easy

Menu Ethnic Cookbooks, covering countries and cultures from around the globe.
Intermediate new reader/pre-GED/ESOL/children's collection.
Subjects: cultural traditions, the Middle East.

Christmas Eve: The Nativity Story in Engravings, Verse, and Song. Salt Lake City, Utah: Gibbs Smith, 2005.

All students who celebrate the Christmas story will marvel at the spare beauty of this book. The text is from the gospels of Matthew and Luke, King James Version, the songs are words and music of familiar Christmas carols, and the engravings picture the events of the gospels in serene simplicity.
Beginning new reader/ABLE/pre-GED/ESOL/adult collection.
Subjects: art collections, religion and spiritual themes.

Ganeri, Anita. ***Out of the Ark: Stories from the World's Religions.*** Illustrated by Jackie Morris. San Diego: Harcourt Brace, 1996.

As Ganeri researched across the spectrum of religious traditions to find the stories for this book, she saw more connections and similarities among the stories than differences, and so she has grouped them not by religion or culture but by theme. Creation stories, flood stories, animals stories, war stories all share certain elements, including a profound sense of wonder and mystery. "Fact files" and a "who's who" list of names and terms add depth of information.
Intermediate new reader/ABLE/pre-GED/ESOL/children's collection.
Subjects: cultural traditions, religious and spiritual themes.

Ganeri, Anita. ***Religions Explained: A Beginner's Guide to World Faiths.*** New York: Henry Holt, 1996.

With photographs of sacred places and practices, pictures of symbols and shrines, and excerpts from holy books, this book discusses the origins, influences, and current practices of religions from all over the world.
Intermediate new reader/ABLE/pre-GED/ESOL/children's collection.
Subjects: international perspectives, religion and spiritual themes.

Kidwai, Azra. *Islam*. Photographs by Thomas L. Kelly, Kabir Khan, and Taj Mohammad. Leicester, England: Silverdale, 2000.

The origins of Islam, its customs and beliefs, and the arts and creativity it inspires are all discussed. Quotations from biblical sources and from the Qur'an show the connections between these religious traditions. Numerous photographs of mosques around the world and the faithful at prayer underscore the world wide reach of Islam.

Intermediate-advanced new reader/ABLE/pre-GED/GED/ESOL/adult collection.

Subjects: international perspectives, religious and spiritual themes.

McQuiston, John II. *A Prayer Book for the 21st Century*. Harrisburg, Pa.: Morehouse, 2004.

Although he comes from a Christian tradition, the prayers McQuiston offers encompass a wider view of God as a spirit or presence in the world. Brief quotes from the Bible, both old and new testaments, as well as from other religious texts are intermingled with his own contemporary prayers.

Intermediate new reader/ABLE/pre-GED/adult collection.

Subjects: international perspectives, religious and spiritual themes.

Mitchell, Stephen. *Bhagavad-Gita*. New York: Harmony, 2000.

Mitchell's translation of this sacred Hindu text, whose title means "The Song of the Blessed One," presents the dialogue between Krishna (God) and Arjuna, the human being to whom he reveals himself, in metrical verse.

Beginning-intermediate new reader/ABLE/pre-GED/ESOL/adult collection.

Subjects: international perspectives, religious and spiritual themes.

Stoddard, Alexandra. *Things I Want My Daughters to Know*. New York: HarperCollins, 2004.

Affirming, humorous, at times controversial, and often profound, these brief essays suggest how to live a life that is both full and fulfilling. With many quotations from a range of inspirational writers, Stoddard encourages her daughters and all readers to embrace what life has to offer with courage, persistence, and joy.

Intermediate-advanced new readers/pre-GED/GED/adult collection.

Subjects: inspirational stories and pictures, religious and spiritual themes.

To Every Thing There is a Season. Illustrated by Leo and Diane Dillon. New York: Scholastic, 1998.

> With slight modification for ease of reading, the text is the familiar verse from the Book of Ecclesiastes, King James Version, a verse that has been a source of solace and faith for many generations across many cultures. The universal appeal of this verse is reflected in the fifteen illustrations, all original but painted in the style of a different culture, including illustrated manuscripts from Ireland, the murals of ancient Egyptian tombs and of the Anasazi people of North America, and the bark paintings of the Australian aborigines.

Beginning new reader/ABLE/pre-GED/ESOL/children's collection.

Subjects: arts and crafts, international perspectives, picture books for all ages, religious and spiritual themes.

Viesti, Joe, and Diane Hall. ***Celebrate! In Central America***. New York: Lothrop, Lee & Shepard, 1997.

> The Day of the Dead, Carnival, and other traditional celebrations of all seven countries in Central America are presented in text and wildly colorful photographs. The same team has also produced *Celebrate! In South Asia* and *Celebrate! In Southeast Asia.*

Beginning-intermediate new reader/ABLE/pre-GED/ESOL/children's collection.

Subjects: cultural traditions.

Religion, Folklore, and Cultural Traditions—Family Literacy

Amado, Elisa. ***Barrilete: A Kite for the Day of the Dead***. Photographs by Joya Hairs. Toronto: A Groundwood Book, 1999.

> Every year, in a little village in Guatemala, three young boys and their grandfather build a barrilete—a kite—to fly on the feast known as The Day of the Dead. But this year, they have an additional challenge. Their grandfather has died, so the boys must create a kite on their own and make it worthy of their grandfather's spirit. Photographs show the village, its people, and the process of creating these large and colorful kites.

Beginning-intermediate new reader/ABLE/pre-GED/ESOL/children's collection.

Subjects: arts and crafts, cultural traditions, family literacy, Latin America and the Caribbean.

Burckhardt, Ann. *The People of Africa and Their Food.* Series title: Multicultural Cookbooks. Mankato: Minn.: Capstone, 1996.

Facts about African countries, including their markets and festivals, are followed by recipes for main dishes, side dishes, soups and salads, and desserts. The simplicity of the recipes and the mouth-watering appeal of the photographs make this a collection of recipes that adults and children will want to try together.

Other titles in the series review the people and food of China, Mexico and Russia.

Beginning-intermediate new reader/ABLE/pre-GED/ESOL/children's collection.
Subjects: Africa, cultural traditions, family literacy.

Bryan, Ashley. *Beautiful Blackbird.* New York: Atheneum, 2003.

When Blackbird is voted the most beautiful bird in the forest, all the other birds ask him to share a touch of his black with them, even though he reminds them that real beauty comes from within. Based on a folktale of the Ila-speaking people of Zambia, this beautifully illustrated book is an allegory about valuing yourself and sharing your heritage.

Beginning-intermediate new reader/ABLE/pre-GED/ESOL/children's collection.
Subjects: Africa, family literacy, cultural traditions, nature and the universe.

English, Karen. *Nadia's Hands.* Illustrated by Jonathan Weiner. Honesdale, Pa.: Boyds Mills, 1999.

Nadia is a Pakistani-American girl, more accustomed to American traditions than to those of her parents' homeland. When she is asked to be a flower girl in her aunt's wedding, she is apprehensive of the practice of having her hands decorated with henna in a traditional style. But all turns out well, and Nadia learns an important lesson about her family heritage.

Intermediate new reader/ABLE/pre-GED/ESOL/children's collection.
Subjects: family literacy, cultural traditions.

Hanson, Regina. *A Season for Mangoes.* Illustrated by Eric Velasquez. New York: Clarion, 2005.

In this story of family bonds and traditions, a young girl finds strength and acceptance in her community. Young Sareen is experiencing her first "sit-up," a Jamaican custom in which friends and relatives sit up all night telling stories about a person who has died. The deceased is Sareen's beloved Nana, and though she is anxious about doing so, she wants to tell how her Nana described happiness as "the taste of a ripe mango," and so each season they would search for a mango that had reached the point of perfect ripeness and share it.

Intermediate new reader/ABLE/pre-GED/ESOL/children's collections.
Subjects: cultural traditions, family literacy, Latin America and the Caribbean.

Hopkins, Lee Bennett. ***Days to Celebrate: A Year full of Poetry, People, Holidays, History, Fascinating Facts, and More.*** Illustrated by Stephen Alcorn. New York: Greenwillow, 2005.

Each chapter represents one month of the year. First, Hopkins presents a complete calendar for the month, noting feasts or facts for each day. Then he highlights a few days for each month with a poem, a brief biography of someone born on that day, a description of an invention celebrated on that day or some other item of interest. Filled with fun facts and amusing illustrations, this is the kind of book that adults and children can browse together. In a grouping of several families, a teacher might ask a few students, adults and children together, to pick a day and create a multimedia presentation for the class. (See Sample Lesson on p. 180.)

Beginning-intermediate new reader/ABLE/pre-GED/ESOL/children's collection.
Subjects: cultural traditions, family literacy.

Ladwig, Tim. ***Psalm Twenty-three.*** New York: Eerdmans, 1997.

Ladwig has illustrated the familiar words of this comforting verse by showing the hope of its message as lived in the daily lives of a family of contemporary African Americans struggling amid the dangers and discomforts of modern urban life.

Beginning new reader/ABLE/pre-GEDESOL/children's collection.
Subjects: African Americans, family literacy, picture books for all ages, religious and spiritual themes, urban life.

Lewis, E.B. ***This Little Light of Mine.*** New York: Simon & Schuster, 2005.

The lyrics of the African American spiritual "This Little Light of Mine" are the only words of the text. Lewis's illustrations tell the story of a young black boy, happy and confident in the love of his family, using his own "light" by befriending a boy who is shunned by other children. The text is easy and will be familiar to many students. ESOL students will be introduced to a well-known American song, the music for which is included at the back of the book.

Beginning new reader/ABLE/ESOL/children's collection.
Subjects: African Americans, family literacy, music, religious and spiritual themes.

Lynch, Tom. *Fables from Aesop*. New York: Viking, 2000.
Lynch introduces yet another generation to the age-old fables of Aesop in language contemporary ears will understand and in fabric collages that tell the stories in graphic and amusing detail. In fact, these illustrations could inspire adults and children to create such "story pictures" of their own, using fabric or paper.

Intermediate new reader/ABLE/pre-GED/ESOL/children's collection.
Subjects: cultural traditions, family literacy, picture books for all ages.

Oppenheim, Shulamith Levey. *Iblis*. Illustrated by Ed Young. San Diego: Harcourt Brace, 1994.
Iblis is the devil in this Islamic version of the story of Adam and Eve's expulsion from the Garden of Eden, a story that bears much similarity to the biblical version, but with fascinating differences of detail. Young's dramatic illustrations add power and beauty to this ancient tale.

Intermediate new reader/ABLE/pre-GED/ESOL/children's collection.
Subjects: family literacy, religious and spiritual themes.

Sports and Leisure

Baddiel, Ivor. *Ultimate Soccer*. New York: DK, 1998. (alternate title on cover: Soccer: The Ultimate World Cup Companion).
DK Publishing produces many books about a variety of subjects that combine text, factual information in charts and graphs, and photographs in a visually appealing format that will attract readers of all levels as well as all ages. This book about the game Americans call soccer but many others call football covers the history of the game from its origins to the 1998 World

Cup match, profiles some of the great teams and great players, and reviews all the World Cup matches from 1930 forward. A page of World Cup Trivia and a Test Your Knowledge Quiz will entertain serious fans; lists of winners and of rules of the game will offer practice at finding information from different forms of textual presentation.

Beginning-advanced new reader/ABLE/pre-GED/ESOL/adult collection.

Subjects: international perspectives, sports.

Blumenthal, Karen. *Let Me Play: The Story of Title IX, the Law that Changed the Future of Girls in America.* New York: Atheneum, 2005.

The law popularly referred to as Title IX is one sentence that says any school receiving government funding cannot discriminate on the basis of gender. It doesn't even mention sports, yet it has had a profound effect on the number and kinds of opportunities available to girls and young women interested in athletics. With a historical overview of the women's rights movement, brief profiles of female athletes as well as influential women who worked to promote their cause, and an engaging combination of cartoons, advertisements, and newspaper stories that reveal changing cultural attitudes, this book helps readers see women's sports in a historical and cultural context.

Advanced new reader/pre-GED/GED/ESOL/children's collection.

Subjects: American history and culture, sports, women.

Curlee, Lynn. *Ballpark: The Story of America's Baseball Fields.* New York: Atheneum, 2005.

As Curlee discusses—and beautifully illustrates with his paintings—the various baseball parks that live in the legends of the game, he also discusses how changes in the location and design of these parks reflected changes in the social structure of the country. Early parks such as Ebbets Field in Brooklyn or Wrigley Field on the north side of Chicago were wedged into city neighborhoods and became part of their cohesive social structure. They were accessible by subway, bus, and foot. As populations moved out of the city and into the suburbs, so did the ballparks like the Astrodome in Houston, surrounded by vast parking lots and accessible only by car. Then in the 1990s came a new trend, a reversal of sorts back to the city and back to the style—with modern facilities—of the older parks. Baltimore's Camden Yards is a prime example. For sports fans, this book offers a familiar lens through which to view a changing America. For ESOL students, it offers an introduction to names and places as familiar to many Americans as the Brooklyn Bridge or the Grand Canyon.

Intermediate-advanced new reader/pre-GED/GED/ESOL/children's collection.

Subjects: American history and culture, picture books for all ages, sports.

———————

Kurkjian, Tim. *America's Game.* New York: Crown, 2000.

The inclusion of facsimiles of documents such as a letter from Jackie Robinson, the first black player to cross the color line in major league baseball, and a scouting report on Mickey Mantle, a player destined to become one of the most famous of the century, makes this book feel like a virtual tour through the National Baseball Hall of Fame. Brief but informative chapters cover many topics, including the somewhat disputed origins of the game. Numerous photographs, including a pictorial review of famous ballparks, add visual appeal. The scrapbook style of this historical overview could serve as a model for a student project to create a memory book about a topic of the student's choosing.

Intermediate-advanced new reader/ABLE/pre-GED/GED/ESOL/children's collection.

Subjects: American history and culture, sports.

———————

Robinson, Sharon. *Promises to Keep: How Jackie Robinson Changed America.* New York: Scholastic, 2004.

Sharon Robinson places her father's stellar baseball career in the context of the segregated world he entered and changed, first by his very presence but eventually by undeniable talent and his courage in the face of hostile opposition. Numerous family photographs as well as archive materials from baseball and from the civil rights movement add to the depth of information not only about Robinson but about the time in which he made his mark.

Intermediate-advanced new reader/pre-GED/GED/ESOL/children's collection.

Subjects: African Americans, African American history and culture, civil rights, sports.

———————

Sports, Leisure—Family Literacy

Adler, David A. *Lou Gehrig: The Luckiest Man*. Illustrated by Terry Widener. San Diego: Harcourt Brace, 1997.

Even folks who don't know much about sports have heard the name Lou Gehrig because of its association with the deadly disease that killed the real Lou Gehrig, widely acclaimed as one of the greatest athletes—and all around good guys—to ever play the game of baseball. This book chronicles his early life and the career that ended all too soon. Wonderful illustrations set a tone of nostalgia for a time long past.

Intermediate new reader/ABLE/pre-GED/ESOL/children's collection.

Subjects: family literacy, sports.

Cooper, Floyd. *Jump! From the Life of Michael Jordan*. New York: Philomel, 2004.

Noted illustrator Cooper is the author here as well, telling the story of basketball legend Michael Jordan's early years growing up in North Carolina. Though he could never seem to best his brother Larry, and he was passed over for his high school basketball team, he kept on trying. His persistence paid off, and today his name is virtually synonymous with the sport he has loved since the day his father bought a basketball hoop for the backyard.

Beginning-intermediate new reader/ABLE/pre-GED/children's collection.

Subjects: African Americans, family literacy, sports.

Horenstein, Henry. *Baseball in the Barrios*. San Diego: Harcourt Brace, 1997.

A young Venezuelan boy takes readers on a tour of his neighborhood, or barrio, showing all the ways in which his favorite game of baseball is played. Sometimes he plays in organized leagues, with uniforms and standard equipment, and sometimes he and his friends play a pickup game using whatever patch of grass is available and whatever will suffice for equipment, even if it's a bottle cap for a baseball. With color photographs on every page and a glossary of baseball terms, in English and in Spanish, this book is a delightful affirmation of baseball's hold on the affection of Venezuelans.

A Spanish language edition of this book is also available.

Intermediate new reader/ABLE/pre-GED/ESOL/children's collection.
Subjects: family literacy, international perspectives, Latin America and the Caribbean, sports.

Otten, Jack. *Soccer.* Series title: *Sports Training.* New York: PowerKids, 2002.
  Clear, direct, and simple sentences explain the basic skills of soccer, accompanied by photographs of a team of young girls practicing with their coach. This book, and other sports-related titles, are part of PowerKids Press's Reading Power series that offer "high-interest subject matter at an accessible reading level." Books in the Reading Power series cover other sports as well as topics related to history, nature, and social issues.
Beginning new reader/ABLE/ESOL/children's collection.
Subjects: family literacy, sports.

Ulmer, Mike. *J is for Jump Shot: A Basketball Alphabet.* Illustrated by Mark Braught. Chelsea Mich.: Sleeping Bear, 2005.
  As each letter introduces a term related to basketball, it also leads to an explanation of some aspect of the game, along with additional terminology, making this book a primer on basketball as well as the alphabet. Beginning level students will find lots of vocabulary words to add to their sight word lists, while more advanced students might use the brief descriptive paragraphs as a model for writing exercises. The illustrations feature boys, girls, men, and women playing the game, so adults will be comfortable with this book, even without a child to share the experience.
Beginning-intermediate new reader/ABLE/pre-GED/ESOL/children's collection.
Subjects: family literacy, picture books for all ages, sports.

Chapter 8

Print and Electronic Reference: Entering the Information Age

Lessons for Information Literacy

In the last chapter, we looked at the library's collection of nonfiction materials with a view toward helping adult new readers move from learning to read to reading to learn. In this chapter we take the next step toward that goal, a step that recognizes that in this Information Age, just knowing how to read is not, in and of itself, enough. If we want our students to become lifelong learners, to be active participants in the intellectual, civic, and cultural life of their communities, they also need to know how to apply their newly developing literacy skills to the task of finding the information and resources they need. They need to become familiar with the way information is organized and with the varied formats in which it is packaged. In short, they need to develop the basic skills of information literacy.

The public library is the perfect learning lab for applying the developing skills of literacy to the tasks of finding information. Libraries offer access to a wealth of information in several formats. They have books, magazines, newspapers, dictionaries, encyclopedias, atlases, and other reference sources in both print and electronic formats. They offer access to electronic databases covering many subject areas including history, literature, health, business, and consumer issues, among others. Many libraries provide public computers equipped with word processing programs, Internet access, and other resources that are available to card-holding patrons. Even the children's department offers computers with entertaining as well as educational software. If adult new readers feel overwhelmed by the number of resources available, reassure them that even experienced library users feel intimidated by the number of choices. Indeed, the choices *are* overwhelming at first, but two basic principles of library service remain as they have always been: librarians and library staff are trained and eager to help patrons access the information resources in their library, and those resources are available to all. The public library believes in and supports information equity.

The Library as Information Central

The focus of this chapter is twofold: first, to suggest some basic information-seeking skills that literacy students should develop; and second, to help them become familiar with the many information resources, both print and electronic, that are available to them in the public library. To accomplish these two goals we will weave sample exercises using information literacy skills into the discussion of library resources. Although electronic resources may get the most attention in this Information Age, we will not neglect print resources which are easily accessible and in some cases already familiar to our students. In addition, becoming familiar with the organizational structure of print information may help students develop a visual image of that organization, an image that will help them as they learn how to navigate the sometimes complex formats of electronic information resources. Let's begin with a tour of the library.

A Tour of the Library

For many of our adult literacy students, the library is not a familiar place. Even the basic vocabulary that we take for granted, terms such as fiction and nonfiction, call numbers, reference area, and circulation desk, may be new to them. Librarians and literacy teachers can work together to organize a simple guided walking tour of different areas of the library, showing examples of the materials and resources found in each section.

Points of Interest

- First and foremost: help is available. Librarians *want* to help patrons. They *like* finding materials that answer questions.
- Libraries are not just about books—or computers. Most libraries offer audio recordings of music, books on tape or CD, and video recordings of popular movies and informative documentaries covering a wide range of subjects.
- Newspapers and magazines are available for browsing. Some libraries have many out of town newspapers and even international newspapers.
- Fiction books are shelved alphabetically by author.
- Biographies are shelved alphabetically by the name of the book's subject.
- Nonfiction books are organized by call numbers, according to their subject.
- Most libraries have a separate reference area with dictionaries, encyclopedias, atlases, statistical sources, and government publications.
- Most libraries offer a bank of computers for public access. Resources will vary, but generally libraries offer e-mail access, word processing and other popular programs, access to electronic reference sources and licensed databases, and access to the Internet. Particular rules limiting the time of use or requiring sign-up will vary.

Alphabetical Indexing and Subject Indexing

Alphabetical and subject indexes are perhaps the most basic methods used to organize information. Many students will actually be familiar with these indexes, although they might not use that term, because we find them in common items we use in our everyday lives. Phone books and building directories, for example, are alphabetical indexes, as are the indexes found in the back of nonfiction books. And anyone who has ever looked in the local Yellow Pages to find a hardware store or a pet sitter has used a subject index.

Sample Exercises Using Alphabetical and Subject Indexes

1. Have students create a list of family members or friends in your local area, then have them look up each person in the phone book and write out their address and phone number.

2. Prepare a list of five services or commodities for which students must find a local merchant in the Yellow Pages: for example, an auto repair shop, a store that sells sports equipment, a plumber, a florist, and an agency that shelters abandoned pets. Have students note the subject term the item they found was listed under.

3. Have students find the listing of restaurants in the Yellow Pages. Ask them to determine if the listings are divided into categories such as by neighborhood or ethnic cuisine.

4. Choose a multivolume encyclopedia covering a subject of interest to students. For example, have students consult *The Gale Encyclopedia of Medicine,* published by the Gale Group, an encyclopedia intended for the lay public and available in many public libraries. Have the students look in the index volume for all the references to diabetes, note the subheadings under diabetes such as symptoms, treatment, etc., then find the correct volume and page for each entry.

The Library's Catalog

To become comfortable library users, to feel that the resources in the library are truly available to them, adult literacy students need to learn to use the library's catalog. In these days of electronic catalogs, that is an easier task than they might think, easier, really—and far more efficient—than using the old card catalogs. At the most basic level, students should be able to find a book by title or author, to find books on a particular topic, and to locate the books or materials they find in the catalog in the various sections of the library. In this electronic age, however, library catalogs provide access to several additional bits of information about a particular book, including such items as a picture of the cover, a summary of the contents, the first line or paragraph, and perhaps even, brief reviews. As students become more confident in their literacy skills, they should also become familiar with using the many "hot links" in a library record that lead to this additional information. The following exercises will help familiarize students with many features of a library catalog. Ideally, a librarian can give students a demonstration of the features of the catalog, then have them do these or a similar set of exercises with the librarian and teacher available to offer assistance.

Sample Exercises Reading the Library's Catalog

Show the students a sample catalog record, then have them complete exercises similar to those suggested below. This exercise is based on a sample record from the catalog of the Columbus Metropolitan Library. Other library catalogs may differ somewhat, but the basic features will be relatively the same. The book used for this example is *With Needle and Thread: A Book about Quilts* by Raymond Bial.

Sample Catalog Record

Discovery Place Libraries

Author: Bial, Raymond
Title: With needle and thread : a book about quilts /
Publishing Information: Boston : Houghton Mifflin, 1996.
9603
Physical Description: 48 p. : col. ill. ; 24 cm.

Click here for summaries, excerpts and more

The system owns 5 copies of this title.

Reserve   Put in Book Bag

Location	# copies		Call Number	Local Information	Volumes
	Owned	Available			
Gahanna	1	1	J 746.46 B576w		
Dublin	1	0	J 746.46 B576w		
Whetstone	1	1	J 746.46 B576w	On Display	
Northwest	1	1	J 746.46 BIA		
Worthington	1	1	J 746.46 BIA		

New Search   Full Description

Points of Interest

- Point out the major features, what librarians call "fields," such as author, title, and publishing information.
- Point out the location information. In this case, five branches of the

system have a copy of the book, and at the Whetstone branch, it is "on display," meaning it's not in its usual place on the shelf so the student may need to ask for help from the library staff.

- Point out the call number of the book, which indicates it will be in nonfiction; the "j" means it will be in children's nonfiction.
- The reserve button enables students to reserve a book located at a different branch from the one where they are searching the record. The book can then be sent to whatever branch is convenient for them.
- Explain that items that are underlined are "hot links" that lead to additional information.
- The "full description" link leads to more information about the subject of the book. Most online catalogs have such links, though the term used may differ.

Suggested Questions

1. Click on the author's name. Name the titles of other books he has written.
2. Where and when was *With Needle and Thread* published?
3. Click on the "full description" link. What additional pieces of information do you find there?
4. On the " full description" page, click on the subject heading "Quilting United States History Juvenile Literature" and note the number of books that are suggested. Name the titles and authors of three other books on quilting.
5. Click on the link "click here for summaries, excerpts and more." What do you find there?

Sample Exercises Searching the Library's Catalog: Basic

Show students the catalog's basic search page.

basic search | advance

Basic Catalog Search

Step 1: Enter your search term(s)

[   ]

Step 2: Click to select the type of search

☐ KEY WORD	☐ AUTHOR	☑ TITLE	☐ SUBJECT
To combine terms	To Find:	To Find:	To Find:
use: AND	Writers/Editors	Book Title	People
OR	Actors/Directors	Movie Name	Places
NOT	Musicians/Composers	CD/Cassette	Things

Optional: Choose a format

Format: [All   ▼]   [Search]   Search Tips

Points of Interest

- You can search by title for a book, movie or CD. You can also search by a *series* title if you're looking for another title in a series.
- If searching by author, enter last name first. You can also search for books by illustrator, using the author search mode. Again, enter the illustrator's name last name first.
- You can search by a specific subject heading (as Quilting United States History Juvenile Literature in the example above.) As this example shows, however, subject headings can be cumbersome. Better to search by keyword, using *and, or,* or *not* as appropriate.
- There is an easier way to search by subject heading, that is by clicking on the link to the full description, then clicking on the subject headings, which are "hot" links.

Suggested Questions

1. Find three titles of books written by Tana Reiff. Where are they located?
2. Find the book *Shutting Out the Sky* by Deborah Hopkinson. Look at the "full description" information. What is this book about?
3. Search for the health care series titled *Just the Facts*. How many titles

did you find that are part of that series? How can you be sure they are part of this series?

4. Do a keyword search for "quilts" and "juvenile." Did Raymond Bial's book *With Needle and Thread* come up in your search? How many other titles came up? Choose one title to investigate the "full description" information and write a sentence or two describing that book.

Sample Exercises Searching the Library's Catalog: Advanced

Show students the advanced search page. Assuming you don't remember the exact title, demonstrate a search for Raymond Bial's book about quilting by entering Bial as author keyword and quilts in title keyword.

Advanced Catalog Searching

Enter your search term(s)   Search Tips

[   ] as   [Author Keyword   ▼]

☉ And ☐ Or ☐ Not

[   ] as   [Title Keyword   ▼]

☉ And ☐ Or ☐ Not

[   ] as   [Subject Keyword   ▼]

☉ And ☐ Or ☐ Not

[   ] as   [Keyword Anywhere ▼]

Limit my search by:
Year of Publication:

Later than [   ]   Earlier than [   ]

- For a single year, enter it in both boxes.
- For a range, enter beginning and ending year.

Format: [All   ▼] Language: [Any   ▼]   [Search]

Points of Interest

- Each of the drop down menus can be changed to author, title, subject, or publisher keyword, or keyword anywhere.
- If you choose to combine the words or phrases you enter in the search boxes with "and," the items retrieved must contain *all* those words or phrases. If you combine terms with "or," the items retrieved will contain *either one of the terms or some of the terms or all of the terms* you entered. In other words, using "and" will limit your search, while using "or" will expand your search.

- You can limit your search by year of publication, by format (clicking on the down arrow will give you choices) or by language (again click on the arrow for choices).

Suggested Questions

1. Find some alphabet books that are about animals.
2. Raymond Bial has written some books about American Indian tribes. Try to find some titles.
3. Find some books about Mexico that have many photographs.
4. Find books about diabetes written in Spanish.
5. Find books about the solar system written after 2003.

Basic Print Reference Sources

Dictionaries

Browsing the shelves of a typical public library Reference Section, students and tutors will find a perhaps surprising collection of dictionaries, encyclopedias, atlases, fact books, and other texts that cover, quite literally, a world of topics. Some of these books will be dense with facts, figures, and discussions, while others will invite browsing through pages of photographs and attractive visual displays of information. Let's look at a few representative examples.

Among dictionaries they will find comprehensive ones such as the *American Heritage Dictionary*, published by Houghton Mifflin and noted for its clear definitions and quotations that illustrate changing patterns of acceptable usage. The *American Heritage Dictionary* also offers many illustrations that enhance its visual appeal as well as add value to its level of information. Even more illustrations can be found in the *DK Illustrated Oxford Dictionary*, from DK Publishing of London and New York. Combined, as its name suggests, with the world-renowned text of the *Oxford English Dictionary*, the publishers describe this dictionary as "appealing to all the family," a description that, from an adult literacy perspective, indicates an appeal across levels of sophistication and reading ability. Remember, too, that most dictionaries include an interesting—almost quirky—array of other kinds of information at the end of the book, such as pictures of the flags of the world's countries, measurement conversion charts, lists of U.S. Presidents, and, in the case of the *DK Illustrated Oxford Dictionary*, a charting comparing U.S., U.K., and European shoe sizes.

Dictionaries can be highly specialized. Consider, for example, the *Abbreviations Dictionary* from CRC Press of Boca Raton, Florida. In this dictionary, students would find the complete term for their car's VIN number, what AM, FM, UHF, and VHF mean, and the full name of United Nations organizations so often referred to in the news such as UNESCO and UNICEF. Teachers of ESOL classes could make much use of dictionaries such as the *Random House Dictionary of America's Popular Proverbs and Sayings*. This work describes the origin, meanings, and usage of sayings with historical roots such as "don't give up the ship," as well as sayings with roots in the popular culture such as "no way, Jose."

Dictionaries can be specialized in another way, profiling people associated with a specific subject. For example, Greenwood Press publishes a multivolume set, each volume covering a major sport such as *A Biographical Dictionary of American Sports: Baseball* (Greenwood, 2000). *The Biographical Dictionary of Black Americans* (Facts on File, 1999, rev. ed.). is an example of a reference book classed as "juvenile literature" yet shelved in the adult collection of many public libraries and found in some college libraries as well.

Encyclopedias and Other Reference Sources

Encyclopedias, too, can be comprehensive, covering virtually every subject of interest to anyone or specialized, offering in-depth information on one particular topic. Among the most popular of the comprehensive encyclopedias is *World Book,* from World Book, Inc. of Chicago, a set of twenty-two volumes in A–Z format that discusses world history and geography, science, the arts and entertainment, and more. Although intended for middle and high school students, this encyclopedia is well suited for adults, especially those at the advanced new reader level. Some libraries shelve the latest edition in the adult reference section and previous editions in the children's section. Also published for the children's market but appropriate for adults, especially at beginning and intermediate new reader levels, is the *Dorling Kindersley Visual Encyclopedia.* Rather than the A–Z approach of *World Book,* the DK book organizes information by subjects, such as the earth, the human body, beliefs and customs, arts and the media, and so on. Each section is brief, but with many photographs, diagrams, and lists of facts, making it a book to browse for the fun of discovering interesting facts rather than one to consult for details about any topic.

Sports: The Visual Reference (Firefly Books), first published in Canada, is an example of a specialized encyclopedia with an international perspective, offering much of its information in a visual format and grouping the contents by categories, such as snow sports, small ball sports, large ball sports, motor sports, and so on.

Books of lists of one kind or another invite browsing and can lead to deeper investigations of topics or events that spark a student's curiosity. One example is a yearly release from DK Publishing called *Top 10 of Everything*. The 16th edition covers the year 2005. The expected lists are here: sports stars, movies, TV shows, but so are some unexpected and intriguing lists such as the 10 countries with the most workers or the top ten occupations by number of workers worldwide or the top ten tea-drinking or coffee-drinking countries. The international perspective of a book such as this one could spark many a conversation and lead to a range of reading, research, and writing projects.

Among the books in a reference collection of any public library will be several texts that discuss a particular subject area in depth. Medical textbooks are a good example, as many public libraries will have copies of medical texts that are comprehensive and authoritative, but published for families or for a general, nonmedical, audience. Some examples of this include *The Mayo Clinic Family Health Book* (HarperResource, 2003), *The American Medical Association Family Medical Guide* (Wiley, 2004), *The New Harvard Guide to Women's Health* (Harvard University Press, 2004), *The Harvard Medical School Guide to Men's Health* (Free Press, 2004), and *The Johns Hopkins Consumer Guide to Drugs* (Medletter Associates, 2005).

Sample Exercises Using Print Reference Sources

1. In the *American Heritage Dictionary,* have students look up the word "loose" and then answer these questions: How many definitions are there for "loose" as an adjective? What example does the dictionary give of "loose" used in an idiom? Can you think of any others? What are synonyms for "loose?" Write three sentences, one using "loose" and the other two using the two synonyms "lax" and "slack."

2. From the *Random House Dictionary of America's Popular Proverbs and Sayings,* or a similar dictionary, ask students to find the meaning of the phrases "the early bird gets the worm" or "don't count your chickens before they are hatched." Ask them to suggest other phrases to look up. In a class with ESOL students, ask them to explain some common sayings from their culture.

3. Give students some examples of abbreviations such as VIN, as in vehicle identification number, or PIN, as in personal identification num-

ber. Ask students to suggest others they know of from their everyday experiences. Then have them look these up in whatever dictionary of abbreviations is available in your library.

4. Using the *World Book,* or a similar general encyclopedia, ask students to look up "basketball" and answer questions such as the following:
   a) Who is credited with inventing basketball?
   b) When did women first play in an NCAA championship round?
   c) Among the men's college teams, which one has won the most NCAA championships?
   d) Choose one player pictured in the discussion of basketball and then find more information about him, either elsewhere in the *World Book* or in a reference book specific to sports.

5. Using a specialized reference work such as *The Biographical Dictionary of Black Americans,* ask students to create a list of people they would expect to find there. Then ask individual students, or a team of students if that is feasible, to choose a person and answer the following questions:
   a) When and where was this person born?
   b) What did you learn about his or her early life?
   c) How did the person become involved in the activity that he or she is known for ?
   d) What did you learn from the profile that you didn't know about the person beforehand?

6. Using one of the medical textbooks prepared for the general public, have students look in the book's index to find answers to questions such as the following:
   a) What is the difference between type 1 and type 2 diabetes?
   b) What are some potential causes of migraine headaches?
   c) When should babies start eating solid foods?
   d) Why should aspirin not be given to young children?
   e) What are the warning signs of a stroke?

Research Databases and the Internet

The availability of research databases and web sites through the Internet has given users of these informational tools to access a range of resources and information unimaginable just a decade or so ago. From finding the health information needed to help care for an aging parent to searching for a reliable used car to reading a review of a recent movie, the use of the Internet has become as much a part of everyday life for many people as reading the local newspaper over morning coffee, and for some, it has replaced that local newspaper.

Not every home has a computer, however, nor does every person have the know-how, confidence, or even the literacy skill to make use of these extraordinary tools, a situation that threatens to widen the gap between those with the means and skills to gain information needed for advancement in their lives and those without those means or skills, a situation some refer to as the "digital divide." But the public library, by adapting its traditional role of providing access to include access to the technological realities of the current age, is leading efforts to erase that so-called "digital divide." Offering a bank of public access computers as well as assistance and, in many cases, classes to help patrons of all educational backgrounds make use of the opportunities that computers afford us, the public library continues to evolve in its role as an educational resource for the whole community.

Not only does the public library offer access to computers and the information they provide, it offers access to *authoritative* information. By choosing research databases created by reputable publishers and reviewed by librarians and scholars, the library leads users to sources of information that have the same weight of authority as the dictionaries, encyclopedias, and other print resources they have sitting on their shelves. There is one more fact that is important to point out in regard to the libraries and the research databases they offer: the libraries must *pay* for them, sometimes rather hefty fees. Many people mistakenly believe that because something is available on the Internet, it is somehow *free*. While it may be *free* to the user, it is not free to the library. Libraries must pay for these databases, just as they do for those books on the shelf.

Let's look first at some of the research databases typically available through public library Web sites and suggest some exercises to help adult literacy students make use of those resources. Then we will look at one specific Internet site, the National Library of Medicine's medlineplus.gov, as an example of an authoritative, reliable, and freely available source of information.

Research Databases

Several of the well known dictionaries and encyclopedias now have online versions as well. The *American Heritage Dictionary* and the *Encyclopedia Britannica* are two examples. Among general interest databases covering a wide range of topics, *Infotrac OneFile,* produced by Thomson Gale, *EBSCOHOST,* produced by EBSCO, and *ProQuest,* from the ProQuest Information and Learning Company are three that are frequently found in public libraries.

For health information, EBSCO offers *Health Source: Consumer Edition,* a database of articles from health journals and pamphlets and other materials from reputable health organizations. Many of these materials will be available in full text and thus can be printed from the computer. Thomson Gale offers a similar database called *Health and Wellness Resource Center.* Both databases also offer access to medical dictionaries and encyclopedias giving detailed descriptions of diseases and disorders.

Other popular databases include *Reference USA* which is like an online telephone book, providing addresses for individuals or for businesses, and *Wilson Biographies Plus Illustrated,* which offers over 72,000 biographies and obituaries of people from pop stars to scientists. Library Web sites will also lead users to resources that will help them find jobs, research consumer products, and find and evaluate collectibles.

Sample Lessons Using Research Databases

1. Use a database such as *Reference USA* to find the addresses of friends or family members.
2. In a class situation with students from different countries, have students create a list of the countries they represent. Add others if the list is not very long. Then have students use an electronic encyclopedia to answer some basic questions such as a) what is the population b) what continent is the country on c) what does its flag look like d) what is its form of government. Ask the students to suggest other questions.
3. Using a general interest database, do a basic search for information on the topic global warming. Note the number of "hits" or responses that come up. Then try doing an advanced search, refining or limiting the original search by adding another concept such as global warming and Greenland or global warming and the Antarctic. Also try limiting the search by the type of article you want to retrieve such as global warming and illustrations to find articles about global warming that include illustrations.
4. Have students list five famous people, then use a biographical database to find basic information about those five people.
5. Have students use the library's Web page to identify a consumer research database and ask them to find information on four different kinds of cars.

The Internet

Most public libraries provide access to the Internet via the World Wide Web. It is important to note to students that searching the Internet via a search engine such as Google or Yahoo is different from searching the research databases the library subscribes to, even though in both cases, searchers are using the Internet. The difference is that the research databases are, in essence, vetted by the library as described above. Not that they are beyond error, but their information is considered authoritative. Searching a topic on the Internet through a search engine, however, will lead to all kinds of "hits," some relevant and some not, some authoritative and some not, some commercially produced and possibly biased, and some just pure junk. The Internet is indeed an extraordinary source of information, much of it worthwhile, but much of it is either not useful, misleading, or downright dangerous, and it isn't always easy to tell the difference. Students need to be wary, to learn to recognize signs that raise at least a yellow if not a red light warning, and to become familiar with sources they know are trustworthy. It is often said that you can find almost anything on the Internet, which is probably close to being true. But the real question is whether or not the information you are finding is authoritative, authentic, and valuable. Librarians can work with literacy teachers to help students become skilled users of Internet resources.

The U. S. government is a source of much authoritative and valuable information on the Internet, and much of it is both freely available to the general public and free of cost. A prime example is MedlinePlus. Produced by the National Library of Medicine and the National Institutes of Health, MedlinePlus offers a wealth of information about health topics in plain English (or Spanish), intended for patients and their families. It discusses over 700 diseases, disorders, and wellness topics. It offers access to drug information, a medical encyclopedia, and a medical dictionary. It offers articles about current research and provides a means of finding doctors in particular specialties and geographical areas. The reading level is not easy, but most advanced new readers will be able to read the materials, especially with the assistance of teachers or tutors. Through the use of the information reading technique, teachers can help to make the information available to less advanced students as well. The homepage of MedlinePlus is reproduced below.

Sample Exercises Using the Internet

Exercises using MedlinePlus.gov

1. Find information on kidney stones. Either enter the term "kidney stones" in the top search box or click on "Health Topics" and go to the list of topics under "K."
2. On the page about kidney stones, link to the information about nutrition.
3. Search the medical encyclopedia for a definition of the term "neonate."
4. In the Directories section, find the name and address of a dentist in your neighborhood.

5. Using the general search box, find articles that discuss whether supplements of zinc help cure the common cold.
6. Click on "Other Resources," then follow the "libraries" links that will lead you to a list of consumer health libraries in your state.
7. Through the "Other Resources" link, explore links that interest you. They will lead to other government sites as well as authoritative sites produced by health care organizations such as the American Cancer Society.
8. Have students suggest topics to research, then work in small groups to find answers to their questions.

Remind students that one of the best ways to become familiar and comfortable with using the resources on the Internet is to "play" around with them, trying various links to see where they take you.

A Note to Librarians
Offer tours of the library to introduce literacy students and their tutors to the many information resources available. Consider offering workshops that demonstrate how to use the library's computerized resources, including the catalog. Create displays which feature a frequently asked question—or just a fun question—along with the answer and the source used to find it. Highlight reference books in your collection that are unusual or that cover "hot" topics such as music or movies or a popular sport. Create displays of sources of information about the countries of origin of immigrants in your community and try to collect materials in those languages. In every way possible, remind literacy students and their teachers that the library is often their best source for information and that in this Information Age, librarians are there to help them navigate through the myriad sources and formats available to find information that is authoritative and valuable to them.

A Note to Literacy Teachers
Model the use of books, electronic resources, and the library as information sources. Make a point of looking things up *with* students when they raise questions. Have some basic reference materials available in the tutoring center. Look for some of these materials at library book sales. Even older editions of encyclopedias, atlases, and dictionaries will contain relevant information, and they are also a record of the way things once were, an interesting subject in itself. Tell your students about information needs you have and the ways

you satisfy them. Arrange with local librarians to have them demonstrate the computer-based resources the library offers, either in the library or in the literacy program, whichever is most convenient. If you are unfamiliar with computer-based information sources, share that with your students and explore these systems together. At every opportunity, help your students develop the skills and, more importantly, the attitude and confidence they will need to function in a society increasingly based on the ability to find and use information.

Part III

Strengthening the Connection

Chapter 9

Building a Literacy Coalition

According to the *Oxford English Dictionary,* the original root of the word *coalition* is the Latin word *coalere,* meaning "to sustain and nourish." That seems a particularly apt image of what a library does for literacy students: sustains and nourishes their developing literacy skills and their participation in a life of reading and learning. For this to happen, however, librarians and literacy providers need to work together. They also need significant support and assistance from the community at large.

Recognizing this need for collaborative efforts, library staff and literacy workers across the country are forming coalitions. In modern usage, the *Oxford English Dictionary* defines *coalition* as "the growing together of separate parts" or "a fusion of parties, principles, and interests." It is this kind of coalition that librarians and literacy providers must aim to build to promote literacy. It must be a fusion of parties: the public library, adult literacy programs, and the community at large. It must be a fusion of principles: a strong belief in the value of learning for each individual and the importance to a free society of a literate, informed, inquisitive citizenry. It must be a fusion of interests: the interests of students who need excellent, well-funded literacy programs to help them learn how to read; the interests of literacy teachers, who seek to provide the best learning opportunities for their students; the interests of the public library, which aims to collect, preserve, and make available to all the rich resources of our culture; and the interests of the community, which works to use, build upon, and transmit that culture to future generations.

The Library Literacy Coalition

Community literacy programs and the public library form the core of the literacy coalition. Literacy programs teach adult students how to read or improve their reading. Libraries offer students opportunities to apply developing reading skills to a wide range of materials. Working together, librarians and literacy teachers strengthen each other's efforts and increase opportunities for students to succeed. Let's look at some specific activities library and literacy personnel can undertake to advance the cause of literacy.

What Library Staff Can Do
Librarians should establish a close working relationship with their local adult literacy programs, by visiting the programs and becoming familiar with staff and students as well as with the general operation of the programs. During their visits to the literacy program, librarians can promote the library literacy connection in numerous ways:

- If the library has a separate new readers collection, explain the collection, indicate where it is located in the library, and show samples of the variety of materials housed there.
- Bring library card applications and explain policies for borrowing materials from the library.
- Give "book talks" at the literacy program, using a range of books from the new readers collection as well as from the general collection. In these book talks, show books that treat the same issues but from different perspectives and at different reading levels. On the topic of sports, for example, show a few biographies of sports figures, including some that will appeal to adults and some that students might share with their children, poetry collections that focus on sports, and photographic collections of particular teams or particular sports.
- Read short stories or an introductory chapter to a longer book and talk with the students about their reactions. For students who are interested, suggest related titles.
- Poll students' interests for suggestions of books or topics to add to the library's collections.
- Invite students to read and review books being considered for the new readers' collection.
- Place rotating deposit collections in adult literacy programs. Include a sampling of all kinds of materials, including books from the general collection.

- Participate in tutor training sessions by preparing information packets for tutors and discussing the various library resources available to new readers.

In the library, librarians can support literacy programs in the following ways:

- Organize tours of the library for each new group of literacy volunteers.
- Build a collection of resource materials for tutors, including training manuals from other programs as well as a comprehensive collection of books on reading, literacy, and adult education.
- Organize tours of the library for literacy students. Maintain an accessible file of book reviews written by literacy students.
- Publish periodic bibliographies of books for new readers and distribute them to literacy programs.
- If the local literacy program publishes a newsletter, ask to have a regular column to highlight materials and activities at the library that will be of interest to new readers.
- Identify books shelved in various sections throughout the library that are appropriate for new readers. Work with literacy staff to create a label for these books that literacy students will recognize and accept.
- Refer potential students to local literacy programs.
- Make library space available for classes or tutoring sessions.
- Invite authors of books that are popular with new readers to discuss their writing and to speak to a larger community about issues surrounding literacy.
- Serve as a clearinghouse for literacy information. This can include maintaining a bulletin board with information about local literacy programs and distributing flyers, brochures, and other information sources about literacy programs.

What Literacy Staff and Volunteers Can Do
Teachers not only teach, they serve as role models for learners. Teachers can encourage library use among students by talking about books they are reading and by linking classroom activities to library books. They can also:

- Take classes or individual students to the library and have the librarian show them the various books and resources available.
- Read stories or poems to classes for brief periods each day. Mention similar books that are available in the library.

- In pre-GED or GED classes, illustrate or supplement specific lessons with a range of books and other materials from the library. For example, enrich a history lesson by displaying biographies of historical figures or collections of photography from the time frame being studied.
- Create a library corner in the classroom with a changing display of books.
- Bring newspapers, magazines, books, and other materials related to current events to the class to stimulate discussions as well as reading and writing activities.
- Ask students for questions or topics they would like to investigate. Bring in library books related to these topics or suggest research databases or Internet searches that might yield information about their topics.
- Work with librarians to create bibliographies of materials for adult new readers.
- Encourage students to write reviews of books they read.
- Distribute library card applications.
- Invite a local librarian to serve on a board of advisors for the literacy program.
- Learn as much as possible about the library: how it is funded, who governs it, and how it views its mission. Look for opportunities for the literacy program to be a supporter and advocate for the library in the community.

What Library and Literacy Staff Can Do Together

- Share ideas for collaborative efforts to support literacy at all levels in the community.
- Develop a jointly sponsored family literacy program. Librarians can offer workshops discussing children's literature, reading to children, and parenting skills. Literacy teachers can help students learn to read children's books that students will later read to their children.
- Conduct training activities to acquaint each other with each agency's services and to develop skills necessary to implement and evaluate jointly planned programs.
- Share promotional materials (flyers, bookmarks, posters, etc.) describing the services of each agency. Include the other agency on your mailing list for newsletters and other communications.
- Sponsor a speaker's bureau through which library staff and literacy tutors can speak to social service agencies and community organizations about literacy services for adults.

- Develop a literacy component of library programs planned for a general audience. For example, if the library is offering a "Let's Talk About It" program, include films related to the topic or organize an oral history project related to the topic and invite literacy students. Also consider a display in the library of materials from the children's collection that are relevant to the topic and appealing to adults.
- Establish a new readers' book discussion club. Librarians can make multiple copies of the books available and lead discussions. Literacy teachers can incorporate excerpts from the books into their classes.
- Encourage students' writing by publishing and disseminating collections of their works.

Reaching Out to the Community at Large

The public library and local literacy programs are at the heart of the literacy coalition. But low literacy levels affect all aspects of community life, and all segments of the community should be involved in efforts to improve those literacy levels. Invite representatives from the business community, social welfare organizations, immigrant and refugee support groups, vocational rehabilitation programs, youth groups, senior citizen agencies, employment agencies, churches, correctional institutions, local universities, and the local media to participate in this effort. This larger coalition can address issues that are fundamental to the success of a literacy program but often beyond the scope of any one literacy program working alone. In particular, a broad-based community literacy coalition can address two issues crucial to the success and viability of any program: funding and the recruitment and retention of students.

A successful literacy program needs solid, long-term financial support. For too many programs, funding is sporadic and insufficient. Staff must spend their time gathering whatever opportunities of financing are available, often competing with other worthy agencies. Changing this situation will require significant change in the way government and businesses view education. Whether these changes will be forthcoming is unpredictable. What is clear is that significant changes will occur only if the literacy community speaks loudly and frequently about the needs of literacy students. Many voices speak louder than one. Broad-based literacy coalitions, representing all segments of the community, can put literacy on the government and business agenda better than any one program director acting alone.

Other than funding, the most significant problem literacy programs face is recruiting the students who need their services and keeping them in the program once they have started. English-speaking ABLE students must overcome the stigma of admitting their lack of reading skill and their own mistrust of "school-like" programs, especially if they have been unsuccessful in past school ventures. For students who do begin a literacy program, staying with it can be harder than admitting the need for help in the first place. The task of learning to read or to improve reading skill is hard and requires a huge commitment of time and energy. For adult students, their efforts are inevitably complicated by pressures from a job, or the lack of one, family responsibilities, physical or learning disabilities, and nagging self-doubt. ESOL students are more forthcoming about seeking help, but they, too, face numerous obstacles of financing, transportation, child care, and overall adjustment to life in a new language as well as a new culture.

Strong community support can help literacy students enter and remain in literacy programs. For that to happen, however, the literacy coalition must include persons who come from the same economic and social circumstances as the students. These community members can reach potential students through local churches, social organizations, and personal contact. They can gain the trust of potential students and recruit other community members to serve as tutors or supporters of literacy.

What the Communitywide Literacy Coalition Can Do

- Organize public relations efforts including newsletters, press releases, business breakfasts, and readathons at local shopping areas, to name a few methods that have been tried.
- Raise the issue through all local media: letters to the editor, editorials in the local newspapers, radio and TV talk shows, and public lectures.
- Research funding opportunities and assist literacy programs in writing grant applications.
- Lobby legislators, both local and national, to provide substantial, long-term support for literacy programs.
- Organize a committee of teachers, librarians, students, and community writers and scholars to write materials for new readers.
- Sponsor community oral history projects involving new readers as well as other members of the community.
- Expand the base of volunteer tutors to include management and workers from area businesses, students from local universities, senior citizens, and retired workers.
- Establish and support an advocacy group of students and former stu-

dents and involve them in planning, implementing, and promoting activities to support literacy programs.

- Organize and maintain ancillary services to support literacy students, such as child care, transportation, and employment counseling.
- Recruit community members to serve as mentors for literacy students.
- Encourage businesses to support literacy by allowing release time for students and tutors to work together, by making on-site tutoring available, and by providing incentives for workers who agree to improve their basic literacy skills and for workers who volunteer to be tutors.
- Arrange large-scale public events, including members of the arts, entertainment, and sports communities to support the efforts of literacy programs and students.

Working together, members of the literacy coalition will sustain and nourish adult literacy students. No one agency can do the job alone. Literacy programs teach students how to read. Public libraries offer students the opportunity to practice newly acquired reading skills by reading books that provide information important to their everyday lives, books that entertain or amuse them, and books that invite them to explore a world of knowledge and ideas beyond their current understanding. The community at large supports literacy students by providing substantial, long-term funding for literacy programs and jobs for students who improve their skills. Sustained and nourished by this coalition, adult literacy students will not only learn how to read. They will become enthusiastic readers and lifelong participants in our learning society.

Appendix A

Chapter Notes
and Suggested Readings

Preface—Cited Source

1. Allende, Isabel. Quoted from *Speaking of Reading,* by Nadine Rosenthal. Portsmouth, NH: Heinemann, 1995.

Chapter 1—Cited Sources

1. American Library Association. Retrieved July 25, 2006 from http://www.ala.org/ala/ourassociation/governingdocs/keyactionareas/keyactionareas.htm.
2. American Library Association. Retrieved July 25, 2006 from http://www.ala.org/ala/olos/outreachresource/servicesnewnonreaders.htm
3. DeCandido, GraceAnne A., ed. 2001. *Literacy & Libraries: Learning from Case Studies.* Chicago: American Library Association.
4. National Center for Education Statistics. National Assessment of Adult Literacy. Retrieved July 26, 2006 from http://nces.ed.gov/NAAL/index.asp?file=KeyFindings/Demographics/Overall.asp&PageId=16.
5. Ranganathan, S. R. 1957. *The Five Laws of Library Science.* London: Blunt & Sons, Ltd.
6. Wedgeworth, Robert. 2004. The Literacy Challenge. *IFLA Journal* 30:14–18.
7. Author visits with Susan O'Connor, Manager of the Literacy Program at the Brooklyn Public Library; Ken English, Literacy Program Director and Terry Sheehan, Site Director for the Seward Park Center for Reading and Writing of the New York Public Library; and Anita Citron, Director of the Adult Learning Center of the Jamaica Branch, Queens Borough Public Library.

Chapter 2—Cited Sources

1. American Medical Association. Retrieved July 26, 2006 from http://www.ama-assn.org/ama/pub/category/8115.html.
2. National Center for Education Statistics. National Assessment of Adult Literacy. Retrieved July 26, 2006 from http://nces.ed.gov/NAAL/index.asp?file=KeyFindings/Demographics/Overall.asp&PageId=16.
3. National Center for Family Literacy. Retrieved July 26, 2006 from http://www.famlit.org/.
4. National Institute for Literacy. Bridges to Practice: the project. Retrieved July 26, 2006 from http://www.nifl.gov/nifl/ld/bridges/about/project.html
5. Wedgeworth, Robert. 2004. The Literacy Challenge. *IFLA Journal* 30: 14–18.
6. Weisel, Laura P. 1998. "PowerPath to Adult Basic Learning: A Diagnostic Screening System for Adults Who Are at High Risk for Being Diagnosed as Having Learning Disabilities." IN: Vogel, Susan A. and Stephen Reder, eds. *Learning Disabilities, Literacy, and Adult Education.* Baltimore: Paul H. Brookes Publishing Co. For additional information about PowerPath, visit http://powerpath.com/.
7. McKinney, Julie, and Sabrina Kurtz-Rossi. *Family Health and Literacy: A Guide to Easy-to-Read Health Education Materials and Web Sites for Families.* Boston: World Education in conjunction with the National Institute for Literacy. May be downloaded from http://www.worlded.org/us/health/docs/family/.

Chapter 2—Additional Resources

1. Chisman, Forrest P. 2002. *Leading from the Middle: The State Role in Adult Education and Literacy.* New York: Council for Advancement of Adult Literacy. Available from www.caalusa.org.

   Adult literacy programs funded by the federal government are administered by state education agencies, and this paper takes a wide-ranging view of the current state of this arrangement and the resulting impact on the programs and their students.
2. Jordan, Dale R. 1996. *Teaching Adults with Learning Disabilities.* Malabar, Fl.: Krieger Publishing Co.

   Jordan offers specific examples and techniques to help adult students with a range of learning disabilities.
3. Rose, Mike. 2004. *The Mind at Work: Valuing the Intelligence of the American Worker.* New York: Viking.

Rose explores the intellectual requirements of what many consider blue collar or physical labor and underscores the value of life experience that adults bring to their efforts to improve their reading ability.

Chapter 3—Cited Sources

1. Dillard, Annie. 1989. *The Writing Life.* New York: Harper & Row.
2. Kruidenier, John. 2002. *Research-Based Principles for Adult Basic Education Reading Instruction.* Washington, DC: The Partnership for Reading (a collaborative effort of the National Institute for Literacy (NIFL), the National Institute of Child Health and Human Development (NICHD), and the U.S. Department of Education).
3. Lyman, Helen H. 1976. *Reading and the Adult New Reader.* Chicago: American Library Association.
4. National Institute of Diabetes and Digestive and Kidney Diseases. Retrieved July 26, 2006 from http://diabetes.niddk.nih.gov/dm/pubs/type1and2/what.htm.
5. Rose, Mike. 1989. *Lives on the Boundary: A Moving Account of the Struggles and Achievements of America's Educational Underclass.* New York: Penguin Books.
6. Sobczak, Alicja. 2005. "Birds." *The Literacy Review* 3, (Spring).
   The Literacy Review is an annual journal of writing by adult students in English for Speakers of Other Languages, Basic Education, and General Education Development programs in New York City. It is published by the Gallatin Writing Program, The Gallatin School of Individualized Study, New York University.

Chapter 3—Additional Resources

1. Comings, John, Barbara Garner and Cristine Smith, eds. 2005. *Review of Adult Learning and Literacy: Connecting Research, Policy, and Practice.* Vol. 6. Mahwah, NJ: Lawrence Erlbaum Associates.
   A project of the National Center for the Study of Adult Learning and Literacy, this book reviews recent research programs and the implications of their findings on the practice of adult literacy education.
2. *Journal of Adolescent and Adult Literacy.* Newark, Del.: International Reading Association.
   This peer-reviewed journal, published eight times per year, offers a wide range of articles from researchers and practitioners discussing the art and science of teaching reading.

3. Knell, Suzanne, and Janet Scogins. 2000. *Adult Literacy Assessment Tool Kit.* Chicago: American Library Association.

    The assessment tools offered in this book attempt to determine students' goals and interests as well as their reading and language skills, and they are appropriate or adaptable to both ABLE and ESOL students.

4. National Center for the Study of Adult Learning and Literacy. *Focus on Basics.* Available from: http://www.ncsall.net/?id=31.

    Focus on Basics is the quarterly publication of the National Center for the Study of Adult Learning and Literacy, presenting articles on best practices, current research on adult learning and literacy, and the application of that research to adult basic education.

5. Reid, Suzanne. 2002. *Book Bridges for ESL Students: Using Young Adult and Children's Literature to Teach ESL.* Lanham, Md.: The Scarecrow Press.

    Using some specific titles as examples, this book offers many suggestions for using YA and children's literature as a basis for language lessons for ESL students. Although not written specifically for adult students, many of the suggested activities will work across ages groups.

6. Rosenthal, Nadine. 1995. *Speaking of Reading.* Portsmouth, NH: Heinemann.

    For this book, Rosenthal interviewed several people about their experience of reading. Some were avid, lifelong readers, some were occasional readers, and others still struggle to improve their reading ability.

7. Rosow, La Vergne. 2006. *Accessing the Classics: Great Reads for Adults, Teens, and English Language Learners.* Westport, Conn.: Libraries Unlimited.

    Rosow offers insights and suggestions for using classic texts to empower students and improve their reading skill.

8. Smith, Frank. 2006. *Reading Without Nonsense.* 4th ed. New York: Teachers College Press.

    Smith continues to promote a holistic approach to teaching reading, emphasizing the use of meaningful materials, whether the students are children or adults.

9. *Teaching Adults: A Literacy Resource Book.* 1994. Syracuse, NY: New Readers Press.

    Teaching Adults: An ESL Resource Book. 1996. Syracuse, NY: New Readers Press.

    Both books were developed by Laubach Literacy Action (now part of ProLiteracy America). Teachers using real-life materials, student-created materials, and library books will find numerous suggestions for incorporating both alphabetic skill-building and comprehension exercises into their reading instruction programs.

10. Viens, Julie, and Silja Kallenbach. 2004. *Multiple Intelligences and Adult Literacy: A Sourcebook for Practitioners.* New York: Teachers College Press.

    After explaining various kinds of intelligence, the authors offer many examples of applying knowledge about the ways people think and learn to particular teaching methods and materials for ABLE and ESOL students.

Chapter 5—Cited Sources

1. Chen, Xiu. *The Literacy Review* 3, (Spring).
2. Connaroe, Joel. 1991. *Six American Poets.* New York: Random House.
3. Dickinson, Emily. 1960. *The Complete Poems of Emily Dickinson.* Edited by Thomas H. Johnson. Boston: Little, Brown.
4. Espada, Martin. 1990. *Rebellion is the Circle of a Lover's Hands.* Willimantic, CT: Curbstone Press.
5. Frost, Robert. 1949. *Complete Poems of Robert Frost.* New York: Henry Holt.
6. Hirsch, Edward. 1999. *How to Read a Poem and Fall in Love with Poetry.* New York: Harcourt Brace.
7. Koch, Kenneth. 1998. *Making Your Own Days: The Pleasures of Reading and Writing Poetry.* New York: Simon & Schuster.
8. Koch, Kenneth. 1973. *Rose, Where Did You Get that Red?: Teaching Great Poetry to Children.* New York: Random House.
9. Lyon, George Ella. 1999. *Where I'm From, Where Poems Come From.* Spring, TX: Absey.
10. Padilla, Miguel. *The Literacy Review* 3 (Spring).
11. Soto, Gary. 1990. *A Fire in My Hands.* New York: Scholastic.
12. Williams, William Carlos. 1988. *The Collected Poems of William Carlos Williams, Volume II 1939–1962.* New York: New Directions.

Chapter 5—Additional Resources

1. Collum, Jack and Sheryl Noethe. 1994. *Poetry Everywhere: Teaching Writing in School and in the Community.* New York: Teachers and Writers Collaborative.

   Collum and Noethe offer excellent advice as well as specific teaching techniques and lesson plans to help students of all ages to read, enjoy, and write poetry.

2. Conarroe, Joel. 1991. *Six American Poets*. New York: Random House.

    Among the six poets Conarroe discusses are four, Emily Dickinson, Robert Frost, Langston Hughes, and William Carlos Williams, whose work includes many poems particularly accessible to adult students new to poetry as well as to reading.

3. Fagin, Larry. 1991. *The List Poem: A Guide to Teaching and Writing Catalog Verse*. New York: Teachers and Writers Collaborative.

    Numerous variations on "the list poem" offer literacy teachers and their students creative ways to use this particular technique, which is an easy, fun, and surprisingly instructive way to become comfortable with writing poetry.

4. Grossman, Florence. 1990. *Listening to the Bells: Learning to Read Poetry by Writing Poetry*. Portsmouth, N.H.: Boynton/Cook Publishers.

    Believing that anyone who has tried to write poetry will experience greater enjoyment and appreciation from reading poetry, Grossman offers numerous suggestions to help students stretch their imaginations as writers and open their eyes and ears to a deeper understanding as readers.

5. Hirsch, Edward. 1999. *How to Read a Poem and Fall in Love with Poetry*. New York: Harcourt Brace.

    Brimming with the author's knowledge and exuberant love of poetry, this book is an immensely readable journey through a wide range of wonderful poetry with Hirsch along to place the works in context and guide the reader to a deeper understanding.

6. Koch, Kenneth. 1977. *I Never Told Anybody: Teaching Poetry in a Nursing Home*. New York: Random House.

    Although more than a quarter of a century old, this book remains an excellent resource for teachers working with adult students unfamiliar with reading or writing poetry. With a class of nursing home residents, most of whom came from immigrant or working-class backgrounds, Koch used many of the strategies and techniques he had developed to engage children in reading and writing poetry (see entry below for *Rose, Where Did You Get That Red?*). The list of poems he used as examples as well as the descriptions of his techniques will provide inspiration for a whole semester's worth of poetry lessons.

7. Koch, Kenneth. 1998. *Making Your Own Days: The Pleasures of Reading and Writing Poetry*. New York: Simon & Schuster.

    A prolific and award-winning poet as well as a renowned teacher of poetry, Koch explores the concept of poetry as a separate language "in which the sound of the words is raised to an importance equal to that of their meaning." In the process of discussing his ideas, he presents several poems as examples, guiding the reader to a deeper appreciation of both the music and meaning of poetry.

8. Koch, Kenneth. 1973. *Rose, Where Did You Get That Red? Teaching Great Poetry to Children.* New York: Random House.

    After thirty years, this book remains a classic in the field of poetry education, and despite its focus on children as the students, Koch's basic philosophy and techniques are highly applicable to adult literacy students in both ABLE and ESOL classes. Koch believed that teaching children only simple, childish poems meant giving them "nothing to understand they have not already understood." In his lessons, he aims to stretch his young students' minds by introducing them to great poetry, mostly written for adults. In yet another volume, *Wishes, Lies, and Dreams: Teaching Children to Write Poetry* (Random House, 1970), Koch outlines his methods for teaching children to write poetry, methods which again are suitable for use with adult students.

9. Lenhart, Gary, ed. 1998. *The Teachers and Writers Guide to William Carlos Williams.* New York: Teachers and Writers Collaborative.

    Several poets and teachers offer their favorite lessons using the rich and varied work of the physician/poet Williams, a poet celebrated for writing about the ordinary and the everyday in a most extraordinary way.

    The Teachers and Writers Collaborative has also produced similar guides to the poetry of Walt Whitman and Frederick Douglass and to Classic American Literature.

10. Morrice, Dave. 1995. *The Adventures of Dr. Alphabet: 104 Unusual Ways to Write Poetry in the Classroom and the Community.* New York: Teachers and Writers Collaborative.

    Morrice teaches poetry writing through various artists-in-the-schools programs and to senior citizens groups. His teaching methods are fun, inventive, and even a bit zany at times, but he gets his students, young and old, involved both mentally and physically with the language and emotion of poetry. Some of his methods may be hard to reproduce exactly, but they are sure to convince teachers that students who've never thought about reading or writing poetry can come to enjoy it immensely.

11. Pinsky, Robert, and Maggie Dietz, eds. 2000. *Americans' Favorite Poems: The Favorite Poem Project.* New York: W.W. Norton, 2000.

    As Poet Laureate of the United States, Pinsky undertook a project to solicit favorite poems from a broad spectrum of Americans. The resulting book is a unique collection of wonderful poems, many accessible to literacy students. But what makes the book truly special are the introductions to each poem in which the person who submitted it recalls the deeply personal memory that he or she connects to the poem. Reading the introduction first, you find yourself reading the poem through the eyes of a stranger whose experience brings the poem to life in a unique way. Even if the poem is familiar to you, your appreciation of it is deepened.

Pinsky and Dietz also published a second and similar volume, *Poems to Read: A New Favorite Poem Project Anthology,* published by Norton in 2002.

Chapter 6—Cited Sources

1. Coles, Robert. 1989. *The Call of Stories: Teaching and the Moral Imagination.* Boston: Houghton Mifflin.
2. Lundin, Anne. "The Company We Keep: Advisory Service for Youth." In *Developing Readers' Advisory Services: Concepts and Commitments*, edited by Kathleen de la Pena McCook and Gary O. Rolstad. New York: Neal-Schuman, 1993.
3. Rylant, Cynthia. 1988. As quoted in *Something About the Author.* Vol. 50. Detroit: Gale Publishing.

Chapter 6—Additional Resources

1. Herz, Sarah K. 1996. ***From Hinton to Hamlet: Building Bridges between Young Adult Literature and the Classics.*** Westport, Conn.: Greenwood Press.

    Herz explores thematic connections between classic literature and popular literature for young adults. Many of the young adult titles will be appropriate for adult new readers or for adults who wish to share the stories of literature with the middle and high school students in their families.
2. Trounstine, Jean. 2001. ***Shakespeare Behind Bars: The Power of Drama in a Women's Prison.*** New York: St. Martin's Press.

    Trounstine recounts her experiences teaching literature in a women's prison and, at the suggestion of a student, producing Shakespeare's plays.

Chapter 8—Additional Resources

1. Duncan, Donna, and Laura Lockhart. 2000. *A How-To-Do-It Manual for Teaching Elementary School Students to Solve Information Problems.* New York: Neal-Schuman Publishers.

   What do I want to know and where can I find the answer? This book suggests techniques for helping children pose questions and then find the answers. It is a model of inquiry that can be easily adapted to adults.

2. Osborne, Robin. www.firstfind.info: Organizing Easy-to-Use Information on the Web. In *From Outreach to Equity: Innovative Models of Library Policy and Practice,* edited by Robin Osborne. Chicago: American Library Association, 2004.

   Osborne describes the development of http://www.firstfind.info, a collection of over 900 websites covering 14 essential topic areas including health, immigration and American government. All of the Web sites have been reviewed by librarians for authority, accuracy, and clarity of language, especially for users with limited reading and/or technical skill. A project of the Westchester (NY) Library System, the Web site is freely available to all.

Chapter 9—Additional Resources

1. The Big Read. http://www.neabigread.org/.

   An initiative of the National Endowment for the Arts in partnership with the Institute of Museum and Library Services, the Big Read is designed to revitalize the role of literature in American popular culture and make reading "a national hobby." Although it grew out of a recognition of the decline in literary reading in America, librarians and literacy teachers can use audio books, community book discussions, author visits and other creative programming to include literacy students in the efforts of this national program to advance the literacy levels of all citizens.

2. The Lindy Boggs National Center for Community Literacy. http://www.boggslit.org/.

   Located in the Monroe Library of Loyola University in New Orleans, the Boggs Center promotes adult literacy as a vehicle for personal, economic, and community development. It sponsors an array of diverse programs that nurture a collaborative partnership between the university and its metropolitan community and between educational research and the practitioners working with students in the community.

3. McCook, Kathleen de la Pena. 2000. *A Place at the Table: Participating in Community Building.* Chicago: American Library Association, 2000.

   In the growing "ageographical" nature of our modern lives, the library's role as a center of community programming is increasingly important, according to McCook, and she urges librarians to play a leadership role in promoting the cultural and educational life of the community. Being a center for literacy development on all levels is one of the critical roles the library can—and should—play.

4. Robertson, Deborah A. 2005. *Cultural Programming for Libraries: Linking Libraries, Communities, and Culture.* Chicago: American Library Association.

   Robertson encourages libraries to expand their community programming beyond traditional literary offerings to "center the library as a cultural hub in the communities they serve." She offers many creative ideas and practical suggestions to help librarians and literacy staff include ABLE, GED and ESOL students and their families in a wide range of community programming.

5. Sumerford, Steve. "Libraries as Community Builders: The Greensboro Experience." In *From Outreach to Equity: Innovative Models of Library Policy and Practice,* edited by Robin Osborne. Chicago: American Library Association, 2004.

   Sumerford describes how the Greensboro Public Library, tired of complaining about not being "invited to the table" to discuss community issues, took a leadership role in identifying and addressing issues of importance, including low literacy levels. Other chapters in this book discuss a variety of library programs developed in the belief that outreach to special and underserved populations should become part of the basic structure of any public library.

Appendix B

Resources for Finding
Books for Adult Literacy Students

The following list suggests books, Web sites, print and electronic bibliographies, and other resources that will help librarians and literacy teachers seeking to identify books from the library's general collection that will be appropriate and appealing to adult literacy students, both ABLE and ESOL. Note that several of the book-length bibliographies listed are reissued on a fairly regular basis. Even the older ones, however, will still lead to titles of interest to students. After all, maintaining access to books long after their time in the spotlight of currency has passed is one of the great services of the public library.

Serendipity, too, is a productive—and enjoyable—means of finding reading materials, and that applies here as well. Searching library shelves or catalogs for the titles suggested in the books listed below will inevitably lead to discovery of additional titles of books by the same authors or on the same subjects. Involving students in this search for books of interest will help them become familiar with libraries, library catalogs, printed bibliographies, and other sources of information retrieval, which is an important aspect of developing literacy.

1. American Library Association. Office for Literacy and Outreach Services. http://www.ala.org/ala/olos/outreachresource/servicesnewnon readers.htm.

   This Web site offers numerous links connecting to a variety of discussions and resources related to literacy, including a Curriculum and Development link that connects users to lessons plans, book lists, and discussions about using a wide range of materials with ABLE and ESOL students.

2. Bloem, Patricia L., Nancy D. Padak, and Connie Spain. *Recommended Trade Books for Adult Literacy Programs.* http://literacy.kent.edu/Oasis/Resc/Trade/.

Continuously updated, this online annotated bibliography from the Ohio Literacy Resource Center offers comprehensive reviews of trade books, many from the children's collection, that can be useful in adult literacy classrooms. Their annotations describe the content of the book as well as identify subject areas and themes, and they suggest ways of incorporating the books into lessons for ABLE, ESOL, GED, workplace, and family literacy programs.

3. Cianciolo, Patricia J. 2000. *Informational Picture Books for Children.* Chicago: American Library Association.

   As noted in Chapter 7, the children's collection of nonfiction books is a significant source of informational materials for adult literacy students. This book suggests many titles that will appeal to adults. What's more, the search for titles mentioned here will inevitably lead to the discovery of an eclectic and enticing range of topics clearly, informatively, and often beautifully presented.

4. Givens, Archie, ed. 1997. *Spirited Minds: African American Books for Our Sons and Our Brothers.* New York: W.W. Norton.

   Focusing on books written by or about African Americans, this annotated bibliography includes books ranging from picture books to books of adult interest. Novels, story collections, biographies, and poetry are among the categories suggested.

5. *Journal of Adolescent and Adult Literacy.* Newark, Del.: International Reading Association.

   In addition to its articles on the theory and practice of teaching reading, this journal includes extensive reviews of books published for adolescents, many of which will appeal to adults as well.

6. Libretto, Ellen V., and Catherine Barr. 2002. *High/Low Handbook: Best Books and Web Sites for Reluctant Teen Readers.* 4th ed. Westport, Conn.: Libraries Unlimited.

   The latest edition of this useful bibliography includes listings of informative Web sites as well as books of fiction, history, and biography, and memoirs, among other categories. The listings also include books by authors such as Tana Reiff and others aimed specifically at adults and teens with limited literacy skill.

7. McCaffery, Laura H. 1998. *Building an ESL Collection for Young Adults: A Bibliography of Recommended Fiction and Nonfiction for Schools and Public Libraries.* Westport, Conn.: Greenwood Press.

   Although the title suggests ESL and young adults, many of the books recommended in this annotated bibliography will appeal to ABLE and

GED students as well. The annotations are informative and the subject groupings, particularly those identifying ethnic interest groups, will be helpful to teachers with students from a range of backgrounds.

8. Rosow, LaVergne. 1996. *Light 'n Lively Reads for ESL, Adult, and Teen Readers.* Englewood, Colo.: Libraries Unlimited.

    Believing strongly in reading *to* students, no matter their age, reading level, or native language, Rosow reviews books from a wide range of subjects and offers creative ideas on how to use particular titles with students in a variety of settings. Although the books mentioned here are ten years old or more, they are high-quality titles that will still be available at many public libraries and will lead librarians and teachers to other titles by the same authors or about the same subjects.

9. Schall, Lucy. 2003. *Booktalks and More: Motivating Teens to Read.* Westport, Conn.: Libraries Unlimited.

    Following an earlier *Booktalks Plus,* Schall offers an annotated and wide-ranging list of titles that will appeal to young adults participating in ABLE or ESOL classes. Many of the titles will cross generational interest lines as well. Perusing lists such as this one with adult literacy students in mind will help librarians and teachers identify not just specific titles but also authors and kinds of books that have a crossover appeal to older students.

10. Schon, Isabel. 2003. *The Best of Latino Heritage 1996–2002: A Guide to the Best Juvenile Books about Latino People and Cultures.* Lanham, Md.: Scarecrow Press.

    This annotated bibliography includes fiction and nonfiction exploring the countries and regions of Latin America. Particularly helpful to librarians and literacy teachers are the "series roundup" reviews of books published in series that present the geography, history, and culture of the various peoples of this large and diverse region.

11. Schwedt, Rachel E., and Janice DeLong. 2002. *Young Adult Poetry: A Survey and Theme Guide.* Westport, Conn.: Greenwood Press.

    This comprehensive resource offers a subject guide to collections of poetry that are marketed to young adults but contain many poems written for and appealing to adults of all ages.

12. Stan, Susan, ed. 2002. *The World through Children's Books.* Lanham, Md.: Scarecrow Press.

    The books in this annotated bibliography are organized first by geographical region and then by country. The lists include picture books, poetry, and fiction and nonfiction titles. This book also specifically reviews the best of the geographical series titles that introduce readers to the geography, history, and culture of countries around the world. Many of these books are excellent sources for ABLE and ESOL students.

13. ***VOYA. The Voice of Youth Advocates.*** Lanham, Md.: Scarecrow Press.

   This bimonthly publication aims to assist librarians and educators who work with students in the middle and high school grades. Reviews of books suggest reading levels and age-related interest levels; they also judge quality of content. Their audio book list will be particularly helpful to librarians and teachers looking for audio books for family reading, some examples of which are listed in the bibliography of Chapter 6.

14. We Learn—Women Expanding/Literacy Education Action Resource Network. http://www.litwomen.org/welearn.html.

   According to their Web site, this non-profit organization "promotes women's literacy as a tool for personal growth and social change." Among the many helpful links on their Web site is a resource list offering extensive reviews of a wide range of books organized by topics and themes.

15. YALSA. http://www.ala.org/ala/yalsa/yalsa.htm.

   YALSA, The Young Adult Library Services Association of the American Library Association, offers an array of resources for librarians working with young adults. Their annual annotated list of the best of the young adult genre will include many titles, both fiction and nonfiction, that will appeal to adults.

Title Index

Author Index

Subject Index

American History and Culture

Health and the Human Body

Immigrants and Immigration

Inspirational Stories and Pictures

About the Author

Marguerite Weibel holds Master's degrees in both adult education and library science. She has promoted the collaboration of public libraries and adult literacy programs for more than twenty-five years by teaching classes in reading and writing for adult literacy students, giving presentations to groups of librarians and groups of adult educators, and offering workshops for volunteer tutors.

She currently serves on the Board of Trustees for the Columbus (Ohio) Literacy Council. Weibel is currently a librarian and associate professor at the Prior Health Sciences Library at Ohio State University.